D1488393

Mark Twain

AND

Southwestern Humor

Mark Twain

AND

Southwestern Humor

by

KENNETH S. LYNN

WITH ILLUSTRATIONS

An Atlantic Monthly Press Book

Little, Brown and Company · Boston · Toronto

The author wishes to thank the following for permission
to reprint copyrighted material:

Houghton Mifflin Company for material reprinted from
Frank Norris's THE OCTOPUS, edited with an introduction
by Kenneth S. Lynn, Houghton Mifflin Company, 1958.
A Riverside Edition.

Yale University Press for "Huck and Jim" by Kenneth S.
Lynn, published in the *Yale Review*, Spring, 1958.

To Valerie

Can we understand at all, ever, where we do not love?

— SHERWOOD ANDERSON

Preface

Wʜᴇɴ Mark Twain prefaced *Huckleberry Finn* with the warning that "Persons attempting to find a motive in this narrative will be prosecuted; persons attempting to find a moral in it will be banished; persons attempting to find a plot in it will be shot," he was, of course, joking. To play the role of a know-nothing never ceased to appeal to Mark Twain's sense of humor. Nevertheless, many of Twain's most fervent admirers have incautiously taken him at his word, thereby confusing the deliberately assumed mask of innocence with the writer behind it. Referring to him with affectionate familiarity as "Mark," they rejoice in his writings as the brilliant improvisations of a man who never really knew what he was doing. My belief, however, is that Mark Twain was a conscious and deliberate creator, and one of the purposes of this book is to treat him as such.

The Southwestern humorists who came before Twain — and whose works comprise the tradition out of which his fiction emerged — have been granted even less artistic awareness. Generally speaking, these authors have been cast in the rude image of their frontier materials: not only did they portray the backwoods mind, we have been told, they exemplified it. Beyond doubt, the notion that Southwestern humor came out of the forest has some truth in it. But this interpretation ignores a great many other truths about the subject, including the influence of Europe, the political exigencies of life in the antebellum South, and above all, the careful craftsmanship that distinguishes Southwestern humor at its best. As with Mark Twain, my primary assumption about the humorous tradition behind him is that it is a self-conscious art, and not an expression of American mindlessness.

Contents

(*Illustrations appear between pages 146 and 147*)

Mark Twain

AND

Southwestern Humor

The Style of a Gentleman

LADY FRUGAL: How! Virginia!
  High Heaven forbid! Remember, sir, I beseech you,
  What creatures are shipped thither.

ANNE: Condemned wretches.
  Forfeited to the law.

MARY: Strumpets and bawds,
  For the abomination of their life,
  Spewed out of their own country.

— MASSINGER

THIN-SKINNED provincials that they were, the colonists of
seventeenth-century America could not stand being laughed
at, particularly by the sophisticates of London. Whenever they
sensed that they were being derided or condescended to, their
invariable response was to boast of the stupendous richness
of the New World.

Tall tales were also good business. The desire of sea cap-
tains for passengers, of land speculators for settlers, of Godly
men for converts, had as much to do with the publication of
such books as *Mourt's Relation,* which detailed the salubrities
of Plymouth, and Thomas Budd's *Good order established in
Pennsylvania & New Jersey,* which did the same for the Middle
Colonies, as did provincial touchiness. The one exception was
Virginia. For the fact that Virginia was responsible for the bulk
of the promotional literature produced in seventeenth-century

3

America was a sign not that the colony was more business-conscious than its neighbors but that it was more acutely susceptible to criticism from the mother country. Many Virginians considered their residence in America as a temporary arrangement; as tobacco-producers, they had commercial relations with England, but in addition they kept up their personal contacts, and talked of returning home for good, once they had made their fortunes in the New World. Hence the Virginians tended to be more aware of English opinion of America than were many other colonists. And along with their greater awareness went a greater sensitivity. Not possessed, as were the Zion builders of Massachusetts Bay, by the belief that their mission to America was Providentially ordained — for the religious dedication of the first-generation Tidewater settlers had faded quickly — the Virginians faced the derision of the London wits without the reassurance of an enthralling dream. For self-justification they had to rely on the tall tales of real estate advertising. From the Reverend Alexander Whitaker's *Good News from Virginia* (1613) to Robert Beverley's insistence in 1705 that "if anyone impartially considers all the Advantages of this Country, as Nature made it, he must allow it to be as fine a Place as any in the Universe," the Virginians defied their critics with glowing accounts of Heaven-on-earth.

In the long run, however, such accounts proved to be an unsatisfactory form of reply. Because it was not so much the brave new world that London liked to make fun of as the people in it, and the jokes which really stung were those which defined the Americans as "a race of convicts," in Doctor Johnson's words, or satirically described the Virginia colonists as

> Strumpets and bawds
> For the abomination of their life,
> Spewed out of their own country.

A change of tactics was clearly called for, and by the 1720s a notable shift in emphasis had taken place in Virginian boasting. In the Reverend Hugh Jones's *The Present State of Vir-*

ginia (1724), for example, which Jones was prompted to write by the familiar provincial desire to correct "the monstrous Thoughts" of certain Englishmen "concerning the Country, Lives, Religion and Government of the *Virginians,*" considerable stress is still placed on the richness of the land. But what is truly striking about Jones's book is the image of a leisurely, cultivated, gentlemanly civilization which it presents. Not only a natural paradise but a heavenly society is insisted on. The social life of the planters is portrayed as an amazingly accurate facsimile of English upper-class ways. In Williamsburg, the fashionable people "live in the same neat Manner, dress after the same Modes, and behave themselves exactly as the *Gentry in London;* most Families of any Note having a *Coach, Chariot, Berlin,* or *Chaise.*" Although Jones admits that the College of William and Mary is poor and the culture of the planters somewhat superficial, he also asserts that these deficiencies will be easily remedied, for the Virginians "have good natural notions and will soon learn arts and sciences." *The Present State,* in sum, sets forth a Virginia that never was — nor would be: "The *Habits, Life, Customs, Computations,* &c. of the *Virginians* are much the same as about London, which they esteem as their *Home.*" The whole effort of the writing is to transform windmills into giants, to dress up agricultural, provincial Virginia in a sophisticated cosmopolitanism. A rural society, so isolated and decentralized that it did not produce even the villages that were springing up everywhere in the colonies to the north, is represented as having a social life as swirlingly active and gay as London itself could offer. Tobacco planters, whose "commercial, agricultural, industrial, and legal obligations" required, as Carl Bridenbaugh has pointed out, "virtually all of . . . [their] waking hours," become in Jones's account splendidly unoccupied aristocrats —"The common Planters, leading easy Lives, don't much admire Labor or any manly Exercise except Horse-racing." Laboring in the name of "perfect Information and true Notions," clergyman Jones in fact set forth a rudimentary version of that gaudy myth on

5

which the Virginians and many other Southerners would increasingly rely. Born in response to that eternal hobgoblin of the Southern mind — criticism from the "outside"— the aristocratic myth would grow in precise proportion to the need of the South to justify itself in the eyes of the world.

ii

Jones's fantasy of Rotten Row sprung up amongst the tobacco fields was certainly an audacious boast. But it was far from convincing. One could not simply *assert* that eighteenth-century Virginia was inhabited by aristocrats and that Williamsburg rivaled the imperial metropolis of London in sophistication. The assertion must be acted out as well, literarily speaking. Which is to say that the emergent Southern myth demanded a propaganda characterized by a certain style as well as by a certain sort of statement; demanded an "aristocratic" tone and point of view that would exemplify — and thereby authenticate — the substantive claims of the Virginians that they were English gentlemen. Hugh Jones's plain and sturdy prose style patently would not do.

Almost inevitably, when the myth-makers of colonial Virginia began to cast about for a more convincing way of expressing themselves, they turned to writing comedy. For the familiar generalization that the comic art views life from above is at least a partial truth, and tells us much about why the Virginia myth-makers were so anxious to laugh. To feel that sense of superiority which Bergson says lurks in every laugher, to look down on the spectacle of life with tolerantly superior amusement, was immensely reassuring to would-be sophisticates. Then, too, in searching for just the right literary model, these nervous provincials naturally turned to London, where as it happened all the right people were laughing at the mild gaiety of Addison and Steele. Light and easy in tone, impressively erudite in their range of reference and allusion, unfailingly urbane, the essays in the *Tatler* and *Spectator* triumphantly vindicated the belief of their readers that they were not parvenus (as so many of them were, in fact), but the truest gentlemen in the world; in the London salons, there was laughter at the latest paper by Mr. Addison, and a renewed complacency.

The possibilities of Addisonian comedy were not lost on Americans who were on the rise. In Boston, a teen-aged Benjamin Franklin aped the urbanity of the *Spectator* by way of proving that he was more sophisticated and worldly-wise than either the Mathers or the young prigs of Harvard College. Meantime, in Virginia, William Byrd II read the papers of Addison and Steele with surpassing care, as indeed he did all the English publications which reached him. When he came to write his *History of the Dividing Line,* a Virginian at last spoke like an English gentleman. With Byrd's book, the literature of what I should like to call "the Southwestern tradition" begins.

Byrd was the grandson of a London goldsmith. The goldsmith established the basis for the family's rise by a judicious marriage; to his son, William Byrd I, fell the enormous problem of wresting a fortune out of the Southern wilderness. Through his mother's brother, the goldsmith's son inherited at the age of eighteen an 1800-acre estate situated near the falls of the James River. With this strategically-located property in his possession, he quickly built up a substantial business as a country merchant and an Indian trader; in time, the caravans of his agents ranged as far as western North Carolina. Speculating in the wildly fluctuating tobacco market, he made more money; whenever he got the chance, he acquired title to more land, until 1800 acres had grown into 25,000. A captain of militia at twenty-four, "Colonel" Byrd at twenty-eight, member of the Council, eventually Auditor and Receiver-General of the colony, this tough, shrewd entrepreneur was by the time of his death one of the richest and most influential men in Virginia.

7

William Byrd II was given all the advantages. He was sent to England for his schooling, and then to Holland for business experience; in 1692, he enrolled, aged eighteen, as a student of law at the Middle Temple in London. In these years, he played the role of the young gentleman about town; he frequented the theaters, and moved easily in what he later recalled as "the Gaity of St. James's"; his friends included Congreve and Wycherley, the Duke of Argyle, Charles Earl of Orrery, and the famous physician, Sir Hans Sloane. Through the good offices of Sir Robert Southwell, he was elected a fellow of the Royal Society. In 1704, his portrait was painted in London by Godfrey Kneller. The painting depicts a young man who carries his elegant clothes with vast assurance; in his look — as Byrd himself was frank to admit — is "a certain cast of pride." But the London dandy who stood for Kneller was not entirely what he appeared, as events immediately proved. In December of 1704, Byrd's father died in Virginia. By the following spring, the dandy had turned into a gentleman farmer. Thirty-one years old, Byrd had spent all but two years of his life since the age of ten in Europe. And Europe was now three thousand miles away.

Byrd inherited more money than business acumen from his father. In 1711, he made a financial agreement that would haunt him for the rest of his life. Out of pride, he was unwilling that certain lands in the estate of his wife's father should be sold to strangers; so as to keep them in the family, Byrd agreed to assume his late father-in-law's debts. The debts proved to be much larger than Byrd had anticipated, and despite all of his efforts he was never able to get free of them. Although he did not yet know it, 1711 sealed Byrd's fate; of the remaining thirty-three years of his life he would spend more than twenty in Virginia, condemned by his debts to a life of exile in what he would more than once call "this silent country."

For a long time, Byrd kept trying to get back to London, and in 1715 he succeeded. Except for one brief visit to Virginia, he managed to stay on until 1726, when he left England forever. These last English years comprise the most crucial period in Byrd's life. His social calendar was more crowded than ever before. He went to assemblies at the Spanish Ambassador's, took dinner with Horace Walpole, and was invited to Petersham by the Duke of Argyle. With Byrd in England was his daughter Evelyn, of legendary wit and beauty, and his own brilliant social career was further illuminated by the reflected light from hers. A frequenter of Will's and Garraway's, of Ozinda's and the Virginia, Byrd began to imitate the literary efforts of the coffeehouse wits. He composed Theophrastian character sketches, translated a story from the *Satyricon* of Petronius in a style which Joseph Addison would have applauded, and tried his hand at literary love letters and *vers de société*. His energy in these years, his zest for the thronging life of the metropolis, was apparently inexhaustible; there was about his activity, indeed, something compulsive. Some desperate feeling seemed to drive Byrd on and on, some well-nigh hysterical dissatisfaction; in the monotonous record he set down in his London diaries of his need for sexual conquest he indirectly revealed the enormous extent of his frustration. A succession of mistresses furnished only the staple of his diet; in these years, he was in the habit of picking up a woman off the London streets every few days, or of dropping by such places as Mrs. Smith's in Queen's Street. The itch of his oat-sowing youth had never hectored Byrd into such a sexual frenzy as overtook him in his middle forties.

What goaded him on from one liaison to the next cannot be established with absolute certainty. Yet one fact about Byrd's London years seems to explain a great deal. He was trying, very hard and very unsuccessfully, to marry an English heiress. Byrd's first wife had died of smallpox in the fall of 1716; from that moment on, he was on the lookout for a lady of property who could pay off his debts and convert his life as a great gentleman in the great world from a temporary into a permanent reality. He courted Mary Smith, daughter of the Commissioner of the Excise, with letters written in invisible ink, and ardent words at clandestine meetings. There is something tragicomic in the spectacle of this middle-aged provincial moving heaven and earth to persuade the wealthy Miss Smith — and her skeptical father — that he would be a better matrimonial bet than his rival, the eminently respectable, and very rich, Sir Edward Des-Bouverie. Byrd promised to live in England always; he ticked off his Virginia assets; he submitted a genealogy; but all in vain. The English knight, not the Virginian, carried the day. Byrd now turned to the rich widow Pierson. She refused three of his proposals of marriage before he gave up. Next on the list was the widow Lady Elizabeth Lee, a granddaughter of Charles II. She would not marry him. (When Edward Young, author of *Night Thoughts,* proposed to her in 1731, she accepted.) Then came a lady known to history only as "Minionet," the name Byrd bestowed on her in his literary love letters. She, too, refused him. Is it any wonder that fair ladies should have been the most consistent target of the literary satires which Byrd turned out in his London years, or that he should have chosen to translate a story by Petronius which with cynical wit exposes the hypocrisies of widows? And is it not possible to see at work in Byrd's compulsive gaiety and his ceaseless seeking-out of whores the terrible despair of a frustrated ambition — the rage of a provincial at being so defeated by the metropolis?

In 1724, Byrd finally succeeded in persuading Maria Taylor of Kensington to marry him, despite the opposition of her mother. Although Maria's late father had been well-to-do, rather than wealthy, Byrd must nevertheless have had hopes that her fortune would be enough, for when he and his wife returned to Virginia two years later, he kept his apartments in Lincoln's Inn. Not for several years, until it became perfectly clear that he was never going back, did he give them up.

The complex duties of managing a great plantation kept Byrd busier than the printing shop did Franklin. In addition, he had political duties as Councillor and Colonial Agent that consumed time and energy. Combining civic responsibility with his insatiable land hunger, he undertook to help run the celebrated surveying project which established the dividing line between Virginia and North Carolina in 1728, and in 1736 he surveyed the Northern Neck. Experimental farmer, militia commander, founder of Richmond and Petersburg, amateur doctor, Byrd in Virginia indeed reminds us, in his energy and versatility, of no one so much as his famous Philadelphia contemporary. Again like Franklin, Byrd was a time saver and a schedule-maker, a man who accomplished all that he did by the clock. With iron discipline, he drove himself through days of rigorous work that often began at four or five o'clock in the morning. His diaries, among the great social documents of colonial American history, reveal a dedicated man. And at the heart of his dedication was an abiding determination to prove that a Virginia colonist could still be a London gentleman. The handsome house he built at Westover; the paintings of his English friends with which he lined its walls; the library he put together of nearly four thousand volumes (the largest — except possibly for Cotton Mather's — in America); these were the props, the stage setting, for the drama of gentlemanhood which he daily acted out. Whether one examines the diaries of the period 1709-1712 — before his last English years — or of the period 1739-1741, the entries almost infallibly begin with one of several variations on the same remorseless refrain: "I rose about 5, read Hebrew and Greek"; "I rose at 4 o'clock this morning and read a chapter in Hebrew and 400 verses in Homer's *Odyssey*"; "I rose at 3 o'clock and read two chapters in Hebrew and some Greek in Josephus"; and occasionally, but only occasionally, "I rose at 7 o'clock and read neither Hebrew nor Greek."

The refrain is impressive, beyond doubt; it is also quite appalling. Something about the literary devotion it describes seems factitious; the performance smacks somehow of a masquerade. Every night Byrd sets down what he has read that morning, but he does not say what he thinks of what he has

11

read, what pleasure Homer's poetry has given him, what reflections the words of Josephus have set in motion. Only the fact of the reading is recorded. Byrd goes to Homer in the morning like a Jew donning phylacteries, or a Christian going to his prayers, or Don Quixote turning to the pages of Feliciano de Silva; his reading is a ritual with him, a way of self-consciously validating, every day, the truth of an illusion. Once again, Benjamin Franklin comes to mind, for Franklin's life was full of equally self-conscious gestures. There was, however, an important difference between their masquerades. For when Franklin burned the light in his shop all night to make people think he was still working, or put on an air of humility in imitation of Jesus and Socrates, he was calculating on a public effect. However provincial Boston and Philadelphia were, they were cities, none the less, and Franklin had the satisfaction of playing his performances before an audience. No corresponding satisfactions existed for William Byrd. Rising at dawn amidst the rural splendors of Westover, he played before an empty house. The public Franklin wished to convince of his humility or his industry lived all about him; the people whom Byrd sought to impress with his devotion to Greek and Hebrew were three thousand miles away. How much easier a time of it Franklin had, knowing at every moment just exactly how he was doing! Doubtless many a Virginia planter believed that William Byrd was a distinguished and cultivated gentleman, but the awe of provincial tobacco-farmers was hardly sufficient for a man who had been the friend of Congreve. As a diarist Byrd invites comparison to Pepys, yet one has only to contrast the colorful variety of Pepys's nocturnal adventures with the evening picture of himself that Byrd presents so often — playing cards in a silent house with his wife, and occasionally cheating whenever she threatened to win — to measure the difference in their situations. Bereft of society, Byrd went through his daily ritual for his own benefit.

There were, of course, the mails. How much correspondence

with English acquaintances meant to Byrd is suggested by his confession that when letters arrived from London "we tear them open as eagerly as a greedy heir tears open a rich father's will." Yet letter-writing was far from satisfactory. On the one hand, he was constrained by his pride to put up a brave front. (Soon after his final return from England he wrote to Charles Earl of Orrery, "Your Ldsp will allow it to be a fair Commendation of a Country that it reconciles a Man to Himself. . . .") On the other hand, what had a Virginia provincial to say that would possibly interest the gossips of the salons? "Tis a great misfortune," he wrote in 1735 to "My Dear Cousen Taylor," "for an Epistolizer not to live near some great city like London or Paris, where people play the fool in a well bred way, and furnish their neighbors with much discourse. In such places, stories rowle about like snowballs, and gather a variety of pretty circumstances in their way until at last they tell very well, and serve as a good entertainment for a country cousen." And country cousins tended to be forgotten by city cousins. "Distance," Byrd said in a *cri de coeur* of 1736, "they reckon the same as death." In 1741, he noticed that his name had been dropped from the rolls of the Royal Society, for which he had diligently collected specimens year in and year out; in words shaking with emotion, he wrote to the President of the Society, "I take it a little unkindly Sir that my name is left out of the yearly List of the Royal Society, of which I have the honour of being one of its ancientest members. I suppose my long absence has made your Secretarys rank me in the number of the Dead; but pray let them know I am alive. . . ."

Living in a silent country, fearful of being forgotten, Byrd desperately desired the attention of the London audience. Since letters were unsatisfactory, perhaps a book would do the trick. His appointment as head of the Virginia Commission to aid in surveying the dividing line between Virginia and North Carolina gave him the literary chance of his life.

iii

During his months in the wilderness, Byrd kept a diary. His *History of the Dividing Line*, however, is very far from being an on-the-spot transcript. As Byrd observed, the diary was "only the skeleton and ground work of what I intend, which may sometime or other come to be filled up with vessels and flesh, and have a decent skin drawn over all, to keep things tight in their places, and prevent their looking frightful." Like *Walden*, the *Dividing Line* does not mirror what really happened in the woods, but the mind of a highly self-conscious artist reflecting on that experience after it had ended. Byrd's ultimate purpose, like Thoreau's, was to establish an image of himself.

The *Dividing Line* went through three separate stages of composition before the finished product was achieved. The diary may be considered Phase One. Phase Two was the so-called *Secret History of the Line*. Rather short, written presumably for private circulation among his closest Virginia friends, this account of Byrd's travels spends most of its satiric ammunition on Virginians — on the foibles of his fellow commissioner, Richard Fitz-William, and on the brutal conduct of some of their men. Quite strikingly, in view of what was to come later, the *Secret History* contains only one slighting reference to North Carolinians.

Phase Three, *The History of the Dividing Line,* was designed for other eyes than those of Virginia friends. Clearly intended for publication in London, this book was to be William Byrd's letter to the world. In rewriting and expanding the manuscript once again, he made many changes. He eliminated derogatory references to Fitz-William and other Virginians, substituting in their stead satiric remarks about other American colonists, particularly the frontiersmen of North Carolina. But the most radical alterations were in the texture of the language, in the tone and diction and point of view of the narrative. To appreciate these changes one has to confront Byrd's prose directly. Here in juxtaposition are two passages, the first from the *Secret History,* the second from the *Dividing Line,* both of which purport to be observations that were made on March 25, 1728. In the *Secret History* account, Byrd and his party are sitting out a northwester in a back-country lodging:

> We killed the Time, by that great help to disagreeable Society, a Pack of Cards. Our Landlord had not the good Fortune to please Firebrand [Richard Fitz-William] with our Dinner, but surely when People do their best, a reasonable Man wou'd be satisfy'd. But he endeavour'd to mend his Entertainment by making hot Love to honest Ruth, who wou'd by no means be charm'd either with his Perswasion, or his Person. While the Master was employ'd in making Love to one Sister, the man made his Passion known to the other, Only he was more boisterous, & employ'd force, when he cou'd not succeed by fair means. Tho' one of the men rescu'd the poor Girl from this violent Lover; but was so much his Friend as to keep the shamefull Secret from those, whose Duty it wou'd have been to punish such Violations of Hospitality. Nor was this the only one this disorderly fellow was guilty of, for he broke open a House where our Landlord kept the Fodder for his own use, upon the belief that it was better than what he allow'd us. This was in compliment to his Master's Horses I hope, & not in blind obedience to any order he receiv'd from him.

In the *Dividing Line* account, Byrd pays no attention to what took place in the landlord's house; instead he describes the countryside roundabout and the frontier people who inhabit it:

> Indian Corn is of so great increase, that a little Pains will Subsist a very large Family with Bread, and then they may have meat without any pains at all, by the Help of the Low Grounds, and the great Variety of Mast that grows on the High-land. The Men, for their Parts, just like the Indians, impose all the Work upon the poor Women. They make their Wives rise out of their Beds early in the Morning, at the same time that they lye and Snore, till the Sun has run one third of his course, and disperst all the unwholesome Damps. Then,

15

after Stretching and Yawning for half an Hour, they light their Pipes, and, under the Protection of a cloud of Smoak, venture out into the open Air; tho', if it happens to be never so little cold, they quickly return Shivering into the Chimney corner. When the weather is mild, they stand leaning with both their arms upon the corn-field fence, and gravely consider whether they had best go and take a Small Heat at the Hough [hoe]: but generally find reasons to put it off till another time.

Thus they loiter away their Lives, like Solomon's Sluggard, with their Arms across, and at the Winding up of the Year Scarcely have Bread to Eat.

The contrast between the two passages is startling. The first scene is cruel and violent. Men who have been out in the wilderness doing an exhausting, dirty job, who have endured cold and mud and reptiles and the enormous emptiness of the forest, are not apt to be polite about taking their pleasures. Fitz-William, a Virginia landholder like Byrd, makes rude remarks to the landlord about his cooking, then tries to seduce one of the women of the house. Meantime, one of Fitz-William's men brutally attempts to rape her sister. The action is vividly immediate — the narrator himself is right there, playing cards. His agitation at what is happening is undisguised. Byrd hates Fitz-William with every fiber in his being, and his prose does not spare him with gentlemanly circumlocutions; in a blunt, jerky style, with a tough, unfooled directness that seems unmistakably American, he tells us precisely what happened in two hundred and fifty outraged words.

The second scene is grotesquely comic, reminiscent in a way of certain Flemish and Dutch paintings of the seventeenth century. Yet the scene possesses a dimension that no pictorial representation could possibly contain, a dimension that establishes the character of the observer through whose eyes we see the picture. If the scene is grotesque, the attitude of the narrator is candid and amused, his diction cultivated, his periodic sentence rhythms vigorous and graceful. Never descending to the crude level of the subject, his humor is not broadly farcical, but coolly sophisticated; its sprightliness is designed to

16

contribute to the gaiety of St. James's and the Spanish Ambassador's, rather than to arouse the belly laugh of the mob. More royalist than the king, the provincial Virginian is in fact a good deal snootier than the *Spectator;* if his comedy is a triumphant American version of the London ideal, Byrd's tone is closer to the élitist hauteur of the Roman comic writer whom he so much admired, Petronius. The passage thus presents a double image: of North Carolina frontiersmen living out their wretched and degraded lives in a lonely and dirty back country, and of a fop from the London salons who has made his way into the wilderness, and who finds the antic and sprawling gestures of the rubes as amusing as a freak show, as diverting as a cockfight. Further emphasizing the detachment of the observer from the observed, the narrator in the second passage is not in the picture he describes; he is completely outside, and above, what is going on. Also, the more generalized time sense of the second passage, as compared with the immediacy of the first, contributes to the sense of spectatorial distance. We hear not merely of what went on on a particular stormy evening, but of how the frontiersmen behave on days when the weather is good, as well as when it is bad. Such is the distance, indeed, that although the movements of the North Carolinians are noted in detail, we do not hear them speak; Byrd's cartoon is animated, but silent.

In not allowing the corrupted accents of the frontiersmen to interrupt his cultivated voice, Byrd once again might have been modeling his work after a Roman literary ideal with which he was familiar: in this case, the ideal of Roman historiography as embodied in the work of Sallust and Tacitus. As Erich Auerbach has shown, these historians looked down from above and judged their subjects by uncompromising moral standards. These standards were borne in upon the reader in many ways, but above all by the narrative style, which in its formality and elevation defined morality in aesthetic terms. Because of the moral purpose of the style, says Professor Auerbach, grotesque or "low" characters could not be allowed to "think, feel, act, and speak out of their own nature," for to do so would allow the subject to obliterate the judgment that was to be passed upon it. Now, the development of a vernacular voice would be one of the most significant achievements of the Southwestern tradition. But as the foregoing passage from the *Dividing Line* suggests, the vernacular voice would not be heard without a struggle, for reasons which Professor Auerbach's discussion of the Roman historians illuminates. From William Byrd to the Civil War, the humorists of the Southwestern tradition by and large remained loyal to the Southern myth, and to the image of themselves as gentlemen. Style was the principal means by which they defined that image, fleshed out their myth, gave the ring of authenticity to fantasy. As much as the Roman historians, they had compelling motives for maintaining the elevation of their language — not even the putative blueness of their blood line ever caused them more anxious concern than the purity of their prose. In the Old South as in ancient Rome, the lower classes were to be seen but not heard. According to Professor Auerbach, the inability of later Roman historians to maintain the traditional style reflects the disintegrating order of the Empire; the decay of the gentlemanly style of Southwestern humor is also symptomatic of a gathering social threat to a gentleman's world — of the Jacksonian revolution which threatened the big planters' political dominance, and of the slavery controversy which ended by destroying the Old South. As the Southwestern humorists were less and less able to control ugly realities by means of myth, the vernacular material of their humor ineluctably mastered the gentlemanly style.

But all this lay in the future. The possibility that rubes might someday have the vote, or that slaves would go free, never disturbed the dreams of the master of Westover. Nevertheless, Byrd in the *Dividing Line* was as concerned with the moral corruption of his subject as was Tacitus, and he depicted the North Carolina frontiersman as a Clown in order to pass judgment on a form of behavior which disturbed him, as well as to set himself off as a Gentleman. The Clown has an intrinsic as well as a comparative significance in the narrative; unless we can understand why Byrd thought him corrupt, half the point of the comedy is lost.

As Byrd portrays him, the dominant characteristic of the North Carolinian is his laziness. Not only in the passage quoted above, but again and again Byrd takes up the theme of the frontiersman's slothfulness and indolence. He theorizes about the warmth of the climate as a cause of laziness. Obviously not satisfied with this explanation, he introduces other theories. Near the Dismal Swamp, he declares, the people "are devoured by musketas all summer and have Agues every Spring and Fall, which corrupt all the Juices of their Bodies, give them a cadaverous complexion, and besides a lazy creeping Habit, which they never get rid of." Or again, a pork diet produces "the Country distemper," which is "apt to improve into the Yaws," and leads to disfigurement, lassitude, and death.

In time, frontier laziness became for Byrd a means of explaining a good deal of American history. In the historical sketch which prefaces the *Dividing Line,* he assails the quixotic dreams of the early colonists that led them to expect "their Coarsest Utensils . . . would be of Massy Silver," because such dreams fostered laziness. Byrd is almost positive he knows why disaster overtook the Roanoke plantation: "The Adventurers were . . . Idle and extravagant, and expected they might live without work in so plentiful a Country." He knows, too, why the Jamestown settlement had trouble: "This Gentleman [Captain John Smith] took some pains to perswade the men to plant Indian corn, but they lookt upon all Labor as a Curse." Starvation, disease and the scalping knife were not so much the primary causes of disaster, in Byrd's view, as consequences of the original sin of sloth.

Such an extravagant concern with the problem of laziness would seem to indicate that Byrd had more than an objective interest in the subject. As his diaries testify, he could hardly be accused of being indolent; which makes it all the more interesting that he himself made the charge. He may have arisen every morning at four or five o'clock to read books, and then have worked without stopping all day long, but William Byrd nevertheless thought of himself as a lazy man. In a prose sketch of his own character (punningly entitled "Inamorato L'Oiseaux"), Byrd declared that "Nature gave him all the Talents in the World for business except Industry, which of all others is the most necessary. This is the spring and life and spirit of all preferment, and makes a man bustle thro all difficulty, and foil all opposition. *Laziness mires a man in the degree in which he was born, and clogs the wheels of the finest qualification.* Fortune may make a Lazy Fellow great: but he will never make himself so. Diligence gives Wings to ambition by which it soars up to to [*sic*] the highest pitch of advancement. These Wings Inamorato wanted. . . ." Since lack of diligence conspicuously fails to describe Byrd's conduct, either in the pursuit of heiresses or in running a plantation, the character sketch can only describe a tendency which he felt in himself, and which he overcame by force of will and effort of mind. The tendency was to be feared for many reasons, but above all because the task of being a gentleman in America demanded so much effort. To give way to laziness was to forfeit his entire conception of himself, and yet the temptation must always have been there. (How many times, as he rose in the dawn light and went to his Greek and Hebrew, did the question, "Why bother?" occur to him?) Fighting the appalling temptation, Byrd put himself through various food and health programs which he hoped would give him more energy; for years he ate ginseng in the belief that it pepped him up. And in the *Dividing Line* he made fun of laziness, over and over again. By thus holding laziness at arm's length, by seeing it as a clownish object of superior amusement, he was perhaps able to bring the subversiveness of his own personality as well as of the frontier under control, admonish them both, restrain them both, and dispel all disillusioning questions with laughter.

iv

In the middle 1730s, an old London friend, Peter Collinson, hearing that Byrd was at work on the manuscript of the *Dividing Line,* wrote him to ask if he could see it. Curiously enough, Byrd refused. "I have one infirmity," he wrote Collinson — "never to venture anything unfinished out of my hands." Had he, after so many years in a silent country, come to dread appearing before the London audience — to the point where he refused to admit that he had finished his book in order to keep it from appearing? A letter of 1737 to an English friend who had seen the rough diary version of the book and complimented him on it suggests, in its embarrassment and confusion, that the provincial now preferred to act out his masquerade in solitude: "I am obliged to you," he wrote, "for the compliment you are pleased to make to my poor Performances. 'Tis a sign you never saw them, that you judge so favourably. . . . It will seem like a joke when I tell you that I have not time to finish that work." *Was* his not having time a joke? An excuse to put off his audience from judging a performance he no longer had the nerve to produce in public, lest it should be found wanting? When Byrd died in 1744, the *Dividing Line* was still unpublished.

It remained so for almost a century; but in 1841 Edmund Ruffin published the book at Petersburg, Virginia, a city that Byrd had founded. Ruffin, too, was a Virginia planter, and he recognized in Byrd's manuscript a magnificent piece of Southern propaganda, although London was scarcely the audience Ruffin desired to impress. For Ruffin was a fire-eating, North-hating hothead, "one of the first and most intense Southern nationalists," Avery Craven has termed him. The dream which consumed Ruffin was grotesque and crazy: the South, he proclaimed, must become a separate nation; once free of the North, Virginia and the other slave states could create the greatest civilization ever known to man. He published the

21

Dividing Line for all America to see that the idea of the South as the home of Cavalier aristocrats was not a myth, but a historical fact. William Byrd's gentlemanly masquerade now served Southern myth-making with a vengeance.

Exactly twenty years after publishing the *Dividing Line,* Ruffin followed his dream to Charleston Harbor, where, an aging knight of sixty-seven years with long white hair hanging down to his shoulders, he was permitted the honor of pulling the lanyard on the first gun fired in the Civil War. Four years later, when the defeated South lay in broken ruins, Ruffin made one final entry in his diary: "With what will be my last breath, I here repeat and would willingly proclaim my unmitigated hatred to Yankee rule — to all political, social and business connections with Yankees, and the perfidious, malignant and vile Yankee race" — then killed himself.

CHAPTER II

The Voice of the Clowns

> Going up that river was like traveling back to the earliest beginnings of the world, when vegetation rioted on the earth and the big trees were kings. An empty stream, a great silence, an impenetrable forest. . . . And this stillness of life did not in the least resemble a peace. It was the stillness of an implacable force brooding over an inscrutable intention.
>
> — CONRAD

TIMOTHY FLINT, New Englander, Harvard graduate, man of God, set out in 1815 to bring Presbyterianism to the Western wilderness. In the course of the next ten years he came to know the Missouri backwoods and the Louisiana bayous, saw both Kentucky and Arkansas, and floated down the broad, flowing rivers from Pittsburgh to New Orleans. In contrast to Byrd's brilliantly unfair caricature of the North Carolinians, Flint's account of the trans-Allegheny frontier was eminently unbiased. The physical splendors of the West impressed him tremendously, while the backwoodsmen seemed to him "a hardy, adventurous, hospitable, rough, but sincere and upright race of people." Yet in the warm and humid river valleys Flint's spare, New England soul could not help being appalled by "the prodigious power of vegetation." "There is with me," he confessed, "in some manner, an association of this thing with the idea of sickness." Somehow, the immense fertility of this Western empire posed an unspeakable challenge to men who ventured into it, calling forth strange curses

23

and dreadful violence: "They claim to be . . . compounded of the horse, alligator, and snapping turtle. . . . I heard them on the bank, entering into the details of their horrible battles, in which they talked with disgusting familiarity about mutilation, as a common result of these combats. Indeed I saw more than one man who wanted an eye. . . ." Lord Byron might envision Daniel Boone amidst the "darling trees" of Kentucky, where "health shrank not from him"; Chateaubriand might aver that the Natchez country was a land of enchantment and frolic, full of "bears, drunken on wild grapes, staggering on the branches of the elms; caribous bathing in a lake; black squirrels frisking in the thick foliage; mocking-birds, Virginia doves, about the size of a sparrow, lighting upon the turf reddened by strawberries"; but Flint understood the power of fertility to appall, and more realistic European writers reinforced his sober words. Charles Dickens's description of the Mississippi Valley as a place where "fatal maladies, seeking whom they might infect, came forth at night, in misty shapes, and, creeping out upon the water, hunted them like spectres until day; where even the blessed sun, shining down on festering elements of corruption and disease, became a horror" thoroughly outraged Valley patriots with its patent distortions of the physical conditions of their life. But part of their outrage stemmed from the fact that in the realm of their suggestible imaginations the West oftentimes *did* resemble the nightmarish landscape of Dickens's account. The "dumb blankness, full of meaning, in a wide landscape of snows," of which Melville spoke in *Moby Dick*, was another of the terrors that the Western frontiersman faced, and so was the silence of the land. Wherever he turned, in sum, the Westerner confronted the passive strength of nature, which simply by its enormous presence took the measure of his helplessness. Stephen Crane's quiet comment on a prairie snowstorm has a general applicability to all of life in the huge demesne beyond the Alleghenies: "One was a coxcomb not to die in it."

A more easily namable threat were the wild animals that

stalked the woods, and the savage Indians whose tomahawks could fly, said Flint, "with unpitying and unsparing fury." In some ways, though, fellow frontiersmen were even more frightening than bears or bobcats or redskins. The men who warped and poled keelboats and broadhorns up the Mississippi from New Orleans were "dirty as Hottentots," said the ornithologist Alexander Wilson, "their dress, a shirt and trousers of canvas, black, greasy, and sometimes in tatters; the skin burned wherever exposed to the sun . . . ; their beards, eighteen days old." Coarsened by the terrific hardships they had endured, these men were capable of a sickening violence. As Carl Sandburg has observed, rough-and-tumble fighting along the Mississippi and Ohio included "gouging of eyes, thumb-chewing, knee-lifting, head-butting, the biting off of noses and ears, and the tearing loose of underlips with the teeth." At New Salem, in the time that Lincoln was growing up, two river toughs decided to fight it out. They stripped off their clothes, "and fought as wolves fight, with claw, tooth, and fang, till men came from over the river, parted them, and made them shake hands. One of the fighters was sick for a year and then died of the wounds and gouges." Even worse than the broadhorn bullies were the renegades and outlaws. Men like the Harpes from East Tennessee began as barnburners and horsethieves, then drifted into murder. Ranging through the wilderness, masquerading as respectable citizens, they killed, and killed again, oftentimes not for profit, but simply for the thrill: "The dog led them back to the sinkhole where the youngster's body lay. Apparently the Harpes . . . had exploded in a very ecstasy of passion. Young Trabue had been shot, kicked, tomahawked, pummeled. His body was macerated by their blows, almost dismembered by their knives. Their whole booty had been a sack of beans and a bushel of flour. And again they had vanished." Or there was Murrell, who liked to travel in the disguise of an itinerant Methodist preacher; who stole slaves by the hundreds, then resold them, and finally murdered the hapless Negroes when they were of no more use to him; who had a vast network of criminal alliances up and down the Mississippi Valley; and who dreamed of a pirate empire. (Faced with explaining how Injun Joe came by the treasure, Tom Sawyer remembered the rumors that the Murrell gang had been around St. Petersburg one summer.)

It is against this background of human violence and physical immensity that the peculiar melancholy and death longing of the Western frontiersman is to be understood. Neither Emerson, with his bland talk of "the central man," nor Carlyle, who mythologized the trans-Allegheny settlers into Homeric heroes "with most *occult,* unsubduable fire in their belly, steering over the Western Mountains, to annihilate the jungle," could see the shadow on the frontiersman's face, but Cooper did in *The Prairie* when he described Natty Bumppo's "look of emaciation, if not of suffering," and so did Melville's Ishmael when he encountered Bulkington, the tall mountaineer from the Alleghenian Ridge: He "stood full six feet in height, with noble shoulders, and a chest like a coffer-dam. I have seldom seen such brawn in a man. His face was deeply brown and burnt, making his white teeth dazzling by the contrast; while in the deep shadows of his eyes floated some reminiscences that did not seem to give him much joy." The promptings of such reminiscences caused many frontiersmen to flee ever deeper into lonely nature. Of those who stayed on to form the raw, new society of the West, many turned for solace to the graveyard poetry of the giftbooks and newspapers — to the sort of mortuary versification that Huck Finn found enshrined in the Grangerford household. For verses about death gave voice to the Westerner's yearning for release from the tough world in which he lived; and because it was sentimental, such poetry enabled him to take a melancholy satisfaction in his fate — to dissolve brutal thoughts and secret sorrows in a warm bath of tears. Abraham Lincoln was only one of many Westerners who clipped verses like "Oh! Why should the spirit of mortal be proud?" from the newspapers, or who wrote poems of the sort he sent to Andrew Johnston in 1846, which in its "mournful song" about insanity and its celebration of death as "thou awe-inspiring prince" employs the language of Emmeline Grangerford's "Ode to Stephen Dowling Bots, Dec'd." to ask the haunting question — can the human mind stand the strain of this existence?

Tearful verses, however, were not the Westerner's only comfort. If one must be a coxcomb in order to survive in this world, then why not deliberately play the coxcomb — and laugh one's head off at the performance? Instead of yearning for death as a surcease to human degradation, why not revel in life by building a fantastic humor about one's brutish uncon-cern? In the spring of 1808, young Christian Schultz, Jr., a New York speculator in Western lands, heard at Natchez two drunken rivermen arguing over a Choctaw woman: "One said, 'I am a man; I am a horse; I am a team. I can whip any man *in all Kentucky*, by G-d.' The other replied, 'I am an alli-gator, half man, half horse; can whip any man on the *Missis-sippi*, by G-d.' The first one again, 'I am a man; have the best horse, best dog, best gun, and the handsomest wife in all Kentucky, by G-d.' The other, 'I am a Mississippi snapping turtle: have bear's claws, alligator's teeth, and the devil's tail; can whip *any man*, by G-d.' This was too much for the first, and at it they went like two bulls. . . ." Traveling in the South a few years later, James K. Paulding heard of a fight be-tween a bateauman and a wagoner that had begun with the latter flapping his hands against his hips and crowing like a cock, to which the former retorted by curving his neck and neighing like a horse. Of these wit-combats Timothy Flint wrote that he was occasionally "compelled to smile, at the readiness or whimsicality of the retorts," but that mainly he was "disgusted with the obscenity, abuse and blasphemy." The frontiersman, however, could not be bound by traditional niceties in his humor, because life itself was neither traditional nor nice. Tall talk that began in whimsicality and ended in blasphemy was necessary to him because it was a way of beat-ing the wilderness at its own game, of converting terror into *joie de vivre* and helplessness into an exhilarating sense of power. With gargantuan boasts, the frontiersman outfaced an overwhelming universe.

Nor was this all that tall talk accomplished. "The backwoodsman," in Melville's words, was "not without some fineness to his nature," a judgment that Mark Twain echoed in his opinion of the keelboatmen as "in the main, honest, trustworthy, faithful to promises and duty," which in turn lends substance to Timothy Flint's insight that for all his roughness, the frontiersman retained in guilty memory the knowledge of gentler ways. Anxiously aware of the difference between his own life and that of most civilized men, the frontiersman mimicked animality in order to deflect a temptation he felt within himself. By burlesquing savage emotion, he remained true to himself as a human being — however obscene his language became — because burlesque turned brutality into a theatrical performance, released the frontiersman into detachment from himself, and allowed him to laugh in the very teeth of his fears. Frontier boasting also served as a device for screwing up one's courage, and as such operated as a further stimulus to violence, but Flint's observation that most combats on the Mississippi and Ohio went no further than words points to the more usual function of tall talk. Men crowed like cocks in order to meet the challenge of the wilderness; they crowed a second time in order to transcend the coxcomb image imposed on them.

Still another factor in the frontiersman's drive toward self-caricature was the presence of increasing numbers of travelers from the Eastern seaboard and from Europe, who came to the West as to a zoo, with notebooks and pens poised to record the mating calls and other bizarre noises of the inhabitants. For these outsiders the frontiersman staged a ludicrously savage exhibition. In part, this was the immemorial shrewdness of the native, who has always made a good business out of giving the tourist what he wanted. By "taking in" the foreigners, the frontiersman gained in addition a splendid revenge on people who considered themselves smarter and more sophisticated than he, thus turning the humorous tables and making would-be laughers laughable. For the Clown, after all, was not impressed by the Gentleman — nor had he ever been: the North Carolinians whom William Byrd disdained must certainly for their parts have considered him an absurdly pretentious figure, with his London manners and aristocratic sneer; by deliberately playing up their own loutishness they may very well have mocked the dandy to his face. Mark Twain's "innocent act" has a long history on the American frontier.

Given the double purpose of Western tall talk — to assert one's toughness and at the same time to mock the whole idea of brutality — it is significant that the most successful humorists were apt to be men whose own physical prowess was unquestioned. Thus Jim Bowie was famous for designing a cruel and deadly knife, but he was also admired for his habit of issuing mock challenges to duel, and if they were accepted, of insisting on extravagant terms — that he and his opponent, so one of his burlesques ran, should fight face to face with knives, seated on a log, with their pants nailed to the wood. If Lincoln's physical strength as a boatman and a wrestler and a railsplitter was an important factor in his early rise to public recognition, so was the humor with which he deprecated belligerency. From New Salem to the White House, Lincoln's jokes ridiculed the chest-thumper. One day a pompous challenger came to him on behalf of a man whom Lincoln had insulted, and informed him that honor would have to be satisfied. "As the challenged party," the man punctiliously asked, "you will have the choice of weapons — what will your weapons be?" "How about cow-dung at five paces?" Lincoln replied. Although far below the level of Lincoln's best, this mediocre joke was considered uproariously funny by those who heard it and was repeated for years. More vividly than a better joke could do, the anecdote illustrates how desperately ready the West was to respond to the man of comic talent.

The Westerner also found pleasure in more fully elaborated stories. Told and retold around campfires and on rafts, interspersed in stump speeches on muster days and in business hagglings in crossroads stores, these comic tales furnished the West with its prime form of social entertainment — for what else, besides an occasional frolic or barbecue, was there? — and thus were instrumental in establishing a sense of community. In a lonely land where all men were strangers, funny stories operated as a form of social glue; by appreciating a story together, self-reliant and solitary men found the basis for other agreements. The stories the Westerners laughed at were sickeningly violent, as exaggeratedly cruel as the tall talk was blasphemous; at their comic heart, to paraphrase Hobbes, lay the apprehension of some fantastically deformed thing — a frontiersman's face, hideously mangled; a Negro or an Indian writhing in pain; the death-agony of a poor animal. Their characteristic hero was some king of the brutes, some champion brawler, crack-shot rifleman, nervy raftsman, prodigious drinker; he was generally ugly and proud of it; Mike Fink was often his name, although as Constance Rourke has pointed out, Mike Fink easily became Mike Finx, Mike Wing, Mike Finch — the name barely mattered. What counted was his savage heart; his habit of introducing himself to a man by beating him up, or of torturing his friends by way of a practical joke; his unlimited appetite for crackskull whisky; his defiant openness, in short, in doing all the things that the Westerner with one impulse wished he had the nerve to do himself, and with another feared that he was already guilty of. On one level, these stories were barely veiled projections of the frontiersman's private fantasies of power; Anthony M. Ludovici's gloomy contention that laughter is man's way of showing his fangs finds ample justification in the humor of the trans-Allegheny West. On another level, though, they worked in the way the boasting burlesques did to keep the Westerner faithful to his humanity. For Mike Fink's exploits were so outrageously violent that the frontiersman could not help but

30

dissociate himself from them. By laughing at Fink, rough men signified to one another what they were loath to say directly: that they were different from this terrible brute, and were relieved and glad about it. In making such communications possible, the humorist established himself at the very center of frontier society. When he spoke, all eyes turned toward him, all other voices fell silent. Is it any wonder that so many of the most gifted humorists in the West were either politicians or revivalist preachers — men who were leaders of the community?

In holding the attention of his audience, the Western humorist depended not only on his ability to mimic and to invent narrative, but on his command of the vernacular idiom of the frontier. "The new times, the new peoples, the new vista," Whitman would sing, "need a tongue according," and in the West traditional English had changed fast. "The average Philadelphian or Bostonian of 1790," Mencken has written, "had not the slightest difficulty making himself understood by a visiting Englishman. But the average Ohio boatman of 1810 or plainsman of 1815 was already speaking a dialect that the Englishman would have shrunk from as barbarous and unintelligible." Along with the new pronunciations, the twang and the drawl, came a marvelously flexible language, powerful, evocative, and fresh. Disdainful of old forms, contemptuous of rules, aggrandizing recklessly from the languages of the Indian, the Frenchman, and the Spaniard, in love with gorgeous and fantastic slang created on the spot, the Western frontiersman irrevocably altered the development of the American language. As a vehicle for the oral humor of the frontier, the new language was perfect; so intimately, in fact, were they bound up together that one can almost say that the humor was the vernacular and the vernacular was the humor: raciness, boldness, and a tendency toward the grotesque were the characteristics of both. For a humor that would outface the universe, what better medium than the exuberant metaphors of the Western idiom? For a language that deliberately flouted polite conventions, what more congenial humor than one which mocked the idea of savagery? The one reinforced the other. A frontiersman who superlatively combined a sense of humor with a mastery of the vernacular possessed a rare power, indeed.

One such frontiersman was Davy Crockett.

ii

Born in the mountains of East Tennessee in 1786, Crockett learned about frontier brutality early. At the age of twelve he was bound out to a cattle drover who tried to detain him by force beyond the completion of his contract. Crockett escaped by walking seven miles through the wilderness in a blinding snowstorm. He was next sent to school, but a brawl with another student, whose face Crockett scratched "all to a flitter jig," ended his attendance after four days. Fearful of the master's punishment, he never returned to the schoolhouse. When his father discovered his son's delinquency, he swore he would beat him; at which point Crockett, like Huck Finn fleeing the wrath of his Pap, ran away from home. He was thirteen years old. Already his personality seemed marked by an inviolable pride.

In 1811, he turned up in the Creek War as a soldier under Jackson. Tearfully, his wife had begged him not to go — "She said she was a stranger in the parts where we lived," he recalled in his autobiography, "had no connexions living near her, and that she and our little children would be left in a lonesome and unhappy situation if I went away." Crockett's grandparents, however, had been murdered by Creeks, and he had to have his revenge. "My dander was up, and nothing but war could bring it right again." After listening to his wife's piteous plea, he took off with his gun. In later years he claimed that killing Indians hadn't been any fun, but the account of the war in his autobiography is so cold-blooded as to suggest that the violence was not nearly so uncongenial to him as he wished people to believe:

> We pursued them until we got near the house, when we saw a squaw sitting in the door, and she placed her feet against the bow she had in her hand, and then took an arrow, and, raising her feet, she drew with all her might, and let fly at us, and she killed a man, whose name, I believe, was Moore. He was a lieutenant, and his death so enraged us all, that she was fired on, and had at least twenty balls blown through her. This was the first man I ever saw killed with a bow and arrow. We now shot them like dogs; and then set the house on fire, and burned it up with the forty-six warriors in it. I recollect seeing a boy who was shot down near the house. His arm and thigh was broken, and he was so near the burning house that the grease was stewing out of him. In this situation he was still trying to crawl along; but not a murmur escaped him, though he was only twelve years old. So sullen is the Indian, when his dander is up, that he had sooner die than make a noise, or ask for quarters.[1]

The war made Crockett a hero, and a few years afterwards he began to move toward a public career. He became a justice of the peace, although he later boasted he had never read a page of a lawbook in his life, and lieutenant colonel of his militia regiment; in 1821 he entered the Tennessee legislature; six years later he campaigned for Congress as a Jacksonian and was elected representative of a district in Western Tennessee.

In his rise to political prominence, Crockett relied heavily on frontier images of power. Besides being a renowned Indian killer, he was famous for his physical endurance and had a great reputation as a bear hunter. It was believed that in the course of only one season he had killed the huge total of one hundred and five bears; and he advertised all over Western Tennessee the claim that he had brought down "in and about" the biggest bear ever seen in North America. To the poor

[1] Although Crockett had the help of a ghost writer in putting the book together, his autobiography undoubtedly reflects his view of life.

Tennessee squatters, Davy Crockett was a mighty man. In the home state of Andrew Jackson, however, Crockett had no monopoly on heroism (his principal opponent in the election of 1827, for example, was the brave Colonel Alexander). But he had one great ability that most of his rivals lacked: he could make the voters laugh. Hard, cold-blooded, and ruthless though he was; a man whose pride was so touchy he could not bear, even as a boy, to be beaten; whose mounting fury at being politically ignored by the President he idolized burst finally into what one of his biographers has termed "a monomaniacal antipathy toward all matters Jacksonian"; who walked out on one wife to kill Indians and walked out on a second to kill Mexicans, because only war could set right his bloody thoughts; whose monumental self-absorption produced in him such an anguish at being badly beaten in the Congressional election of 1835 that he seems almost deliberately to have courted the fate that overtook him at the Alamo the following year; to whom every defeat, big or small, was an unforgivable insult; who, although not mad, even at the end, forcibly reminds us of Captain Ahab; Crockett nevertheless possessed — just as Ahab had his humanities — the gift of laughter.

The gift, it is true, deserted him soon enough; as early as 1831, a blackness began to descend upon his humor and finally swallowed it up. Frustrated by his inability to push through a land bill he had sponsored on behalf of the squatters, and hurt politically by his break with Jackson, he took out his bitterness in vile denunciations of his enemies, real and imagined. Victimized by a persecution complex (the Democratic newspapers and "every little pin-hook lawyer" were hunting him down, he said, "like a varment"), he came to rely for his humor on the spurious folksiness of Eastern ghost writers; the man who gasped out at the end of a terrifyingly bitter speech, "I can't stand it any longer — I won't," found it difficult, indeed, to tell even the jokes that other men had invented for him. Beaten in 1831, he came back strongly in the Congressional election of 1833, but the defeat of 1835 was the final blow. After that, nothing was left of Crockett save rage and self-pity:

> I am grattifyed that I have Spoken the truth to the people of my Distrect regardless of Consequences I would not be compeled to bow to the Idol for a Seat in Congress during life I have never knew what it was to Sacrafice my own Judgment to grattify any party and I have no doubt of the time being Close to hand when I will be rewarded for letting my tongue Speake what my hart thinks I have Suffered my Self to be politically Sacrafised to Save my Country from ruin & disgrace and if I am never a gain elected I will have the grattification to know that I have done my duty. . . .

But Davy Crockett, in the decade between 1821 and 1831, was a master of frontier humor; in these years he was able to give vent to the feelings generated by a hard and lonely life, and yet by humorously exaggerating them to explode their savagery in laughter; through ingenious expressions he relieved an inner pressure. By all accounts, he was a superlative mimic. Like Lincoln, he could caricature an opponent's manner with merciless accuracy. He was also an accomplished storyteller. His speech was slangy and fresh and natural, full of savory expressions and unprecedented images that breathed new life into familiar jokes. For a long time he was unaware of the political possibilities of his talent — or so, at least, he claimed — until one day during the campaign of 1821 he suddenly forgot, as he rose to make a speech, what he was going to say. Stalling for time, he told a joke: "They all roared out in a mighty laugh, and I told some other anecdotes, equally amusing to them, and believing I had them in a first-rate way, I quit and got down, thanking the people for their attention." It was a lesson he remembered. From then on, humor was his primary political weapon; as long as his light touch lasted, he was a tough man to beat. Listening to Crockett telling stories, the back-country people of Tennessee came to regard his words as expressive of everything they felt about life, translated into a comic hyperbole. He was immensely reassuring;

his humor seemed to make everything all right. When he joked, as he often did, about how stupid he was, he damped down both his own insecurity and theirs as well. (Crockett's bill to provide schools for the people of his district was the other side of his ignorance joke.) A story about how he frightened a city lawyer almost out of his wits inevitably pleased a populace that felt itself the victim of legal discrimination. Gratefully, the voters sent him to Congress three times. Even their final rejection of Crockett in 1835 was a tribute in some sense to his ruined talent, for in giving its votes to a certain Adam Huntsman the Western District elected another humorist.

iii

The delight that Tennessee squatters took in Crockett was far from a universal reaction. Many Southerners who liked to think of themselves as aristocrats considered the Congressman from the Tennessee canebrake something less than a wit. When he sprang to national fame at the beginning of the 1830s, they were appalled. Here was a backwoods oaf, who should have been kept firmly in his place, being feted at dinners, quoted in all the newspapers — and even mentioned as a Presidential candidate! William J. Grayson, a South Carolina politician and the future author of *The Hireling and the Slave* — one of the cleverest Southern counterattacks on *Uncle Tom's Cabin* — sat in Congress at the same time that Crockett did. His opinion of the Tennessee bear hunter was murderously disapproving: "A dull, heavy, almost stupid man, in appearance. I never heard him utter a word that savoured of wit or sense. To judge from his features one would have supposed such an event impossible. Yet by some freak or fortune he became the reputed author of innumerable queer sayings and stories, a man of infinite joke, an incarnation of frontier oddity, a sort of Western Joe Miller. . . . he was the last man in the house that a stranger would have pitched upon as a wit and humourist." That Grayson wrote this description some years after his own Congressional career had ended in crushing defeat at the hands of a Crockett-like campaigner undoubtedly accounts for much of his bitterness. Further contributing to Grayson's cup of gall was his knowledge of how it was that Crockett's fabulous rise had been accomplished. For the ironic truth was that the rube from Tennessee had been deliberately made famous by men who believed as firmly as Grayson did that a democracy should be led by an élite. In ascribing Crockett's rise to "freak or fortune," Grayson was simply hitting out at what seemed to him the monumental stupidity of certain conservatives in publicizing a man who stood for the triumph of ignorance and bad manners.

James K. Paulding, for instance, had chosen to write a play about Crockett. Although a New Yorker born and bred, Paulding was a writer who "understood the South" and admired its institutions — even the "peculiar" one. For the slavocracy stood in Paulding's mind for the grand simplicity and moral dignity of the "Old Republic." This was an important symbolism to Paulding, because, like Fenimore Cooper, he believed that modern America was being swiftly corrupted by what the former called "the struggles for place, the heartburnings and jealousies of contending families, and the influence of mere money." "All principles," Cooper wrote in *Home as Found,* "are being swallowed up in the absorbing desire for gain — national honor, permanent security, the ordinary rules of society, law, the constitution . . . are forgotten, or are perverted." Only the leadership of a republican aristocracy, Cooper and Paulding believed, could save the nation. For Cooper, this aristocracy was cast in the image of the New York State landed gentry; for Paulding, in the image of the plantation South. (Having grown up in rural poverty in the Hudson River Valley, Paulding was apparently unable to duplicate Cooper's easy identification of an ideal America with the region of his birth.) Thus in 1816, when he was permitted to read the manuscript of Byrd's *Dividing Line,* his response to

37

this "proof" of the aristocratic myth was as unquestioning as the jingoistic Edmund Ruffin's. When he examined the issue of the "peculiar institution" in *Slavery in the United States* (1836), Paulding's conclusion that it was better to be a slave in the leisurely atmosphere of a Southern plantation than to be trapped for life in one of New England's hellish factories unfalteringly repeated the slavocracy's propaganda line, as did his novel, *The Puritan and His Daughter* (1849), which found Virginia to be morally superior to New England. By any sort of loyalty test, Paulding was a true son of the Old South. How could such a man have ever brought himself to glorify the likes of Davy Crockett?

The explanation of Paulding's aberration begins with the difference between the Virginia he visited for the first time in 1816 and the Old Dominion of William Byrd. The master of Westover had been burdened with debts, but Virginia planters in the post-Revolutionary era were ruined by them. Two years before Paulding's visit, John Randolph — whom Paulding idolized as "the most extraordinary personage" he ever knew — had pronounced a requiem on the aristocratic way of life which he himself had fought so hard to keep alive: "I made a late visit to my birthplace. At the end of a journey through a wilderness. I found desolation & stillness as if of death — the fires of hospitality long since quenched — the hearth cold — & the parish church tumbling to pieces, not more from natural decay than sacrilegious violence. This is a faithful picture of this state from the falls of the great river to the seaboard." Unwilling to face the question whether a greedy concentration on one-crop agriculture had contributed to the ruin he encountered, Paulding preferred the more glamorous explanation offered by Randolph: that the indolence which William Byrd had feared in himself had become the *"maladie du pays* (of Virginia)" — that there was something soft and debilitating about Southern culture which caused gentlemen to throw away their lives and fortunes on drink, gambling and foolish investments. In order to keep his faith in the plantation aristocracy alive, Paulding had to find a newer, fresher South to replace corrupted and ruined Virginia. He found what he was looking for beyond the Alleghenies.

In his three-volume novel, *Westward Ho!* (1832), Paulding presently told the story of Colonel Cuthbert Dangerfield, the scion of an old Virginia family, whose dissipation and gambling finally force him to sell his estate. Removed to the "dark and bloody ground" of Kentucky, Cuthbert's character undergoes a sea-change, and amidst the "rural beauties" of the little settlement of Dangerfieldville, he and his family find lasting happiness. If their life is simpler, it is none the less aristocratic — "rustic opulence" are Paulding's words for it. Cuthbert is still a colonel; his lady still has slaves to do her bidding; their parties are charming as of yore. Paulding's fictional Kentucky is Virginia all over again, only healthier: Athens plus Sparta.

By the eagerness with which Paulding seized on the idea that Kentucky could become a newer and better Old Dominion, he revealed that he had managed to resolve the frontier problem which he himself had posed some years before — the problem of bateaumen who crowed like cocks and wagoners who neighed like horses. Otherwise, how could Paulding have accepted the proposition that the West could restore the character and fortune of a dissipated Cuthbert Dangerfield? If the wilderness was full of spectral evils which degraded self-reliant pioneers into savages, then ladies and gentlemen could hardly be expected to thrive there. Patently, the moral nature of the frontiersman held the key to Paulding's entire vision of the trans-Allegheny West as the birthplace of a new South. It was, therefore, not any disloyalty to the planter aristocracy that caused Paulding, a year or so before he published *Westward Ho!* to confront the problem of frontier wildness in a play about Davy Crockett.

Nimrod Wildfire, the protagonist of *The Lion of the West*, is a Kentucky boatman, not a Tennessee bear hunter; nevertheless, the references in the play to an impending Congressional election, as well as the fact that Wildfire is a colonel, betray his true identity. (In a letter to Crockett, Paulding swore that the Congressman was definitely not the prototype of his hero, but he did so only to emphasize that he was. Benjamin Perley Poore recalled that, when the play opened in Washington, Crockett was ushered to a front seat while the audience cheered. The first time Wildfire — played by the actor-producer, James Hackett — appeared on the stage, he bowed to the paying guests and then to Crockett; at which point Crockett rose and bowed to Hackett.) The dramatic characterization is fond — and immensely patronizing. (It is significant that although Crockett was vainglorious enough to lend himself to the promotion of *The Lion of the West,* the play affronted Western audiences and was distinctly unpopular beyond the Alleghenies.) Paulding's Crockett is both ludicrous and harmless. If he is ignorant, his heart is nevertheless in the right place; if he rants and raves, it is not because he must somehow relieve a savage, inner pressure, but merely because the big ape doesn't know any better. While his uncouth speech thoroughly appalls the foolish British lady, Mrs. Wollope (in honor of Frances Trollope, the author of *Domestic Manners of the Americans*),[2] he in fact speaks in a synthetic vernacular that bears little relation to the anarchically powerful and rule-disdaining idiom of the Western frontiersman. And for all his backwoodsy rodomontade, Wildfire never lays a paw on anyone. His threats may scare the gullible and unmask foreign hypocrites, but Wildfire is not actually wild at all; he is, rather, a natural gentleman, whose opinions on Negro slaves, the barbarous antics of religious revivalists, and the myopia of British travelers in America instinctively coincide with those of all right-thinking people. All that this delightfully colorful character needs is a little learning and he will become perfectly well-behaved. As Wildfire's final speech

[2] The characterization was Paulding's, but the lady was probably named by Hackett, inasmuch as Mrs. Trollope's book was published after the play had become a part of Hackett's repertory.

makes clear, the lion is almost pathetically eager to become a lamb: "Look here, ladies and gentlemen, strangers, I know I'm a pretty hard sample of a white man, but I don't want to skeer nobody; and as you see I'm in want of a little more genteel education, I hope I may be indulged occasionally in 'a trip to New York.'" So much for the alleged brutishness of the Western frontiersman: the "dark and bloody ground" of Kentucky was going to be safe for Dangerfields after all.

Nicholas Biddle, president of the Second Bank of the United States, also had his reasons for publicizing the squatters' Congressman. When Crockett broke with Jackson, Biddle and his anti-Jackson allies saw their chance to match the political appeal of Old Hickory with a Western hero of their own. The wheels of Whig propaganda mills were caused to be turned, and a flood of newspaper stories and a series of books came out, one a biography of Crockett, the others purportedly by him. In appropriating Crockett as a mouthpiece for their political program, the Whigs also remade him in their own image, with the result that a wild man became the exemplary hero of a conservative mythology, whose model behavior the Whigs prayerfully hoped a rank-rabble democracy would emulate. Even more than Paulding had done, the Whig propagandists portrayed their half-horse, half-alligator hero as thoroughly housebroken. (When various newspapers printed a story that Crockett on his first visit to the White House had been guilty of a gross breach of manners, two of his Whig friends sent letters to the papers testifying to his infallibly polite behavior.) The backwoods darling of the Whigs was simply another version of pastoral — a homebody, a family man, a believer in Constitutional government, Daniel Webster, and the soundness of central banking. He was amazingly free of the frontiersman's faults that the Whig leaders feared in Andrew Jackson — vindictiveness, arrogance, and self-will were alien to his personality. Yet along with his reassuringly safe, pastoral qualities he somehow represented a reasonable facsimile of those dynamic qualities which, as John William

41

Ward has demonstrated, made Andrew Jackson such a compelling figure to his age: the ability to rise from poverty and obscurity to a high station in society; the military power which made it possible for America to defeat Europe, and the vigor of the West which guaranteed the future glory of American civilization. In the Whig image, Crockett was less than a wild man, but more than a farmer: he was, in some miraculous way, both Jackson and the anti-Jackson. Crockett's own life indicated that there were certain tensions between frontier vigor and good manners, between being an Indian-killer and a family man, but as the Whigs projected him in the books they fabricated in his name, such tensions are nowhere in evidence. In what Arthur M. Schlesinger, Jr., has called the "counter-reformation" of 1840, the Whigs responded to the Jacksonian appeal by dressing up General Harrison in a coonskin cap and supplying him with a log cabin birthplace; the trial run for that shrewd maneuver, however, had been made in reverse six or seven years before, when Biddle and his friends conjured up a bear hunter whose ugliness was only skin deep.

For sufficient reasons, then, both Paulding and the Whig propagandists chose to publicize the words of the bear hunter from Tennessee. However, it was not the hard, cold, killer's voice of Crockett's autobiography that they allowed to be heard, but rather the sham voice of a ventriloquist's dummy. Underneath the pseudo-vernacular of this kept Clown were the accents of a Gentleman.

But in making the Western genie do their bidding, Paulding and the Whigs also released him from the bottle — much to the distress of William J. Grayson, among others. Both *The Lion of the West*, which Hackett kept in his repertory for twenty years, and the publicity stunts of Biddle's strategists gave an enormous impetus to Crockett's reputation. Throughout the West, storytellers began to tell tales about fabulously heroic hunters, raftsmen, rail-splitters and wrestlers, all named Davy Crockett. George Washington Dixon included some

Crockett verses in his "Zip Coon" minstrel, as did Thomas D. Rice when he sang "Jim Crow." A *Davy Crockett's Almanack* was published in 1835 by a Nashville firm, instantly establishing a fad; in the years following his death at the Alamo, Crockett almanacs were issued in New York, Boston, Philadelphia and Baltimore. If some of these publications clung to imitations of Nimrod Wildfire, the hero of the more impolite almanacs was a far cry from the quaint rustic conjured up by the author of *The Lion of the West*. Speaking in a grotesquely vivid vernacular, this man flung brutal boasts in the face of a brutal world:

He grit his teeth at me, and poked out his tongue about six inches. With that I told him I was a pickaxe and would dig him out of his stumps. He said he was a flint image cut out of a big rock. I told him my gizzard was a wasp's nest and I breathed rifle balls. He said he could double up a streak o' lightning and thrash me with one eend of it.

Then I was pesky oneasy and spit at him so hard that if he hadn't dodged it, he'd have had his nose knocked flat. He came to me feet foremost, and I caught the great toe in my mouth, but the nail came off very lucky for him, and he got his toe back again. But while he was bringing his foot to the ground, I caught the slack of his breeches in my teeth and lifted him up in the air, swinging like a scale beam, as if he didn't know which eend it was best to light on. But his trousers tore through in a minnit, and he come down sprawling.

He jumped up speechless, and looked around as amazed as if he war just born into the world. He seed I war jist ready to lay my paw on him again, and his skin crawled. He turned as pale as a scalded nigger, and told the people that was looking on how they better interfere as he wus afraid he should be the death of me, if we come to the scratch agin. I told the lying sarpint to own he war chawed up, or I would make fiddle-strings of his tripe. So he squat low and felt mean. He sneaked off like an Injun in a clearing.

At times the sheer energy of his language touched his humor with lyric beauty. The bear who "come breaching from the tree like a steamboat," or the rattlesnake that shook its rattles "to have some music to go to war with," were as lovely as they were terrible. And at the very top of his bent he displayed a comic eloquence that was worthy of Melville's imagination:

> Well, arter I had walked about twenty miles up the peak o' Daybreak Hill I soon discovered what war the matter. The airth had actually friz fast on her axes, and couldn't turn round; the sun had got jammed between two cakes o' ice under the wheels, an' thar he had been shinin' an' workin' to get loose till he friz fast in his cold sweat. C-r-e-a-t-i-o-n! thought I, this ar the toughest sort of suspension, an' it mustn't be endured. Somethin' must be done, or human creation is done for. It war then so anteluvian an' premature cold that my upper and lower teeth an' tongue war all collapsed together as tight as a friz oyster; but I took a fresh twenty-pound bear off my back that I'd picked up on my road, and beat the animal agin the ice till the hot ile began to walk out on him at all sides. I then took an' held him over the airth's axes an' squeezed him till I'd thawed 'em loose, poured about a ton on't over the sun's face, give the airth's cogwheel one kick backward till I got the sun loose — whistled "Push along, keep movin'!" an' in about fifteen seconds the airth gave a grunt, an' began movin'. The sun walked up beautiful, salutin' me with sich a wind o' gratitude that it made me sneeze. I lit my pipe by the blaze o' his top-knot, shouldered my bear, an' walked home, introducin' people to the fresh daylight with a piece of sunrise in my pocket.

Superbly in command of an authentic American idiom, an unknown writer — a semiprofessional hack, in all likelihood, sublimely unconcerned with the gentilities of English prose — here summoned up the vision of Davy Crockett as a comic Captain Ahab, who delighted in cosmic challenges.

What had happened was that the factitious literature of Paulding and the Whigs had somehow touched a vital nerve, calling forth a surprising response. The toothless wild man of a conservative mythology had, as it turned out, an *alter ego* — a raffish, reckless fellow, fully determined to be more than a

44

brute, but only in his own wild way and on his own terms. The barbaric yawp of the Crockett almanacs was the voice of a new America, welling up into the national literature from below.

CHAPTER III

The Politics of a Literary Movement

> This Mob . . . is said to have been one of the most odious of all men that ever encumbered the earth. He was a giant in stature — insolent, rapacious, filthy; had the gall of a bullock with the heart of a hyena and the brains of a peacock.
>
> — POE

THE BEAUTIES of Westover had never reconciled William Byrd to his absence from the London swim, but to the Tidewater planters who came of age in the years after Byrd's death life in Virginia seemed very sweet and very certain. While they still felt something of Byrd's nostalgia for England (where many of them had been educated), these younger men had somehow grown accustomed to their colonial fate. Memories of the faraway metropolis were less real to them than the solid gratifications of provincialdom. In Virginia, their social prestige was unquestioned; they found local problems interesting, and their aristocratic authority to decide them highly satisfying; regarding themselves as loyal Englishmen, they had become Virginians almost without realizing it. During the Revolution, the planter class in Virginia produced far fewer Tories than did the upper classes in the Northern colonies. For their serene mastery of the Old Dominion gave the planters a greater confidence in the Colonies' capacity for independence, and in their ability to dominate the new nation, than was felt by many of the merchants and landowners of New York and New England.

One of the most revealing registrations of the Virginia aristocracy's confident state of mind in the middle of the eighteenth century is Robert Munford's comedy, *The Candidates; or, The Humours of a Virginia Election.* Born in 1730 or thereabouts (the date is uncertain), a planter, a slaveowner, and a prominent figure in Virginia politics, Munford was a dilettante author who apparently did not care whether or not his plays were produced. As William Byrd had done, Munford sought through his writings to serve a private conception of himself as an English gentleman, a type with which he was personally familiar from his schoolboy days. Loving England as he did, he found the growing estrangement between the Colonies and the mother country deeply distressing, and he remained loyal to the Crown until the last possible moment. (As late as April 20, 1775, he could still write to his old military commander, Colonel William Byrd III — the son of the *Dividing Line* author — of his determination to bring the people of his home county "to a due Sense of obligations both of Duty and allegiance that bind them to their Sovereign and to the preservation of civil order," unaware that the events of the day before at Concord had made his words obsolete before they were ever written.) When, however, the moment for decision came, he found that Virginia meant more to him than England, and Munford chose for the Revolution. The decision was undoubtedly painful, and may even have surprised him, although *The Candidates*, written in 1770, had long since foreshadowed which way the cat would jump.

The play has two heroes — Wou'dbe, who is seeking re-election to the House of Burgesses, and Worthy, who chooses not to run until the last minute. Both men are lofty aristocrats, cultivated, well-educated, fully aware of their social and intellectual superiority to the common run. They are, indeed, very much like the Gentleman who is the narrator of the *Dividing Line* — with one significant difference. Byrd had represented

himself as a traveler in a far country, as an aloof and disaffili-
ated dandy who had only an anthropological interest in the
bizarre people he encountered in the course of his wilderness
journey. For all their loftiness, Worthy and Wou'dbe are
deeply involved in the American scene. The Olympian Worthy
seems not to care about being elected — his prestige is already
so considerable that it needs no further enhancement — while
Wou'dbe campaigns on the platform that gentlemen in office
obviously cannot be bound by the will of the people; nevertheless, their victory at the polls is the triumphant climax of the
play. One feels, in *The Candidates*, a sense of community, of
ties that bind men together, no matter what their social station.
If the play patronizes "the people," the humor is fundamentally sympathetic; as opposed to the disdainful point of view
maintained in the *Dividing Line*, there is a saving affection in
Munford's caricatures. The voters may be naïve enough to ap-
plaud demagogues, but in the end their basic good sense is
affirmed: they re-elect their aristocratic representatives by ac-
clamation.

More than anything else, it is the language of Munford's
comedy that reveals why the planter aristocrats found life in
Virginia so attractive. "Mimesis" is the name that Toynbee has
given to the sharing of ideals between the privileged and lower
classes of a society, and in *The Candidates* the fact of social
mimesis is reflected in mimetic conversations. The diction of
the two heroes is polite and measured; the bluster of the opposition candidates, although meant to be ridiculous, has a
gentlemanly elegance, none the less; even the expression of
the "low" characters is well-bred (Ralpho, for instance, the
first stage Negro in American literature, does not speak out of
his own nature, but in the voice of a sensible, right-thinking
Englishman, given to occasional malapropisms). Munford may
simply have been aping a convention of the London stage in
making his characters speak alike, yet in eighteenth-century
Virginia the convention mirrored reality. In a harmony of
speaking styles — each one sufficiently different to suggest a

48

particular gradation in a fixed social hierarchy, but all alike in orderly spirit — can be heard the confidence of the great planters that an insurgent democracy would never turn against their leadership. The people were to be trusted because they in turn infallibly placed their trust in gentlemen. *The Candidates* sets forth a world that seemed as stable and orderly and well-regulated as Newton's laws of the universe.

The tone of *The Patriots* — Munford's second play — is much less assured. Written during the turmoil of the Revolution, the comedy depicts a society in upheaval: normal political controls have lapsed and Committees of Safety have taken over. The time would come in the United States when conservatives would remain silent in the face of the zeal of populist witchhunters; although Munford was blind to the necessary role played by the Committees in handing over power to the Revolutionists, his second play deftly satirizes the stupidities of superpatriotism.

In an atmosphere charged with suspicion, a number of Committees had made political scapegoats out of the Scotch merchants of Virginia, who as a "foreign" minority were vulnerable to the charge of disloyalty, even when it came from men who were in debt to the merchants and were patently trying to destroy their creditors. At the beginning of the second act of *The Patriots*, three Scotsmen — M'Flint, M'Squeeze and M'Gripe — are denounced as enemies of the Revolution. When M'Flint asks what they have done, he receives from Colonel Strut, a vainglorious braggart, the classic answer of guilt-by-association. "The nature of their offence, gentlemen, is, that they are Scotchmen; every Scotchman being an enemy, and these men being Scotchmen, they come under the ordinance which directs an oath to be tendered to all those against whom there is just cause to suspect they are enemies." M'Gripe's demand for proof of his disloyalty merely prompts the loudmouthed Brazen to exclaim, "Proof, sir! we have proof enough. We suspect any Scotchman: suspicion is proof, sir." Feeling their power, the witchhunters move on from the merchants to far bigger game. Trueman and Meanwell, who are to *The Patriots* what Worthy and Wou'dbe are to *The Candidates,* also fall under suspicion of Toryism. It is at this point that the agitation of the playwright becomes unmistakably apparent. Such an imputation against the grand aristocrats of Munford's earlier play would have been inconceivable, nor would Brazen have had the nerve to address his sneering remark, "I hate your high flown speeches, Mr. Trueman," to the august Worthy. Trueman, for his part, displays a resentful animus, in exclaiming "I hate these little democracies," that is quite out of keeping with the Munford hero's usual pose of unruffled superiority.

The Patriots is far more amusing than *The Candidates*. Its humor, in fact, is superior to that of any other eighteenth-century American play, including Royall Tyler's *The Contrast* (1787), generally thought of as the first American comedy of any consequence. The vividness of the play can be explained by the intensity of Munford's concern with its subject. Time and again, Munford's uneasy feeling that the energies unleashed by the Revolution might bring down the entire social order comes flickering up through the surface assurances of his prose, charging his dialogues with extraordinary tension. "What a pity it is," gibes Meanwell, "that all heads are not capable of receiving the benign influence of the principles of liberty." Read one way, his words seem to patronize an ever-humble, ever-obedient electorate; read another, they envisage the doom of an aristocratic republic at the hands of a mindless mob.

ii

For almost half a century following Munford's death in 1784, nothing of consequence was added to the literature of the Southwestern tradition. If one would read a noteworthy humorist of this period, one must turn away from imaginative writing to the letters and speeches of John Randolph, the "wittiest man of his age." For a generation and more, Randolph defended his vision of the "Old Republic" with brilliantly sarcastic characterizations of the men who, he felt, were wrecking it. Thomas Jefferson was "that prince of projectors, St. Thomas of Cantingbury." John Quincy Adams and Henry Clay were "Blifil and Black George — the Puritan and the blackleg." The lawyer and merchant Edward Livingston was "a man of splendid abilities, but utterly corrupt. Like rotten mackerel by moonlight, he shines and stinks." Fighting with his back to the wall, lashing out in all directions, Randolph was a man whose enemies (this was his proudest boast) were legion. If he had friends, they were apt to be amongst the Jacksonians — men like Thomas Hart Benton, for instance — who respected Randolph's intransigent republicanism. In the eyes of conservative Southerners of the next generation, however, Randolph's states' rights philosophy made him the martyred hero of a sacred cause. Under attack in a hostile House of Representatives, this wealthy, brilliant man, known to be sexually impotent and rumored to be insane, arose from his seat and sneered at his enemies:

> "The little dogs and all,
> Tray, Blanch and Sweetheart,
> See, they bark at me!"

In the South, in days to come, that moment would be recalled and cherished.

Appropriately enough, it was in or around the year that Randolph died, 1833, that the long drought in humorous writing in the South came to an end, almost as if his death had been required to produce the literary movement that would so often invoke his name. All at once, almost in chorus, men all over the South — but most particularly in the region between the Alleghenies and the Mississippi, which was then called the Southwest — began to write comic sketches. It was a movement without a manifesto or a capital city; which had neither

51

a recognized elder statesman nor an official journal. Yet the Southwestern humorists of the antebellum period were more cohesive in spirit, and more readily definable as a group, than the Transcendentalists, say, who were their contemporaries, and they were destined to influence later American writing in precisely definable ways. Scattered and out of touch with one another as they were, the Southwestern humorists were nevertheless bound together by all the things that counted: by a devotion to the same literary gods; by a common set of literary principles; and by the similarity of their social views. These writers were in fact so much alike that it is even possible to construct a biographical archetype that bears a fair resemblance to the lives of all of them. The ideal Southwestern humorist was a professional man — a lawyer or a newspaperman, usually, although sometimes a doctor or an actor. He was actively interested in politics, either as a party propagandist or as a candidate for office. He was well educated, relatively speaking, and well traveled, although he knew America better than Europe. He had a sense of humor, naturally enough, and in a surprising number of cases a notoriously bad temper. Wherever he had been born, and a few were of Northern origin, the ideal humorist was a Southern patriot — and this was important. Above all, he was a conservative, identified either with the aristocratic faction in state politics, or with the banker-oriented Whig party in national politics, or with both. To call the roll of the best-known Southwestern humorists in the twenty-year period from 1833 to 1853 — Longstreet, Thompson, Kennedy, Noland, Pike, Cobb, Thorpe, Baldwin, Hooper — is to call in vain for a supporter of Andrew Jackson. No other fact about these writers is quite so significant.

In the 1820s, the men who would become humorists a decade later had fervently believed in Jackson. They yearned, as did most Southerners, for the end of the Adams administration and the accession of Jackson to the Presidency. The squire of the Hermitage would surely furnish the South a measure of relief from the unfavorably high tariff of 1828. The high tariff legislation of 1832 was thus a considerable shock; when South Carolina, under Calhoun's direction, declared the bill null and void, it was even more shocking to see Jackson push a bill through Congress empowering him to force compliance. Out of such shocks came, among other things, a new form of American literature. For it is not merely coincidental that the outpouring of Southwestern humor after 1830 began at the very moment that the Nullification crisis was reaching fever pitch, or that the most influential of all the humorists of the antebellum South, Augustus Baldwin Longstreet, idolized John C. Calhoun and was a diehard Nullifier. The fantastically bitter dispute over the tariff, beginning with Calhoun's famous Exposition of strict constructionist theories in 1828 and culminating with the Force Bill five years later, had momentous literary consequences because it inaugurated — even in those states where sympathy for South Carolina's extremism was not strong — the South's consciousness of itself as a collective entity, as a region that was apart and different from the rest of the nation. William Byrd had thought of himself as an English gentleman; Randolph had proclaimed that "When I speak of my country I mean the Commonwealth of Virginia," a sentiment in which Robert Munford would have concurred. But the flowering of Southwestern humor in the 1830s was the product of a new awareness. The humorous customs of local people in Georgia and Arkansas, and in Tennessee and Alabama and Mississippi, were to be recorded in literature because they were *Southern* customs, aspects of the life of a separate civilization, and therefore highly significant.

When to the tariff fight one adds the fact that the early 1830s saw the beginnings of a new and energetic abolitionist movement in the North, as well as a dramatic upturn in profits from slave-breeding and cotton culture, the defensive self-consciousness that inspired Southwestern humor becomes even more understandable. Many Southern writers turned, of course, to the "plantation novel" in order to justify the slavocracy, as if by pointing with pride to Greek Revival houses they hoped to

53

make the world forget Uncle Tom's unspeakable cabin. Looting the novels of Walter Scott for a feudalistic symbolism, the plantation novelists amplified and extended the gentlemanly myth of Hugh Jones and William Byrd to gigantic proportions. Little more than a hundred years after Jones had implied that Williamsburg was another London, the plantation novelists suggested that the only proper comparison to the civilization of the cotton kingdom was the courtly life of the medieval lords. Launcelot and Guinevere, Ivanhoe and Rowena, now loomed in the Southern mind as the heroes of the Golden Age had in Don Quixote's. The humorists were equally fascinated by Scott — for they, too, were myth-makers. (Indeed, at least one Southern author, John Pendleton Kennedy, wrote both novels *and* comic stories in order to promote the Southern myth.) What the humorists learned from Scott was, first of all, the uses of history. Beginning with Longstreet, who subtitled a collection of sketches *Characters, Incidents, &c., in the First Half Century of the Republic,* the humorists attempted to foster a sense of the Southern past for the same reason that Scott had recorded Scotland's past: it was a means of asserting a national identity. Scott further taught them that "low" characters could serve their mythology as readily as could chivalrous heroes. Scott had turned to Scotch peasants and servants for his comic materials because the special flavor and peculiarity of, say, Andrew Fairservice, the gardener in *Rob Roy*, or of Jenny Dennison, Miss Bellenden's maid in *Old Mortality*, helped to define Scotland's distinctiveness; by being humorously "low," such characters also made Scott's aristocrats seem more grand by contrast. The Southwestern writers exploited the antic life of the poor white with analogous ends in view. Thanks in considerable part to the example of Scott, humor as well as romance was enlisted in the Southern cause.

As the symbol of an encroaching national power, then, Andrew Jackson came to be hated and feared by the new generation of humorists. There were other reasons, however, why Old Hickory loomed like a demon in their minds, reasons which perhaps go even further toward accounting for the startling exfoliation of Southwestern humor that began while Jackson was in the White House.

Describing, in *The Valley of Shenandoah* (1824), what life in Virginia had been like in the 1790s, the Virginia aristocrat George Tucker depicted a group of common roughnecks blocking the roads and insolently upsetting every carriage that attempts to pass. To conservative Southerners of the middle 1820s, this was not simply an isolated incident in the remote past; it was also the terrible image of what might happen to them at any moment, if they were not careful. Behind their insecurity lay certain hard facts. From the day that Jefferson had entered the White House in 1800, popular agitation had begun to build up in the Southern states for constitutional reforms to abolish religious and property qualifications for voting and holding office; to base representation on population rather than on county units; to widen popular control, in sum, over all the instruments of government. These changes could be accomplished, the reformers felt, only by means of specially summoned state conventions. For thirty years, efforts were made to call such conventions into being; and for thirty years, the conservative ruling class in the several states managed to hold the reformers at bay. Then, quite suddenly, the reformers could no longer be denied. In 1829, a constitutional convention was called in Virginia; in 1833, a convention met in Georgia, and another in 1839; there was a convention in North Carolina in 1835, and a "Revolution of 1836" in Maryland. The democratic movement that swept Andrew Jackson into the White House in 1828 also penetrated the local defenses of the old order from Tidewater Virginia to the Gulf of Mexico. By 1860, every Southern state except South Carolina would have a democratic constitution.

The rise of Jacksonian democracy transformed Southern politics. The planter-politician who in Munford's time had condescended to the electorate now had to scramble for votes, inasmuch as in most contests the margin between victory and defeat was slim. According to one student of the subject, the vote of the Southern states was very nearly equally divided between the Whig and Democratic parties in every Presidential election from 1836 to 1852; according to another, Southern Democrats won an aggregate total of 234 seats in the five Congressional elections between 1832 and 1842, as opposed to 263 for their opponents, a difference of less than thirty seats in a ten-year period. Not until the slavery controversy reached the height of its fury in the 1850s did the South become anything like the monolithic society of legend.

In the economic sphere, life became equally competitive. Jackson's destruction of the Bank inspired other struggles against corporate privilege, until the "race for the top" had been blown wide open. Especially in the Southwest, a new breed of men emerged. Small-time stock speculators; clerks knowledgeable in the mysteries of paper money and land prices; courthouse loungers with glib tongues and a smattering of law: they seemed to come out of nowhere, these men, even as Faulkner's Snopes clan would do after the Civil War. Bold, imaginative, oftentimes ruthless, sometimes unscrupulous, they were more at home in the flush-times atmosphere of Alabama or Mississippi than many a well-born *émigré* from South Carolina or Virginia, while even the cleverest and toughest *nouveau* banker or planter dared not grow soft or careless, lest he find himself no longer *riche*. The historian Richard Hildreth noted in 1836 that the poor whites in the South "are at once feared and hated by the select aristocracy of the rich planters," and these emotions were generated to a great degree by the terrific emotional cost of remaining king of the mountain in a wide-open economy devoid of rules or even precedents. Joseph G. Baldwin, one of the most accomplished of the Southwestern humorists, has left a memoir of the era which nicely captures the anxiety felt by many sons of the planter class that they simply could not compete in business with men who did not play the game the gentlemanly way. Baldwin is speaking of Mississippi and Alabama in the mid-1830s:

Superior to many of the settlers in elegance of manners and general intelligence, it was the weakness of the Virginian to imagine he was superior too in the essential art of being able to hold his hand and make his way in a new country, and especially *such* a country, and at *such* a time. What a mistake that was! . . . . All the habits of his life, his taste, his associations, his education — everything — the trustingness of his disposition — his want of business qualifications — his sanguine temper — all that was Virginian in him, made him the prey, if not of imposture, at least of unfortunate speculations. . . . If he made a bad bargain, how could he expect to get rid of it? *He* knew nothing of the elaborate machinery of ingenious chicane, — such as feigning bankruptcy — fraudulent conveyances — making over to his wife — running property — and had never heard of such tricks of trade as sending out coffins to the graveyard, with negroes inside, carried off by sudden spells of imaginary disease, to be "resurrected," in due time, grinning, on the banks of the Brazos.

To hold on to a world that seemed in danger of slipping from their grasp, Southern conservatives flocked into the newly-formed Whig party. Generally speaking, the merchants and bankers of the towns became Whigs, as did the majority of the planter class.[1] Their allies among the professional groups, particularly the lawyers and newspaper editors who depended for their livelihood on the fees and good will of the merchants and planters, also joined the party. Inasmuch as the typical Southwestern humorist was a professional man, it is not surprising that the overwhelming percentage of those about whom political data exist were Whigs. As for the minority who were not, they might be called Whigs *manqués:* anti-Jacksonians who were too deeply committed to low tariffs and states' rights to accept the nationalist, high tariff policies fastened into

[1] Except in South Carolina, where the upper classes followed John C. Calhoun toward the Whig party and then away again, when personal ambition prompted him to become a Democrat once more. Having withstood the threat of constitutional reform, South Carolina conservatives did not regard the Democratic party in the same hostile light as did their counterparts elsewhere in the South.

the Whig platform by the Northern wing of the party. The Whiggery of the humorists is worth insisting on, for it tells us much about their entire cast of mind, including their comic imagination. In a preeminently political era, political allegiance was as important a key to American writing as religious belief once had been. About no group of American writers in the age of Jackson is this generalization more true than it is about the Southwestern humorists.

To the Whig mind, the quality of violence inherent in Jacksonianism was what made the movement so disturbing. The quality could be sensed at once in Democratic rhetoric. Taking up arms against Nicholas Biddle, the Democrats denounced his Bank as a "Monster," spewed out upon it the same sky-vaunting threats and curses, the same hyperbolic humor, that had appalled a generation of well-bred visitors to the trans-Allegheny West. The Democratic program was as violent in its effect as the oratory which put it across; wherever the Democrats touched American life, they galvanized the entire nation. There was a boldness about Democratic ideas, a pragmatic willingness to take risks, to commit the nation to untrod paths, that the Whigs found frightening. ("They desire," cried the *American Whig Review,* "a freedom larger than the Constitution.") Hoping to avoid a repetition of the Panic of 1837, Jacksonians in the Southwest audaciously called for the abolition of *all* bank charters, not merely Biddle's. In the 1840s, the Democrats took up the daring theme of an American imperium that would extend southward into Mexico and as far west as the Pacific, while Whig orators timorously invoked the specter of Caesarism and the doom of all empires. The schemes of the Democrats, whatever their shortcomings, had a reckless grandeur; Whig ideas, by contrast, were prudential and cautious.

They might even be said to have been nonexistent. Henry Adams has remarked that "Of all the parties that have existed in the United States, the famous Whig party was the most feeble in ideas." To fight against economic and social mobility by means of ideas was, after all, excruciatingly difficult for a party composed largely of self-made men who agreed with Webster that "intelligence and industry ask only for fair play and an open field." Hamstrung intellectually, the Whigs counted on a series of emotional appeals to overcome the rampant Democracy. In an America made anxious, as Tocqueville observed, by the ceaseless competition of equals, the Whigs celebrated harmony and unity; denying reality, they offered the nation psychological relief in the genial vision of America as one big, happy family. In the North, the Whigs answered the class conflict analysis of a Seth Luther or an Orestes Brownson by preaching an identity of interest between merchant and mechanic (did not the Lowell mills, as Edward Everett suggested, have all the comforts of home?). In the South, the Whigs depicted gentle masters, happy yeomen, and grinning darkies living together in an atmosphere of domestic bliss. The log cabin and the white-pillared mansion were in the Whig iconology the two faces of the same charismatic image, for if the former signified democratic aspiration and the latter aristocratic pretension, both stood for the American Past, when conflicts of interest had been unknown, and both were Homes.[2] Amidst the gathering storm of the slavery controversy,

[2] For an effusion typical of both Northern and Southern Whigs on the subject of the Home, see Daniel Webster's speech at Saratoga, New York, on August 19, 1840: "Gentlemen, it did not happen to me to be born in a log cabin; but my elder brothers and sisters were born in a log cabin, raised amid the snowdrifts of New Hampshire, at a period so early that, when the smoke first rose from its rude chimney, and curled over the frozen hills, there was no similar evidence of a white man's habitation between it and the settlements on the rivers of Canada. Its remains still exist. I make to it an annual visit. I carry my children to it, to teach them the hardships endured by the generations which have gone before them. I love to dwell on the tender recollections, the kindred ties, the early affections, and the touching narratives and incidents, which mingle with all I know of this primitive family abode. I weep. . . ." So filled were Webster's "noble explosions of sound," as Emerson called his speeches, with invocations of Home and Mother and Late Lamented Loved Ones that Mark Twain, who as the son of a Whig knew the sentimentalism of the movement from the inside, could conclude his account of the Examination Evening in *Tom Sawyer*, with its compositions on "Is this, then, Life?" and "Melancholy" and "Heart

the Whigs insisted that the Union itself was a family; differences of opinion existed, of course, but as long as both North and South could go on loving the Flag and the Constitution, as long as both could look to Mount Vernon, which that fine Whig lady, Sarah Josepha Hale — author of *The Good Housekeeper,* sponsor of Thanksgiving Day, and editor of *Godey's Lady's Book* — was busily trying to have declared a national shrine, there was no sectional split that could not be healed. As for the manifold problems engendered by the headlong development of the country, the Jacksonians might agitate if they wished for political and economic reforms; the Whigs preferred to get behind the Infant School movement, do charity work, and above all, campaign for temperance. Because, to the Whig mind, the temperance movement was not simply a battle against alcoholism; it was a character ideal and a way of life. If temperance workers took George Washington as their patron saint — if somehow the Constitution crept into their discussions of juvenile drinking — if a Whig lawyer (it was Abraham Lincoln) could suddenly broaden the scope of a speech to the temperance society of Springfield, Illinois, and imagine a "Happy day, when, all appetites controlled, all passions subdued, all matters subjected, *mind,* all conquering *mind,* shall live and move the monarch of the world. Glorious consummation! Hail, fall of Fury: Reign of Reason, all hail!" — the reason was that the temperance campaign, to the political conservatives who were engaged in it, was the battle for America in microcosm. The checks and balances of the Constitution; the calm orderliness of George Washington's Virginia; the unity of the family — wild men had endangered this sacred heritage, but temperance would preserve it. Seeking to contain the violence of Jacksonian America, the Whigs spoke in praise of moderation in all things.

Longings," by having the mayor of St. Petersburg praise the prize-winning address with the remark that "Daniel Webster himself might well be proud of it."

iii

By now it should be clear why the literary hero developed by the Southwestern humorists was a Self-controlled Gentleman — the very model of Whiggery's ideals. His first notable appearance occurs in the comic sketches of A. B. Longstreet.

Born in Augusta, Georgia, Augustus Baldwin Longstreet had grown up in comfortable circumstances. He was educated at Moses Waddel's fashionable academy in Willington, South Carolina, where Calhoun had been a student, and then followed in the footsteps of his idol to Yale and to Tapping Reeve's law school at Litchfield, Connecticut. Like his father, William Longstreet, the graduate of Yale and Litchfield had a savage temper. When an actor in a Georgia theater sang a song one night which made light of William Longstreet's belief that he was a talented inventor, the subject of the parody, who was in the audience, got up from his seat, blind with rage, and stalked out. Angry withdrawals became one of his son's most conspicuous habits. Campaigning for Congress in 1824, he suddenly withdrew his candidacy, and eight years later he canceled his plans to run for the state legislature with equal abruptness. All during his later years as president of the Georgia temperance society and of various academic institutions, Longstreet constantly held above his trustees' heads the threat of resignation. Even as an old man, he issued warnings to his family that he was about to walk out of the house for good. That he backed Calhoun during the Nullification crisis, was a fervent supporter of states' rights, and eventually a convert to the cause of secessionism, only completes the pattern of vindictive withdrawals that shaped Longstreet's whole life.

His first sketches appeared in a newspaper in Milledgeville, Georgia, until Longstreet himself bought a paper. In 1833, the political faction in Georgia that supported Jackson and the Union had emerged more strongly than ever before. Longstreet, an aristocrat, a states' righter, and never a man to hide his opinions, decided to go into the newspaper business to defend his principles. Purchasing a paper in Augusta, he renamed it the *State Rights Sentinel*. Literary critics have often remarked the Southern vindictiveness of Poe's journalistic criticism, and Mark Twain's sketch of "Journalism in Tennessee" makes it abundantly clear that the tone of newspaper editorializing in the antebellum South was, as Twain said, "peppery and to the point," to say the least.[3] Yet even when the journalistic temper of the times has been taken into account, one stands amazed in the furious presence of Longstreet's editorials. Corruption and filth — the words are Longstreet's — were all about him, and he attacked them with every verbal weapon he could muster, including defamation of character. One citizen who had incurred the editor's wrath found himself described in the *Sentinel* as having "two negro wives." As Longstreet's biographer has rightly observed, such editorials were the work of a fanatic.

By way of comic relief to the fury of his opinions, Longstreet supplied his newspaper with humorous sketches of Georgia life, culled mainly from his recollections of the days

[3] Exaggerating within an inch of his life, but catching the essential truth by doing so, Twain quoted what he swore was a typical paragraph from the *Morning Glory and Johnson County War-Whoop:*

"The inveterate liars of the *Semi-Weekly Earthquake* are evidently endeavoring to palm off upon a noble and chivalrous people another of their vile and brutal falsehoods with regard to that most glorious conception of the nineteenth century, the Ballyhack railroad. The idea that Buzzardville was to be left off at one side originated in their own fulsome brains — or rather in the settlings which *they* regard as brains. They had better swallow this lie if they want to save their abandoned reptile carcasses the cowhiding they so richly deserve."

The lives of Southern newspaper editors were often as violent as their columns. Twain's tall tale of mayhem in the *Morning Glory* offices does not exceed by much Edward Ingle's factual recollection of what life had been like as an editor in Vicksburg, Mississippi, before the Civil War: "The founder of the paper, after being involved in several street-fights and a duel, was killed. Of his successors, four were killed in duel or street-fight, one by a rival editor, one drowned himself, and one, after killing his man, was himself killed in Texas."

when, as a young lawyer, he had ridden circuit in the back-woods of Middle Georgia. As had been true of Fielding, whose vocation as Justice of the Peace for Westminster and Middle-sex had taken him out of the cultivated world of Eton and Ley-den where he had been educated and exposed him to what Maynard Mack has called the "vivid and barbarous life of country inns and alehouses" — an experience which formed the basis for both *Joseph Andrews* and *Tom Jones* — Long-street the Yale man discovered in the strongly colored, highly flavored speech of the piney woods people, in their grotesque expressions and cruel sense of fun, a rich source of humor. No more than Fielding is to be equated with Black George, is Longstreet to be identified with the life he described, despite the careless confusions of numerous critics. The work of a highly self-conscious man, Longstreet's sketches were a comic version of the remorseless editorials beside which they ap-peared, an integral part of a continuing effort to impose the political opinions of the author and his aristocratic friends on the Georgia community, and beyond Georgia, on the whole South. Whatever its defects as a general theory, Bergson's in-sistence that comedy stands midway between life and the "disinterestedness" of most art in that it "accepts social life as a natural environment," and even has a "scarcely conscious in-tention to correct and instruct," says a good deal about Long-street's sketches. As well as William Byrd did, Longstreet knew his Addison, the purpose of whose *Spectator* had been "to banish vice and ignorance out of the territories of Great Britain"; destined to become a Methodist minister in later years, Longstreet in the early 1830s believed with the creator of Sir Roger de Coverley that laughter could guide the moral destiny of society as effectively as a sermon.

When George Bancroft observed in 1840 that Joseph Addi-son belonged by rights to the party of Daniel Webster, he was thinking not merely of the number of conservative writers in America who called the Englishman master, but of Addison's "reasonableness," which was so closely akin to the temperate ideals of American Whiggery. Certainly the Self-controlled Gentleman of Southwestern humor is the American cousin of Addison's Man of Reason, and the fact of the Gentleman's moderate nature is established by a variety of Addisonian means.[4] The most important of them is the use of a "frame." The literary device of introducing a speaker who then tells us a story that comes to his mind was not new when Addison employed it, nor even when Boccaccio did, but Addison was the writer from whom Longstreet borrowed it. That the frame device eventually became the structural trademark of Southwestern humor is because it suited so very well the myth-making purposes of the humorists. For Longstreet and his successors found that the frame was a convenient way of keeping their first-person narrators outside and above the comic action, thereby drawing a *cordon sanitaire,* so to speak, between the morally irreproachable Gentleman and the tainted life he described. Thus the fact that the Gentleman found recollections of violence and cruelty both interesting and amusing did not imply anything ambiguous about his own life and character. However hot-tempered the author might be in private life, the literary mask of the Southwestern humorists was that of a cool and collected personality whose own emotions were thoroughly in hand.

By containing their stories within a frame, the humorists also assured their conservative readers of something they had to believe in before they could find such humor amusing, namely, that the Gentleman was as completely in control of the situation he described as he was of himself. As Maynard Mack has shrewdly observed, "even a rabbit, were it suddenly to materialize before us, . . . could be a frightening event. What makes

---

[4] For a Northern equivalent of the South's Addisonian hero, compare the praise of Daniel Webster by that organ of New York Whiggery, the *Knickerbocker:* "As the most impetuous sweeps of passion in him are pervaded and informed and guided by intellect, so the most earnest struggles of intellect seem to be calmed and made gentle in their vehemence, by a more essential rationality of taste." Quoted in Perry Miller, *The Raven and the Whale* (New York, 1956), 23.

us laugh is our secure consciousness of the magician and his hat." The frame device furnished an equivalent consciousness. When Longstreet concluded "The Fight," a particularly violent sketch, by saying, "Thanks to the Christian religion, to schools, colleges, and benevolent associations, such scenes of barbarism and cruelty as that which I have been just describing are now of rare occurrence," he reassured his readers that all was well. By asserting that barbarism was a thing of the past, the Gentleman tacitly affirmed that temperate Whig institutions were in control of the present, and in so doing released the laughter of those who might otherwise have shuddered at the comic spectacle. Finally, the frame device was a way of driving home, explicitly and directly, the social values of the author. "The peace officers," reads the last sentence of "The Fight," "who countenance . . . [barbarism and cruelty] deserve a place in the Penitentiary." To convert the entire community to the temperate values of Whiggery was the ultimate purpose of Southwestern humor, and the frame was the place where those values were most overtly insisted on.

The least successful of Longstreet's sketches are those in which his impulse to lecture the community in explicit terms carries over from the frame to the story itself. The same tendency mars much of the work of his successors as well. In "Darby, the Politician" for instance, Longstreet has barely thought through his story, or reflected on his characters; like John Pendleton Kennedy's *Quodlibet*, a dull, endless tale about good Whigs and bad Democrats, "Darby" comes closer to being a political speech than a short story. Darby Anvil is a blacksmith, "the first man who, without any qualifications for the place, was elected to the Legislature of Georgia." Instances of his ignorance and of the drunkenness of his supporters are cited with the mechanical regularity of the points in a lawyer's brief; in the end, the blacksmith is shown to be much worse off in every way than before he overreached himself by presuming to run against a Gentleman for office. One hardly needs to know that Longstreet's own political ambitions had come to naught in order to sense that "Darby" is the work of a man bent entirely on self-justification, and not at all on creating a meaningful fiction.[5]

In his best work, however, Longstreet buries his meanings deep within the concrete action of the comedy. His finest stories are parables, not tracts. As Longstreet finally understood, the Self-controlled Gentleman was defined more convincingly by his ability to perceive eccentricity than by his habit of condemning it, and "Georgia Theatrics," "The Horse-Swap," "The Fight," and two or three other sketches which constitute the Longstreet canon, are distinguished by an intense observation of character.

In "Georgia Theatrics," the briefest of the sketches in *Georgia Scenes* (the collection of his humor that Longstreet published in 1835), the Self-controlled Gentleman is a minister of the cloth who tells us of a trip he once took through the backwoods county of Lincoln in the year 1809. Speaking in a calm and elevated tone, he remembers that the natural (although, alas, not the moral) condition of the county in those bygone days had been a thing of splendor, and he recalls his initial delight in the "undulating grounds, luxuriant woodlands . . . sportive streams . . . [and] blushing flowers." His mood of enchantment, however, had been suddenly broken by the sound

---

[5] Longstreet's political failure was typical of the Southwestern humorists who sought elective office. Thorpe, Cobb, and Baldwin, for example, were rejected by the voters, and Pike probably would have been if he had not realized the futility of running as a Whig in the preponderantly Democratic state of Arkansas. Longstreet's sneering remark, in "Darby," that to win in Georgia a candidate had to "attend every gathering in the county, treat liberally, ape dignity here, crack obscene jokes there, sing vulgar songs in one place, talk gravely in another, tell long, dry stories, give short mean toasts, jest with the women and play with the children, grow liberal in suretyships, pay promptly and dun nobody, and ask everybody to vote for you," expresses the political frustration felt by many of his fellow humorists. See also Pike's bitter confession: "I am weary of Arkansas . . . sick of the . . . antediluvian notions of Boobydom. The government of the State is in the fullest sense of the word a booby-ocracy, and itself lies supine like a lean sow in the gutter."

coming from behind a clump of bushes of what seemed to be a terrible fight:

> "You kin, kin you?"
> "Yes, I kin, and am able to do it! Boo-oo-oo! Oh, wake snakes, and walk your chalks! Brimstone and — fire! Don't hold me, Nick Stoval! The fight's made up, and let's go at it. — my soul if I don't jump down his throat, and gallop every chitterling out of him before you can say 'quit!' "

The humor of the story is contained in the revelation that the commotion was not what it sounded like. Instead of the two brutes whom the minister had expected to find tearing each other apart, he had found instead a single eighteen-year-old boy, "jist seein' how I could 'a' *fout*." The story ends with the minister recollecting how he had examined the ground from which the boy had risen — "and there were the prints of his two thumbs, plunged up to the balls in the mellow earth, about the distance of a man's eyes apart; and the ground around was broken up as if two stags had been engaged upon it."

The minister's illusory contentment with the sylvan scene, his startled disillusionment, and finally his realization that his disillusionment is also an illusion, are represented with skill and economy. It is the youth, however, who makes the story. As he claws at the earth, he is a ridiculously quixotic figure, and we laugh, but the knowledge that Poe was fond of this story helps to call our attention to the darkness in the boy's life that it exposes. Victimized by the violent society of which he is a member, the boy's mind is thronged with images of violence; his fantasies of gouging out some ruffian's eyeballs with his fingernails are so real to him that he must take to the lonely woods to act them out. The subject of "Georgia Theatrics," as of Poe's "The Black Cat," is the psychology of aggression.

Did such a story have a political purpose? By its very artistry, "Georgia Theatrics" challenges the hypothesis that politics is the key to Southwestern humor. Yet the fact is that the conservative political allegory inherent in the sketch was recognized at once. Two years after the publication of *Georgia Scenes,* the Whig author of *Colonel Crockett's Exploits and Adventures in Texas* reproduced "Georgia Theatrics" as one of the episodes in the life of Whiggery's favorite backwoodsman. The author's sole adornment of Longstreet's tale was to suggest that the boy's assault on the mellow earth rather closely paralleled Andrew Jackson's ridiculous war on Biddle's Bank. The underlying political strategy of Longstreet's humor was thus clearly revealed by the more obvious literary intelligence which created *Crockett's Exploits:* if this author's allegorization reduced the richness of Longstreet's sketch, he nevertheless brought its political energies out into the open, enabling us to understand that just as the Self-controlled Gentleman who tells the story embodies a conservative political ideal, so the violent boy represents what to the Whig mind was the central quality of Jacksonism.

The moral contrast between the Gentleman and the youthful Clown is brought out in several ways. First of all, by the *cordon sanitaire* of the frame; secondly, by the superior point of view from which the story is told, a device which coerces the reader into laughing at — rather than sympathizing with — the boy; and finally — and most importantly — by the language. The language of the narrator is as urbane as Addison's; the cool elegance of the diction, the measured rhythms, the familiar yet reserved tone, are the credentials of an impeccably civilized man. Exemplifying a whole constellation of values, the narrative style speaks to us of order and rationality, of good taste, and of optimism tempered by wisdom; it is the style of "Christianity and the colleges," of sobersided and temperate adulthood — of Whiggery, in a word. The backwoods child, on the other hand, speaks in the vernacular. His idiom is not the hoked-up, synthetic mixture which the Whig propagandists represented Davy Crockett as speaking, but a barbarously authentic dialect, for Longstreet's purpose in employing the vernacular was to demonstrate the social and political incapacities of the barbarous Democracy, rather than to affirm the natural gentlemanliness of a backwoods Whig, as Crockett's ghost writers were attempting to do. By the same logic that compelled the Crockett myth-makers to be dishonest about how their pet backwoodsman talked, the myth-making humorists were encouraged to be blisteringly accurate in their representations of popular speech. The exigencies of Southern Whig politics, which forced the writers of the Southwestern tradition to lift the ban on the vernacular, thus precipitated the linguistic revolution that led eventually to *Huckleberry Finn*. The sole consideration which restrained the Southwestern humorists in their use of the vernacular was the one which had caused William Byrd to keep the Clowns of North Carolina quiet: if the backwoodsman was too often allowed to speak out of his own grotesque nature, then perforce the language of the story would no longer present quite so clear an image of the Gentleman's values. That the vernacular menaced the moral didacticism of his style was clearly recognized by Longstreet. Trained in the classics of Roman antiquity as well as steeped in the literature of Augustan England, he did not need to be told what the reasons were for holding firm to a formal narrative mode. The formula worked out by Longstreet was to use the vernacular sparingly, and never to allow its uncouth accents to interrupt for very long the bland flow of the narrator's language. The Clown in "Georgia Theatrics," therefore, has fewer lines than the Self-controlled Gentleman, but when he does speak we hear a genuine backwoods voice. The language of the youth is a language of cruelty and violence; it tells of quixotic hallucinations and irrational fears; it is full of misspellings, bad grammar and crude expressions. In other words, it beautifully exemplifies what, to the Whig mind, were the reckless spirit and childish ignorance of Jacksonian America. Someday Mark Twain would rewrite "Georgia Theatrics" as one of the scenes in *Tom Sawyer* — which reminds us not only of how well he knew A. B. Longstreet's work, but also of how much the comic symbols of the Southwestern tradition meant to Twain's art, albeit he radically altered their moral evaluations.

Longstreet's best story is "The Fight," which Poe praised as "unsurpassed in dramatic vigor and vivid truth to nature." This sketch introduces Longstreet's most intensely observed character: first of a long line of unforgettable Southern grotesques, Ransy Sniffle anticipates — in the satiric brilliance of his name, in the comic ugliness of his appearance, and in the utter malevolence of his soul — Faulkner's Flem Snopes. He was "a sprout of Richmond," says Longstreet's narrator,

> who, in his earlier days, had fed copiously upon red clay and blackberries. This diet had given to Ransy a complexion that a corpse would have disdained to own, and an abdominal rotundity that was quite unprepossessing. Long spells of the fever and ague, too, in Ransy's youth, had conspired with clay and blackberries to throw him quite out of the order of nature. His shoulders were fleshless and elevated; his head large and flat; his neck slim and translucent; and his arms, hands, fingers, and feet were lengthened out of all proportion to the rest of his frame. His joints were large and his limbs small; and as for flesh, he could not, with propriety, be said to have any. Those parts which nature usually supplies with the most of this article — the calves of the legs, for example — presented in him the appearance of so many well-drawn blisters. His height was just five feet nothing; and his average weight in blackberry season, ninety-five.

At the end of the description comes the most telling detail of all: "He never seemed fairly alive except when he was witnessing, fomenting, or talking about a fight. Then, indeed, his deep-sunken gray eye assumed something of a living fire, and his tongue acquired a volubility that bordered upon eloquence." Infinitely more degraded than the youth of "Georgia Theatrics," Ransy Sniffle cannot set his mind at rest with mock violence; blood must flow in order to satisfy this back-country sadist. Living only for violence, he willingly subverts the stability of society to satisfy his thirst for blood.

The figure of a sinister subversive who engineers the destruction of peaceful communities recurs often in Southwestern humor, indeed in all pre-Civil War Southern literature. As abolitionist pressure mounted, this subversive came more and more to be identified as a Yankee, and Southern variations on "The Legend of Sleepy Hollow" quickly multiplied toward infinity. As a Nullifier, Longstreet was early into the field with a story of a Yankee, called "The Village Editor." The sketch begins with a description of the "harmony" of life in Natville, the "good feeling" that prevails, the "temperate character" of all discussions, the presence in all families of "all the good things, and sweet things, and pretty things, that were found in one family." Into this Whig Utopia drifts a Connecticut Yankee named Asaph Doolittle; establishing a newspaper, he so agitates the townspeople with his editorials that soon good friends are at one another's throats. Before he is finally forced to leave Natville, "the village was completely revolutionized. The street meetings were broken up, the social parties discontinued, and many long years passed away before the citizens of Natville returned to their former friendship." The story makes its editorial point — that the North has no business interfering with the South — with awesome vigor; but as a study of character it is a failure. Doolittle derives from Longstreet's acquaintance with Ichabod Crane, rather than from his own observation. When, however, Longstreet turned from "foreign" to local subversives, he created the first memorable Clown in the Southwestern tradition. Kennedy's Flan Sucker, the "distinguished loafer"; Thompson's cadaverously ugly Sammy Stonestreet; Johnson Hooper's Simon Suggs; G. W. Harris's Sut Lovingood — these are the great Clowns of the tradition, and they all trace their ancestry back to Ransy Sniffle.

The Georgia county depicted by the gentlemanly narrator of "The Fight" is unified and peaceful — until Ransy Sniffle finds a way to tap its latent violence. Skillfully playing on hot Southern tempers, Sniffle provokes a fight between the two strongest men in the county, who previous to his machinations had had a "wonderful attachment" to one another. Soon the entire community is divided into two hostile camps. In the course of the ensuing battle, the two combatants, whose very names — Billy Stallions and Bob Durham — suggest their colossal strength, claw and tear at one another until one of the fighters has lost his left ear and a large piece of his cheek, and the other is minus a third of his nose. Ransy Sniffle is obviously well pleased by the bloodshed; but to the Self-controlled Gentleman the brawl has been a "hideous spectacle," and he concludes his story with a strong paragraph of moral condemnation. As for us, we emerge from "The Fight" as from a bad dream. Through the Gentleman's eyes, we have been witness to a vision of evil, a vision at once realistic and incredible, and made so largely by the character of the demonic Ransy Sniffle. While the clay-eater is in some basic sense a "true to life" character, as Asaph Doolittle was not, he can hardly be described as the fictionalized version of some backwoods lout whom the author had encountered during his circuit days. His weight of ninety-five pounds, for instance, is as much of a tall tale as is the fabulous strength of Durham and Stallions. Although decked out in realistic detail, Sniffle is a creature of fantasy, like Poe's nightmarish Mob. No more than Simon Suggs would be, is Longstreet's Clown a detached and objective study of the Southern poor white; he is, rather, a projection, in outrageous caricature, of a political conservative's exacerbation. Behind the Self-controlled Gentleman's cool and collected pose was an outraged editorialist who savagely despised the new Democracy for the divisions that its upsurge had created in Southern life; and the strange story of a sadistic clay-eater who split the community in two is the product of that savage feeling. To the Whig humorists who came after Longstreet, the diabolic humor of *Georgia Scenes* would be a source of inspiration in the hard political years ahead.

CHAPTER IV

The Confidence Man, the Soldier, and the Mighty Hunter

"IT IS GOOD TO BE SHIFTY IN A NEW COUNTRY."

— SIMON SUGGS

"Where's the fun, the frolicking, the fighting? Gone! Gone!"

— MIKE FINK

Georgia Scenes proved to be a surprisingly popular book, both in the North and the South. The discovery that there was a national audience for Southwestern humor gave a shrewd New York magazine editor an idea. He began combing through his newspaper exchanges from the Southwest to see if there were any other humorists of the caliber of Longstreet who were wasting their comic talents on a local sheet, rather than helping to boost the circulation of a metropolitan publication. In the early 1830s, William T. Porter had occasionally included a Southwestern sketch in his magazine, the *Spirit of the Times*, but not until after the publication of Longstreet's book did he really begin to sense the possibilities of this sort of humor. By the middle '40s, Porter was publishing the work of Thorpe, Hooper, Noland and Pike, among many others. In furnishing such writers with a nationwide outlet, he encouraged them to become more carefully professional about their work, at the same time providing the literati of the Eastern seaboard with what for most of them was their first contact with a vital movement in contemporary American letters. Few magazine editors have played a more important role in the history of American literature than William Trotter Porter.

Porter had been brought up on estates in Vermont, where he had acquired the passion for sports, especially horse racing, that eventually inspired him to found the *Spirit of the Times*, the resounding subtitle of which — *A Chronicle of the Turf, Agriculture, Field Sports, Literature and the Stage* — made its interests crystal clear. As befitted a sporting journal, the *Spirit* was officially nonpartisan in politics. Porter, however, was the grandson of a wealthy Tory, the son of a man who counted Daniel Webster as a personal friend, and a member in his own right of the Whig literary set in New York (Lewis Gaylord Clark of the *Knickerbocker* was a particular friend). If the *Spirit* avoided taking an explicit position on most issues of the day, the conservative bias of the editor was not hard to discern. A full-length, front-page tribute to Webster shortly after his death was only the most conspicuous instance of the *Spirit*'s unflagging devotion to Whig principles.

Nor did Porter make any bones about the type of reader he sought for his publication, announcing that the *Spirit* was "designed to promote the views and interests of an infinitesimal division of those classes of society composing the great mass." "We are addressing ourselves," he continued, "to gentlemen of standing, wealth and intelligence — the very corinthian columns of the community." Curiously enough for a Vermonter, the gentlemen to whom Porter most assiduously addressed himself were Southern aristocrats — as perhaps the metaphor of the corinthian columns implied. In part, this was because most of the active horse fanciers and breeders in the United States, to whom Porter naturally looked for readers, lived on plantations in the South. But it was not merely the lure of paid subscriptions that caused Porter to woo the planter class. To Porter as to James K. Paulding, the stability, amplitude and graciousness that the Southern aristocrat's life connoted were enormously compelling. So much did Porter admire such friends as Colonel Wade Hampton, the owner of a famous racing stable and the proprietor of one of the richest plantations in the South, that despite his Yankee ancestry he identified himself almost totally with the social and political views of the planter class. In line with the national Whig policy of playing down sectional disagreements in favor of accentuations of harmony, Porter did not flaunt his pro-Southern prejudices in the pages of the *Spirit*, although occasionally his feelings boiled over and the magazine came out hard against "the Abolition-Super-Philanthropic-Monster: Whom bigotry and fanaticism have rendered a knave and who hopes to cheat heaven into a belief of his 'good will to man' by cutting the throats of his neighbors, and marrying his daughter to his footman Cuffee." Such intemperate blasts, however, were untypical; in general, the *Spirit*'s editorials displayed an aristocratic, but not a particularly sectional, bias. Where Porter courted the planters was in the Southwestern humor that he published. In these stories, with their symbolic representation of the opinions and prejudices of the Southern Whig mind, Porter revealed how deeply he was committed to the planter's cause.

The Southwestern humorists who wrote for the *Spirit* were, most of them, newspapermen and lawyers trying to get on in the world, men allied with, but not of, the planter class. But as Porter puffed them up in his editorial introductions to their work, they were all men of learning and culture, scions of ancient families, inheritors of vast wealth. Albert Pike, Porter reminded his readers, was a Harvard graduate; C. F. M. Noland was a gentleman of infinite sophistication; the writer who signed himself THE TURKEY RUNNER was, if the truth could be told, one of the most distinguished statesmen of the South. The cumulative impression of these introductions was similar to that created by the plantation novels: in his easy, snobbish way, Porter summoned up a vision of an age-old, hierarchical South, unchanged for generations and unchangeable for many more. Yet, ironically, the very fact that Porter was publishing the work of these humorous writers was itself symptomatic of how swiftly the South was changing. All through the 1830s, the sport of bigtime horse racing had been rapidly declining in the South. The exhaustion of land in the seaboard states, and the rising cost of the slave labor that was necessary to man the vast, new plantations of the Southwest, forced more and more planters to sell their thoroughbreds and give up their subsidies of the famous tracks. The panic of 1837 accelerated the decline. Confronted, consequently, with a dearth of racing news, Porter elected to fill the pages of his magazine with reprints from *Punch* and *Blackwood's,* serializations of Dickens and Thackeray, improving essays, and sentimental poetry. In a gesture that aped the legendary extravagances of Colonel Cuthbert Dangerfield and the debt-ridden Virginia heroes of a dozen other plantation novels, Porter also met the challenge of adversity by spending more money. All America might still be groggy from the 1837 panic, but no engravings were too costly or elaborate for a magazine which aimed to be "complete in its design and in all its appointments elegant," an ideal which in 1842 forced Porter to cede financial, although not editorial, control of the *Spirit* to a publisher with less aristocratic tastes. Finally (and to his glory), Porter took the imaginative step of publishing the nationally unknown humorists whose work he had come across in Dixie newspapers.

While the heyday of bigtime racing faded into memory, the readers of the *Spirit* were consoled by humorous stories that mocked the efforts of the mob to make the sport of kings a pastime of its own. Perhaps the best of them was "A Quarter Race in Kentucky," by Thomas Kirkman, the owner of the celebrated race horse, Peytona, and a gentleman, in the admiring words of Porter, "of immense fortune." Stung by the swiftness with which roughnecks had moved in on the sport that the gentry could no longer afford, Kirkman composed a satiric sketch of the violence, ignorance and dishonesty of a crowd of gamblers and white trash bullies, come together in upcountry Kentucky for a horse race. Self-conscious about the nuances of social decorum, the *Spirit*'s stable of humorists spent more time writing about democratic manners than about any other subject. C. F. M. Noland, for example, the editor of a Whig newspaper in Arkansas, ridiculed the clumsy efforts of a backwoods character named Pete Whetstone to do his fighting according to the rules of the code duello. To Noland, who in his time had killed a man in a gentlemanly way, Pete Whetstone's awkward imitation of his betters was uproariously funny. Meanwhile, Governor Alexander McNutt of Mississippi (it was he who signed himself THE TURKEY RUNNER) contributed a series of hunting yarns about a pair of hardbitten frontier types named Jim and Chunkey, who had a bizarre fondness for killing animals with knives or their bare hands, rather than according to the elaborate protocol of gentlemen-sportsmen. By the early 1840s, every issue of the *Spirit* contained its vignette of a racing meeting, its anecdote of the card table, its tall tale of a military campaign or a hunting trip, its "factual" account of a backwoods duel, frolic, or practical joke.

Out of the crowd of literary Clowns who became the familiars of the *Spirit*'s pages, three basic types emerged.

THE CONFIDENCE MAN. His first appearance in Porter's magazine was as a loafer and pickpocket, hanging around nameless and dusty race tracks all across the Southwest. When he showed up again, he was a fixer, knowledgeable in the ways of tampering with horseflesh: the saddle burr, the cut rein, and various pills and sirups were now as familiar to him as the palm of his hand. On the rare occasions when he was caught out on a bet, he knew how to vanish into thin air. Sometimes, too, he was a trader in horses; on other occasions, a card-sharp, full of sly tricks. Along with his marked decks and extra aces he brought to the card table an air of amazed innocence: the mask of the greenhorn was the perfect disguise for the professional cheater. Soon he had other disguises as well. A born actor and boldly self-assured, he swaggered through a dazzling variety of parts, becoming by turns a doctor, lawyer, banker, long-lost relative. His favorite stage for acting his roles was the deck of a Mississippi steamboat. Another of his frequent haunts was the camp meeting revival, where he either played the ranting preacher or the sweaty sinner who "got religion"— whichever masquerade led most directly to the collection plate. From ignorant revivalists he moved on to bankers. Great gentlemen accustomed to deriving a handsome return from speculations in land or dealings in commercial paper found themselves outsmarted by his unscrupulous tactics. Avaricious, cruel, and utterly ruthless, always operating on the edge of the law, he moved through the land like a flight of seven-year locusts, leaving empty wallets behind him.

In his supreme incarnation he was known as Simon Suggs, the character created by Johnson J. Hooper. The editor of a struggling Whig newspaper in Chambers County, Alabama, Hooper was unknown as a humorist outside of Alabama until Porter reprinted one of his stories with the prefatory note, "This Hooper is a clever man, and we must enlist him among the correspondents of the *Spirit of the Times*." From that initial recognition, Hooper went on to become one of the magazine's most popular writers. When, in the mid-'40s, Hooper brought out a collection of Suggs's adventures in book form, he dedicated the volume to Porter, to whom he owed so much.

Some Adventures of Captain Simon Suggs (1845) is cast in the form of a campaign biography. Hooper's Confidence Man is running for office, we are informed by the Self-controlled Gentleman who is the narrator of the story, and the book is purportedly an *apologia pro vita sua*. In a tone of carefully extravagant admiration, the Gentleman introduces us to his candidate. He describes Suggs's gruesome face in minute and enthusiastic detail, mentioning in particular his four-inch mouth, on which "an ever-present sneer — not all malice, however — draws down the corners," and his "long and skinny, but muscular, neck." The Self-controlled Gentleman appears slightly embarrassed that the sample of Suggs's autograph which he wishes to describe to the voters was "only produced unblotted and in orthographical correctness, after three several efforts, 'from a rest,' on the counter of Bill Griffin's confectionary," but this momentary uneasiness is more than made up for by his apparent appreciation of the Suggsian wit: "His whole ethical system lies snugly in his favourite aphorism — 'IT IS GOOD TO BE SHIFTY IN A NEW COUNTRY.' " Nature, the narrator says in fond summation, made Suggs "ready to cope with his kind, from his infancy, in all the arts by which men 'get along' in the world; if she made him, in respect to his moral conformation, a beast of prey, she did not refine the cruelty by denying him the fangs and the claws." Murderously ironic as these quotations are, they by no means get to the heart of Hooper's destructive humor. To appreciate the introductory "frame" to the full, one has to understand why Hooper chose to model his book on a political campaign biography.

It is by means of campaign biographies, the Self-controlled Gentleman explains, that "all the country has in its mind's eye, an image of a little gentleman with a round, oily face — sleek, bald pate, delicate whiskers, and foxy smile. . . . [called] Martin Van Buren; and future generations of naughty children who will persist in sitting up when they should be a-bed, will be frightened to their cribs by the lithograph of 'Major General Andrew Jackson,' which their mammas will declare to be a faithful representation of the Evil One — an atrocious slander, by the bye, on the potent, and comparatively well-favoured, prince of the infernal world." The comparison of the Devil's physiognomy to Jackson's prompts a second glance at the Gentleman's description of Suggs's diabolic appearance, and sure enough, in the hang of the nose, the slit of the mouth, and the hardness of the eyes we see who it is that Hooper's caricature resembles. Later references in the course of Suggs's adventures to Amos Kendall of Jackson's Kitchen Cabinet, and to the honorary degree that Harvard awarded Old Hickory, serve to keep Suggs's prototype lively in the mind: "Would that thy pen, O! Kendall, were ours! Then would thy hero and ours — the nation's Jackson and the country's Suggs — go

down to posterity, equal in fame and honors, as in deeds! . . .
Would that, like Caesar, he could write himself! Then, indeed,
should Harvard yield him honors, and his country — justice!"
In thus linking his Confidence Man with the idol of the Democracy, Hooper invited his audience to read political and cultural meanings of the broadest significance into the despicable
life and times of Simon Suggs.

The son of a pious, austere, and "very avaricious" Baptist
preacher, Simon has grown up in a home that has never been
sanctified, to say the least, by the Whig harmonies. Watching
his father administer a vicious lashing to a Negro boy, Simon
says to himself, " 'Drot it! what do boys have daddies for,
anyhow? 'Tain't for nuthin' but jist to beat 'em and work 'em.
— There's some use in mammies — I kin poke my finger right
in the old 'oman's eye, and keep it thar, and if I say, it ain't
thar, she'll say so, too." Deciding that his parents are of no use
to him, Simon wins his father's horse from him by cheating at
cards, and as he rides off in search of adventure he laughs
aloud at the thought that he has secretly stuffed his mother's
pipe with gunpowder instead of tobacco, and that soon she
will be lighting it. The comedy in this opening sequence is in
many ways reminiscent of Longstreet's work of the previous
decade. Frame, point of view, and narrative style establish an
aristocratic standard against which the antics of this Jacksonian
boor are measured and evaluated. The differences between
Hooper and Longstreet, between the Southwestern humor of
the '40s and of the '30s, are as striking, however, as the
similarities. Ransy Sniffle, to begin with, had been a solitary
sadist in a fundamentally decent community; his victims, Stallions and Durham, had been upright and admirable men. The
people whom Simon Suggs triumphs over, commencing with
his parents, are a gross and greedy lot. Following the adventures of Simon Suggs, one is oppressed by the sense of moving
through a darkening world, populated by dehumanized grotesques. Sensual and superstitious, gray with fear and green
with envy, the people who are taken in by Hooper's Confi-

dence Man are as morally degraded as he is. The perspective in which we view Simon Suggs is altered considerably as a result. The alteration is particularly evident in Simon Suggs's best-known adventure, the one which Mark Twain would draw upon for an episode in *Huckleberry Finn:* "Simon Suggs Attends a Camp-Meeting."

Camp meetings were one of the prime targets of the Southwestern humorists throughout the antebellum period. As Longstreet's remark about the Christian religion at the end of "The Fight" implied, the Whigs looked to the churches for allies in their battle against the Democracy. The Episcopalian minister and Whig propagandist, Calvin Colton, spoke for his class when he said that "Christian morality and piety, in connexion with the intelligence of the common people, are the last hope of the American Republic, and the only adequate means of bridling and holding in salutary check that rampant freedom, which is so characteristic of the American people." The one trouble with this pious hope was that by 1839, the year in which Colton voiced it, even the most myopic conservative, even Calvin Colton, must have realized that "the last hope of the American Republic" could no longer be counted on as a bulwark against rampant freedom. For in the voluntaristic denominations, at least, the techniques of revivalism were serving the cause of Jacksonism. Inviting all sinners to forget about doctrinal and ministerial guidance and save themselves by their own initiative, the revivalists bolstered the notion that "converted men by choice create the church" — an idea which, as Sidney E. Mead has seen, was "paralleled in the political realm by the notion that the people create the government." The religious emotion generated in the camp meetings was the political emotion of Jacksonian rallies in another form. Testifying to the Whigs' awareness of this fact was the amount of ammunition expended by the Southwestern humorists on demagogic preachers and their hallelujah-shouting congregations. When Simon Suggs rides into the camp meeting at Sandy Creek he enters an atmosphere that conservative Christians regarded with a mixture of contempt and extreme disquietude:

> The excitement was intense. Men and women rolled about on the ground, or lay sobbing or shouting in promiscuous heaps. More than all, the negroes sang and screamed and prayed. Several, under the influence of what is technically called "the jerks," were plunging and pitching about with convulsive energy. The great object of all seemed to be, to see who could make the greatest noise. . . . "Bless my poor old soul!" screamed the preacher in the pulpit; . . . "Keep the thing warm!" roared a sensual seeming man, of stout mould and florid countenance, who was exhorting among a bevy of young women, upon whom he was lavishing caresses. "Keep the thing warm, breethring! — come to the Lord, honey!" he added, as he vigorously hugged one of the damsels he sought to save.

In this luridly lit scene of mendacity and sexuality, Simon Suggs is no longer a Clown in the sense that Ransy Sniffle had been: a puppet to be held at arm's length and laughed at. Hooper's Confidence Man is, rather, a comic hero, who — to a degree at least — enlists our sympathies on his side. Although he is a supreme hypocrite, we paradoxically admire his honesty, for unlike anyone else at the camp meeting, Simon Suggs admits his shiftiness; thus his cynical masquerade as a sinner who gets saved wins our surreptitious approval, while the censorship that would ordinarily prevent us from laughing along with him as he extracts a "handsome sum" from the congregation is lifted by the knowledge that the money would otherwise have lined the pockets of that fake religioso, the Reverend Bela Bugg. In a world of Buggs, we prefer Suggs.

The degradation of the society in which he moves is by no means the only factor responsible for the shift in comic perspective toward Simon Suggs. To compare Longstreet's book with Hooper's is to see that the clumps of vernacular dialogue judiciously planted by Longstreet in the early 1830s have grown rank and wild in the course of a decade. Once we are past Hooper's marvelously executed introduction, the gentlemanly style is kept up much less consistently than in Long-street's sketches. For long periods, only the vernacular voices of the Confidence Man and the other Clowns can be heard. One effect of Hooper's increased use of the vernacular is to lend his scenes of Southwestern life a vitality unequaled by any humorist of the '30s. The sensory vividness of popular speech quickens his comedy with a ferocious energy; if the appearance and gestures of the poor whites are still described in the Gentleman's bland style, the extended use of quoted dialogue charges their characterizations with new life. The most important effect, however, is to blur the moral outlines of the comedy. As we listen to Hooper's characters "speak out of their own nature," the temperate voice of the Self-controlled Gentleman fades and we drift loose from the familiar assurances of the Whig universe into a featureless world of nightmarish sounds. Amidst the ecstatic screams of God-drunk revivalists, the shrieks of frontier settlers, their teeth chattering with fear at the prospect of an Indian attack, and the howls of pain of mothers, fathers, and slaves, it is no longer possible to pass a moral judgment when we hear the lying, cunning voice of the Confidence Man, because the very existence of a moral tradition in this world seems problematic. The triumph of the vernacular over the gentlemanly style is by no means definitive in *Simon Suggs*. When the Confidence Man and his victims are finished talking, the Self-controlled Gentleman is heard once again, as disdainfully unruffled and impeccably refined as ever. Nevertheless, the total effect of the book's nervous alternation between two drastically different modes of expression is to obscure the comedy's didactic intent and to cause the reader's judgment of the central character to waver. Is Simon Suggs's motto, "IT IS GOOD TO BE SHIFTY IN A NEW COUNTRY," a despicable ethic, or the only one that makes survival possible? A. B. Longstreet would never have left such a question hanging fire.

As with language, so with point of view: there are times in Hooper's book when we leave the Gentleman's vantage point and enter the warped and vengeful mind of Simon Suggs. If the Gentleman quickly leads us out again and re-establishes his own distantly superior point of view, the momentary transposition is as shocking as though a puppeteer were temporarily to relinquish the direction of his show to Punch or Judy. For when we view men and events through the glittering eye of the Confidence Man, we are *in his world*, where no moral reference points exist; seen through the glass of the Suggsian consciousness, humanity has not the slightest dignity, while such terms as harmony, unity, stability — all the Whig shibboleths — are exposed as empty mockeries. The Gentleman, in Hooper's book, is no longer the supreme master, no longer quite so firmly in control of things. Our awareness of his presence is less vivid than previously, and so is our sense that the stories he tells have taken place in the past. In a footnote inserted in the "Camp-Meeting" story, Hooper attempted to assure his readers that "the scenes described in this story are not *now* to be witnessed," but the very fact that he felt constrained to add the footnote suggests his own awareness of the moral obscurities of his humor. When William Dean Howells deplored pre-Civil War Southwestern humor as being on the side of slavery, drunkenness and irreligion, he was almost certainly thinking of Hooper as a prime example, for no more famous character was ever produced by the tradition than Simon Suggs. Yet if slavery was defended by Hooper, drunkenness and irreligion were about as far from his temperate Whig precepts as possible. That a perceptive reader like Howells could have been so wide of the mark is eloquent testimony to Hooper's ambivalence. Wavering between two points of view as well as between two linguistic modes, Hooper's humor is above all a nervous humor, brilliantly funny at times, but with no secure base anywhere.

The nervousness of *Simon Suggs* is the quality which beyond any other makes the book such an interesting documentation of the state of mind of conservative Southerners in a crucial decade in American history. For the vacillations of

Hooper's book track the wide swings between optimism and pessimism to which the Southern Whigs were subject in the 1840s. Nothing in life seemed certain to them. If the Whigs won two out of three Presidential elections during the decade, both their candidates, being infirm generals, sickened and died in office. Their success in blunting the more radical reforms proposed in the constitutional conventions of the 1830s was scant solace in a decade which produced a new wave of populist agitation, including a scheme — pressed with particular fervor in Hooper's Alabama — for basing representation on white population alone, whereby the political strength of the slave-populated plantation counties would be severely reduced. And if slavery and cotton were bringing in bigger profits than ever, the world-wide outcry against the "peculiar institution" mounted ever higher in the '40s. Conservatives in the '30s had had their ups and downs, but the peaks had never been so sharp, nor the valleys so deep, and it is this psychological unsureness which *Simon Suggs* reflects. As his remarks about Andrew Jackson in his introduction indicated, Hooper desired with a fervor equal to Longstreet's to make his humor the instrument of political enlightenment. Like Longstreet, therefore, he turned to the serenely didactic Addison for his literary model. The complacent optimism of the *Spectator* manner was also admirably suited to express the sense of power and confidence that represented one strain of the Southern Whig mind in the '40s. But the Hooper who shared the well-nigh apocalyptic judgment of the *American Whig Review* in the mid-'40s that Jacksonism had brought America to the brink of "degradation and ruin" — and whose own editorials voiced the guilt, the indignation and the fear of the planters at the increasing fury of the slavery controversy — could not give vent to his feelings in the round tones of Joseph Addison. When Hooper confronted the Jacksonian saturnalia of the camp meeting, he was, consequently, a man divided against himself. In one guise, Hooper at Sandy Creek was the Self-controlled Gentleman, pointing with mild ridicule at violent excesses; in another, he was the Confidence Man, making war on a rotten world. In a decade of confusion, doubt, and growing uneasiness, halfway between the wide-open '30s and the dark and hate-filled '50s, Hooper's Jekyll-and-Hyde humor perfectly caught the ambivalent mood of Southern Whiggery.

THE SOLDIER. Local militia leaders in the South, so John Hope Franklin has told us in his study of Southern violence, were one of the chief reasons why the temperature of ante-bellum Dixie habitually ran at fever heat. Although the Indian menace was the official business of these men, their trigger-happy tendencies had a way of leading to bloody embroilments with fellow whites. When to their violent habits was added their hero-worship of General Andrew Jackson — *vide* Colonel Crockett in the 1820s — it is not surprising that militia officers should have seemed to the Whig mind the incarnate spirit of Jacksonism, or that the comic possibilities of Southern military life were capitalized upon by conservative humorists from the early '30s on. In dozens of sketches, back-country officers were depicted as militarily inept braggarts, incapable even of drilling soldiers, let alone of leading them into battle. One of the best was by Longstreet's friend, Oliver Hillhouse Prince, who told of a militia company drill that began in soldierly pomp and ended in a tanglefooted mess. (Longstreet thought so well of Prince's sketch that he included it as a chapter in *Georgia Scenes;* years later, it inspired one of the episodes in Thomas Hardy's novel, *The Trumpet Major*.) When they were not ridiculing the militia officer, the Whig humorists portrayed him as a variant on Nimrod Wildfire: awkward, rude, but fundamentally sound, and susceptible to the improving admonishments of his betters. Major Jones, the main character in several of William Tappan Thompson's books, is a fair sample of this toothless type: "I haint got no very grate opinion of myself," Major Jones confesses, "but I've always tried to live a honest man, and what little character I is got I want to keep." The proof that Major Jones has a good Whig heart beneath his Jacksonian exterior is signified by his choice of a name for his baby boy: "How do you think Henry Clay Jones would do for a name? I go for Mr. Clay, tooth and toe nail, myself, and 'tween you and me he's jest as good for President next fall as thrip is for a ginger-cake."

In the early '40s, however, as the drums of Manifest Destiny began to beat louder and louder, a new version of the Soldier appeared. A corrupt and cynical gunman, he talked a better war than he fought; but even though a coward at heart, he was a far more fearsome figure than he had ever been before. One of the principal masquerades of Simon Suggs, the Confidence Man, was that of "Capting of the Tallapoosy Vollantares," whose ruthless use of the Creek War crisis as an excuse for looting his neighbors' possessions was understood by Whig readers to be a commentary on the Democrats' manipulation of the Texas question as a means of winning power. (Perhaps the most significant thing that can be said about Simon Suggs is that he made his first appearance in the *Spirit of the Times* in December of 1844, one month following the victorious conclusion of Polk's campaign for the Presidency on a platform of Manifest Destiny.) Hooper's Soldier was a Whig response to the challenge of Democratic expansionism.

As was true of his Confidence Man stories, however, Hooper's view of Simon Suggs, the ruthless bully boy with a gun in his hand, was curiously shifty; once again, Suggs was half Clown, half comic hero — at once far more evil than the stumblebums in Oliver Prince's sketch, and yet more capable of stirring our sympathy than such housebroken wild men as Thompson's Major Jones. Reflected in Hooper's wavering attitude toward his Soldier was a profound split in the Southern Whig attitude toward military adventuring in the 1840s.

The commercial interests behind Northern Whiggery would have nothing to do with Manifest Destiny. The Southern wing of the party, however, was not nearly so sure of its position. There were many reasons why the Southern Whigs feared expansionism: they were afraid of upsetting the delicate balance of power in the nation between slave states and free states; the planters of the Delta were uneasy at the thought of competition from Texas cotton; the idea of war with Mexico conjured up the faceless image of the Caesar who would win it, and who might not listen to conservative advisers with any more patience than had the diabolic Jackson. On the other hand, the thought of a new Southern empire, lying at the very doorstep of New Orleans, had an economic and political appeal to the Southern Whigs that could not be denied. Struggling to resolve their conflicting emotions, the merchants and planters of the South listened eagerly to Henry Clay's lame formulation in his second Alabama letter: "The efforts of the opposite party to use the [Texas] question for their own political advantage would merely delay a consummation which the Whigs intended — in the proper way and at the proper time — to bring about." *In the proper way and at the proper time.* Empire would come to America, the Southern Whigs proclaimed, in the fullness of time, automatically, like a ripe apple dropping in a maiden's lap. There was no necessity for reckless adventuring below the Rio Grande, as certain demagogues were urging. Keep cool, the Southern Whigs said in effect, and all would be ours. Or would it? They were never quite as satisfied with this complacent doctrine as they made out. How many Southern Whigs quietly cast their ballots for Polk in 1844 remains a matter for speculation, but in the half-condemned, half-surreptitiously-admired military career of Captain Simon Suggs we have a public record of the troubled spirit of the planter class as it confronted the major political question of the day.

THE MIGHTY HUNTER. In a decade of tension, the Mighty Hunter loomed up in Southwestern humor like a malevolent Quixote. Mounted on a spavined horse, a rifle across his saddle, he rode the lonely paths from Natchez to the Cumberland, on the lookout for bears and Indians — and solitary travelers with golden watch chains. The pessimism that produced this vindictive portrait also eventuated in a yearning for an unrecapturable past, when life had been simpler and the future bright with promise. The Mighty Hunter, telling gorgeous lies of his brave deeds — of the crocodile that almost swallowed him, or the bear that got away — voiced the nostalgia of the Southwestern humorists for a vanished America. He may have been a vainglorious braggart, this Hunter, or even a killer; he was certainly a Clown, to be laughed to scorn. But he was also a Pagliacci figure, whose lies were charged with heartbreak, and to whom a certain dignity clung, as is sometimes true of men who have lived to recognize their own defeat. The Mighty Hunter's boasts were elegies addressed to a dying frontier.

Of all the humorists in the *Spirit of the Times* who wrote of this poetic figure, incomparably the most talented was a transplanted Northerner named Thomas Bangs Thorpe. Born the son of a Methodist minister in Westfield, Massachusetts (his father rode the circuit that included Litchfield, Connecticut, in the days when Longstreet was a law student there), Thorpe went to New York as a young man to study painting. For a time, too, he was a student at Wesleyan College, until a trip through the South decided him to quit the North, partly because his health could not stand the rigors of the New England climate, but also because, like his future publisher, his Yankee soul had been stirred by the gaudy vision of an aristocratic South. Settling in Louisiana in the 1830s, in a region of the state where parvenu "Cotton Snobs" — as the Charleston lawyer, Daniel R. Hundley, would someday call them — were busily carving out vast plantations and throwing up elegant (and heavily mortgaged) mansions, Thorpe earned his living by painting the portraits of those who were eager to acquire a sense of history, ready-made. Although his profession brought him into exciting contact with some of the most powerful men in Louisiana, the pay was poor, and Thorpe shifted to newspaper work, becoming associated with the New Orleans

Tropic, a Whig daily. In the course of three years, Thorpe had
bad luck with five different newspapers. A flier at politics
proved even more unsatisfying. During the campaign of 1844,
he worked actively for the Whig ticket, only to see Louisiana
go Democratic by a narrow margin. Despite Thorpe's early
and energetic support of Zachary Taylor for the Presidency
(which included painting a portrait of his candidate), he
never received the political appointment he expected after
Taylor reached the White House. In 1852, Thorpe ran for
State Superintendent of Education — and went down to
overwhelming defeat along with the entire Whig ticket.

As the resident of a predominantly rural, predominantly
Anglo-Saxon section of Louisiana, Thorpe easily became convinced that Catholic New Orleans was the cause of his disappointments, both political and journalistic, a conviction that
in the mid-1850s would be a strong factor in his decision to
join the xenophobic Know-Nothing party. Frustration also led
to a turning-away from the present. Like the flare-ups of racial
and religious bigotry in the 1890s and the 1920s, the anti-
Catholicism and anti-foreignism of Thorpe and his *nouveaux
riches* planter friends went hand in hand with a nostalgia for
an America that was fast disappearing. In the tense and tu-
multuous '40s, insecure aristocrats gazed out past the corinthian columns that did not, after all, seem to be the guarantee
of a stable society, toward the receding image of a more heroic Southwest, the land of the first pioneers — of the raftsman, the hunter, and the Indian scout. Those days had been
the best days. Writing accounts of hunting trips for the *Spirit*
was a means of caricaturing the uncouth manners of backwoods bullies — and of escaping from the disillusionments
of the present into the Utopia of the woods. Harmony and
unity existed in nature, at least, if not in society.

In Thorpe's mind, hunting trips were voyages into the past.
The numerous sketches he wrote of his expeditions to the
woods and prairies of the Southwest are all colored by a deep,
emotional attachment to an undespoiled, undefiled, natural

world. With the sensitive eye of a painter, he recorded what he called the "mysteries" of nature — the silence of the big trees and of the wide, lonely, Mississippi, the special look of the sky over the prairie, the awesome grandeur of the buffalo. The traveler from the outside could never hope to understand these mysteries; their secrets had been given only to old-timers like Tom Owen, the bee-hunter, or Mike Fink, the famous king of the broadhorns. Possessed of a magic knowledge, these denizens of the woods commanded respect as well as inviting patronization. Mike Fink, as depicted by Thorpe in a story called "The Disgraced Scalp-Lock," was undoubtedly a wild and brutish man; his idea of a good joke was to shoot off an Indian's scalp lock with his rifle. Yet he was also the heroic representative of a bygone American type, a type characterized, said Thorpe, by "sterling common sense — the manner modest, yet full of self-reliance; the language forcible, from superiority of mind, rather than from education. . . ." Here was a comic hero to be sympathized with, even identified with; when Thorpe made Fink exclaim, "What's the use of improvements? When did cutting down trees make deer more plenty? Who ever found wild buffalo or a brave Indian in the city? Where's the fun, the frolicking, the fighting? Gone! Gone!" the frontiersman expressed his creator's suspicion of New Orleans, and of other modern bewilderments. Thorpe's point of view toward his vernacular material was thus ambivalent. On the one hand, he presented Mike Fink with the detachment of an outsider and a would-be aristocrat; on the other hand, Fink's subjective emotions, expressed in his own rough language, were Thorpe's as well. In Southwestern humor, the traditional mask for the Whig author was that of a Self-controlled Gentleman, yet how could Thorpe voice his frustrations in a language which breathed optimism and hope and the triumph of the moral light over the moral dark? As a medium for conveying the emotions that lay behind Thorpe's nostalgia for the past, the Gentleman's style was inappropriate. Consequently, Thorpe spoke through the mask of Mike Fink, because only by speaking in the vernacular, the language of violence and unreason, could he communicate his sense of impotence and defeat. Thorpe's employment of the gentlemanly style throughout much of "The Disgraced Scalp-Lock" mirrored one facet of his mind: the perseverance of his ambitions. Energetic, well-connected, an influential member of a powerful political party, he still entertained high hopes, as did his planter friends in their brand-new houses. But the voice of the doomed raftsman echoed the Southern Whigs' uneasy feeling that somehow history was against them.

Thorpe's most exquisitely poised combination of urbane confidence and intense uneasiness is "The Big Bear of Arkansas," the most famous story the *Spirit* ever published. The scene of the story is a Mississippi steamboat. Its crowded, jostling atmosphere is presented to us in the familiar, elevated style. As the gentlemanly narrator hurries on board, he observes — in his sharp-eyed, condescending fashion — that the other travelers are as heterogeneous as they are picturesque. Disdaining to speak to anyone, he settles down in the cabin with a newspaper. With the refinement of the puppeteer's personality incontestably established, the puppet show now begins. An Indian war whoop is heard issuing from the bar, followed by a loud crowing sound, culminating in an exultant halloo — "Hurra for the Big Bar of Arkansaw!" With a fine theatricality, the "hero of these windy accomplishments" strides into the cabin. As the conversation drops, he takes a chair, puts his feet on the stove, "and looking back over his shoulder, passed the general and familiar salute of 'Strangers, how are you?'" Except for an occasional question or gibe addressed to him by other passengers, the big bear hunter (whose real name is Jim Doggett — an echo possibly of Davy Crockett) dominates the room with a series of tall tales about the wonders of Arkansas. In this "creation state," the soil runs down to the center of the earth, the wild turkeys weigh up to forty pounds, the bears are fat the year round, and the beets grow as large as cedar stumps. Suddenly, this boisterous hyperbole becomes curiously grim around the edges. Beets the size of cedar stumps are useless and constitute a warning as well as a boast: *"Planting in Arkansaw is dangerous."* By way of further illustration of this text, Doggett recalls an old sow who stole an ear of corn, left a grain or two on the ground, and lay down on them; "before morning the corn shot up, and the percussion killed her dead." In a voice full of surprising feelings, he declares, "I don't plant any more; natur intended Arkansaw for a hunting ground and I go according to natur." On this mixed emotional note, his harangue abruptly ends, for the Gentleman now breaks in to say that "In this manner the evening was spent" — an announcement which in effect rings down the curtain on the first act of the show. Thus far, the story seems only a superior version of a familiar formula in the *Spirit of the Times:* a Gentleman is reproducing for the delectation of a self-consciously aristocratic readership the crude but vivid garrulities of a Mighty Hunter. The final speech of the Hunter seems to hint at something else, but it is only a hint. Not until the second half of the narrative is the double perspective of Thorpe's story revealed.

Part Two begins with the Gentleman narrator asking Doggett to give a description of a bear hunt. With the assertion that "in bar hunts *I am numerous,*" the backwoods boaster once again launches into an extravagant monologue, this time without any interruptions from his listeners. Until the final two paragraphs of the story, only Jim Doggett's voice is heard.

The adventure of the bear hunt, then, is presented through what may be termed the "Jacksonian perception" of the Mighty Hunter. As Jim Doggett begins his tale, we are no longer merely listening to vernacular dialogue, but to a vernacular *narration,* to a native American speech on the way to becoming a literary style. If the narration does not last very long, we nevertheless see the world through the mind of the Clown for a much more sustained period of time than in any of Johnson Hooper's stories. The Gentleman's purpose in drawing out Doggett and allowing him to tell his own story in his own way has the ostensible purpose of amusing us with the "great peculiarity" of the bear hunter's lingo. As we listen to Doggett talk on, however, a subjective reality is also created — the mystery of the woods, and of the bear, as they are intensely remembered by the backwoodsman. The puppeteer invites us to laugh at this Clown, but Doggett's drawling voice makes us see things his way as well. Our point of view is, therefore, both within and without the tall tale that Doggett spins. Seen from the inside, witnessed through the vernacular imagination of the Mighty Hunter, the adventure takes on unexpected dimensions. Depths of meaning are revealed that would never have become apparent if our viewpoint had remained exclusively identified with the Gentleman's. The "Jacksonian perception" of Jim Doggett penetrates far below the comic surfaces that are the province of the gentlemanly spectator.

To Thorpe, one of the profoundest "mysteries" of nature in the Southwest was the presence in the woods and rivers and on the prairies of certain illusory creatures of fabulous size or special marking. Other writers were fascinated by these creatures, too. In the same year that the *Spirit* published "The Big Bear" — 1841 — the Southwestern humorist George Wilkins Kendall heard tall tales in Texas about a mysterious White Steed of the Prairies; five years later, James Hall reported that the tales were still going strong in the West, a statement that may have prompted Melville to remark in one of his descriptions of Moby Dick that the White Steed was "most famous in our Western annals and Indian traditions." Equally renowned was the white whale of the Pacific that J. B. Reynolds described in 1839, at the very moment when the Crockett almanacs were offering up dozens of prodigious bears and cunning alligators as home-grown versions of Mocha Dick. These stories must have stirred Thorpe's imagination to the very bottom, as surely they did Poe's and Melville's; for such animals seemed to contain in their very hugeness some fundamental secret of life, which meant that hunting them down might bring the answer to Faustian questions.

The bear Jim Doggett tells of is as fantastically big for its kind as Moby Dick, and its size constitutes a challenge to him, even as the gigantic whale goaded Ahab's pride. "Says I, 'here is something a-purpose for me: that bar is mine, or I give up the hunting business.'" As the mammoth creature continues to elude him, his proud vow turns into an obsession. The humor of the yarn becomes less gay — and then sardonic; the comic extravagance of his early speeches finally gives way to the hyperbole of monomania. Like the hatred that would crack the sinews and cake the brain of the captain of the *Pequod*, driving him to pile on Moby Dick's white hump "the sum of all the general rage and hate felt by his whole race from Adam down; and then, as if his chest had been a mortar. . . . burst his hot heart's shell upon it," the bear-hunter's rage consumes him. "Missing that bar so often took hold of my vitals, and I wasted away," Doggett says. "The thing had been carried too far, and it reduced me in flesh faster than an ager." He begins to believe that the bear is "the Devil" and is hunting the hunter — or can it be that the hunter is hunting himself? For "I loved [the bear]," he says in a strange burst, "like a brother." The further he pursues the beast, the more fully he is enveloped in his nightmare. Bullets bounce off the bear's head; a male animal, it disappears into a lake and comes out female; "the thing was killing me," Doggett cries, "and I determined to catch that bar, go to Texas, or die."

With that mighty oath, however, so ludicrously undercut by the mention of Texas, Jim Doggett's good humor comes back, dissolving terror and the sense of evil in comic travesty. Doggett's final, all-out assault on the bear is not destined to end like the third day of the chase in *Moby Dick* — is in fact not even to be launched at all. For the bear who had consistently eluded the pursuit of a bloodthirsty monomaniac succumbs ahead of schedule to a prat-falling comedian:

> I made my preparations accordin'. I had the pack shut up and rested. I took my rifle to pieces and iled it. I put caps in every pocket about my person, for *fear of the lining*. I then told my

neighbours, that on Monday morning — naming the day — I would start THAT BAR, and bring him home with me, or they might divide my settlement among them, the owner having disappeared. Well, stranger, on the morning previous to the great day of my hunting expedition, I went into the woods near the house, taking my gun and Bowie-knife along, just *from habit,* and there sitting down also from habit, what should I see, getting over my fence, but *the bar!* Yes, the old varmint was within a hundred yards of me, and the way he walked *over that fence* — stranger, he loomed up like a *black mist,* he seemed so large, and he walked right towards me. I raised myself, took deliberate aim, and fired. Instantly the varmint wheeled, gave a yell, and *walked through the fence* like a falling tree would through a cobweb. I started after, but was tripped up by my inexpressibles, which either from habit, or the excitement of the moment, were about my heels, and before I had really gathered myself up, I heard the old varmint groaning in a thicket near by, like a thousand sinners, and by the time I reached him he was a corpse.

The tragic dénouement of the novel that Melville had not yet written becomes in Thorpe's story a comically happy ending.

Underneath the burlesque, however, the diapason of a deeper feeling can be sensed. If travesty has successfully dispelled the furious emotions which shape and color the first two thirds of the yarn, it cannot exorcise the conclusion's haunted mood of loss. The action of the passage quoted above makes us laugh at the comic triumph of Jim Doggett, but the language in which he tells of that triumph forces us into a new and sobering appreciation of the grandeur of the bear. With his painter's sensibility, Thorpe in this passage made the vernacular into something more than the medium of violence. That Mark Twain would come to understand how he might use the speech of an ignorant river waif to impart a new loveliness to the hackneyed subject of a sunrise was a momentous discovery in American literature, but behind that discovery was Thomas B. Thorpe's achievement in opening up the poetic potentiality of the vernacular. Seven years before the publication of "The Big Bear of Arkansas," Emerson had prophesied in his journal, "I suppose the evil [of America's cultural dependence on England] may be cured by this rank-rabble party, the Jacksonism of the country, heedless of English and all literature — a stone cut out of the ground without hands: — they may root out the hollow dilettantism of our civilization in the coarsest way, and the newborn may begin again, to frame their world with greater advantage." In saying that the bear loomed up "like a black mist," and that it walked through a fence "like a falling tree would through a cobweb," Jim Doggett found the native materials in which to frame a new world. And having "caught" the bear in a metaphorical sense, the Hunter suddenly understands what it is that he has literally captured. In framing his world with greater advantage, he has comprehended not only its grandeur, but its doom:

> 'Twould astonish you to know how big he was: I made a *bedspread of his skin,* and the way it used to cover my bar mattress, and leave several feet on each side to tuck up, would have delighted you. It was in fact a creation bar, and if it had lived in Samson's time, and had met him, in a fair fight, it would have licked him in the twinkling of a dice-box. But, strangers, I never liked the way I hunted, and *missed him.* There is something curious about it, I could never understand, — and I never was satisfied at his giving in so easy at last. Perhaps, he had heard of my preparations to hunt him the next day, so he jist come in, like Capt. Scott's coon, to save his wind to grunt with in dying; but that ain't likely. My private opinion is, that that bar was an *unhuntable bar, and died when his time come.*

Overcome by somber thoughts, the bear hunter stops talking; and the Gentleman narrator notes that for some minutes he sat "in a grave silence." "I saw," the narrator continues, "that there was a mystery to him connected with the bear whose death he had just related, that had evidently made a strong impression on his mind." Attempting to dissipate the surprising gloom that the end of the tale has engendered, the Gentleman briskly deprecates the bear hunter's melancholy as

the sort of "superstitious awe . . . common with all 'children
of the wood.'" With this reminder that Doggett is a Clown and
his tale the amusing revelation of a childlike mind, the puppeteer swiftly brings the story to a close. Stepping back at the
end into the character of the Self-controlled Gentleman,
Thorpe breaks the sorrowful mood of his backwoods narrator
and reaffirms the familiar optimism of the Southwestern tradition.

But condescending remarks cannot conceal what the bear
hunter's story has revealed. We recall, in the light of his
tall tale, certain facts about "The Big Bear of Arkansas" that
have not previously seemed significant. The name, for instance,
of the steamboat on which the story is told is the *Invincible;*
and we further remember that the Gentleman narrator had
particularly emphasized the heterogeneity of the typical steamboat crowd: "The wealthy Southern planter, and the pedlar of
tinware from New England — the Northern merchant, and the
Southern jockey — a venerable bishop, and a desperate gambler
— the land speculator, and the honest farmer — professional
men of all creeds and characters — Wolvereens, Suckers,
Hoosiers, Buckeyes, and Corncrackers. . . . " "The Big Bear of
Arkansas," like Melville's *The Confidence Man,* pictures the
United States as a side-wheeler on the Mississippi River. In
Melville's novel, the ship ironically proclaims America's trust-
worthiness to all the world in the name *Fidèle;* in Thorpe's
story, the ship similarly advertises America's physical strength.
A product of the moral crisis of the middle '50s, *The Confidence
Man* bids what Perry Miller has called a "long farewell to national greatness." In the early '40s, Thorpe bade a less definitive
adieu. The death of the "creation bar" symbolizes the death of
Arkansas as the "creation state," and the end of the pioneer era
in the Old Southwest. Like the fabulous creature in Faulkner's
"The Bear," a story which to some extent at least was inspired
by "The Big Bear," the mighty animal of Jim Doggett's imagination stands for the strength and simplicity of an older America, and its death bespeaks a larger defeat. In hunting the bear,

Jim Doggett has in truth been hunting himself. Yet the irony of his telling the story of the death of an unhuntable bear while on board a ship misnamed the *Invincible* is not altogether crushing. If the bear hunter sits in "grave silence" confronting death, the Gentleman narrator is unshakably jaunty. An Addisonian optimist, he is, to be sure, incapable of understanding, let alone of accepting, Jim Doggett's vernacular vision. On the other hand, to the Thorpe of 1841 the Self-controlled Gentleman was still a figure to be believed in. "The Big Bear of Arkansas" ends as it began, in the gentlemanly style.

CHAPTER V

The Volcano — Part I

Might not the San Dominick, like a slumbering volcano,
suddenly let loose energies now hid?

— MELVILLE

As the woods of the Southwest were rolled back into broad
cotton fields, Mike Fink's whoop and holler rose into a curious
falsetto cackle. The sound was the synthetically high-pitched
guffaw of the Negro slave, going through the motions of his
desperate comic act. This black Clown called himself "nigger," although he hated the term; he grinned; he danced; and
he laughed and laughed. No image of self-abasement was beneath the dignity of this harried actor. By turns he played the
irresponsible child, the happy-go-lucky fool, the patient and
grateful animal. The wages of his masquerade were miserable:
mostly he was trying to build up indulgences against the evil
day when he would be caught in the act of loafing or stealing;
nevertheless, they were sufficient to drive him on in a lifelong
performance. By every word and gesture he sought to furnish
his master with an image of his utter contentment in being a
slave, for that was an image, he knew, that the white man
liked to believe in.

To lighten the boredom of his drab and empty life, the slave
sang songs, keeping time by clapping his hands or stamping
his feet, his loosened voice wailing or shouting against the in-
terminable, chanting chorus, and when he ran out of words,

humming or whistling. When he found that white men paused to listen to his music, he sang all the more, being careful as to which songs he let them hear. In the evenings, the house servant or field hand became a court jester, if he had talent, invited up to the veranda where the master and his guests were sitting and encouraged to tell jokes, act up, and rip off his gayest and most rhythmic tunes. Through the medium of these nocturnal entertainments, staged as they were in an atmosphere of friendliness and relaxation, and creating a lasting impression on all who heard them, the slave's comic masquerade became fixed in the white Southern consciousness. Before too long, the masquerade had transcended the plantation and become a national stereotype. For the command performances of the captive court jester largely inspired the Happy Darky character of the plantation novels. Echoes from the veranda were heard, too, by Northern white men who had never ventured further south than Louisville, but who would grow famous by blacking their faces with burnt cork and singing minstrels in a Negro accent, thereby creating a white imitation of a black imitation of a contented slave. As the profits from the slave system and the volume of abolitionist propaganda both began climbing upwards in the 1830s, there shuffled forth in dozens of novels and on a hundred stages a white-toothed, dehumanized buffoon, impervious to pain, incapable of anger — a harmless, empty-headed figure of fun who wouldn't have the sense to revolt even if he cared to, which he didn't. Here, indeed, was a characterization to soothe a guilt-stricken nation.

The Happy Darky image probably convinced more Northerners, it must be said, than Southerners, though doubtless this was not for any lack of Southern will to believe. Living amongst slaves, many Southerners found the image patently incredible, whereas most Northerners had only the denunciations of the abolitionist press to instruct them in its fraudulence. It was precisely this gullibility of the Northern innocent, with his appalling willingness to be "taken in" by the masquerade of the contented slave, that Melville characterized in "Benito Cereno" in the person of "sappy" Captain Delano from Duxbury, Massachusetts, who, thinking of Negroes as so many amiable Newfoundland dogs, considers the master-slave relationship, as he first encounters it on board the *San Dominick,* a beautiful one. On the other hand, the gathering disquietude that Melville creates in the minds of his readers, our agonizing unsureness, right up to the moment of shattering revelation, as to whether or not the smiling surface of life on the *San Dominick* is but the mask of a "slumbering volcano" of revolt, brilliantly reproduces the uncertain psychological atmosphere of the plantation South. For the white master class could never be sure that the very obsequiousness of the slave was not in some insidious way a mockery; that the flash of white teeth in the Negro's wide-grinning face was not somehow a challenge and a warning. When a highly intelligent Southern woman, the mistress of a large plantation, confided to her diary that she could never penetrate the "black masks" of her slaves' faces, she voiced the general anxiety of white Southerners that they were being victimized by a humor so subtle and devious they could not even begin to see the joke, let alone determine whether the invisible man behind the mask was really smiling. To many Southerners, the Nat Turner uprising of 1831, which took sixty white lives, and the bloody insurrection of Toussaint L'Ouverture, lent the substance of reality to their worst suspicions. Magnified and distorted by white fear, a more sinister image of the black emerged side by side with the Happy Darky in antebellum Southern literature.

In the writings of the most subtle Southern authors, this dreadful, half-savage beast, with a smile on his face and murder in his heart, appears only for an instant — as in that startling moment at the end of Simms's *The Yemassee* when we suddenly glimpse armed Negroes running through the darkness — or in symbolic disguise, as in the stories of Poe. When Poe explicitly portrayed the American Negro slave, he came up with the grinning, loyal Jupiter of "The Gold Bug," but, as

Harry Levin has pointed out, when he presented the Negro symbolically, Poe gave us a Jupiter transmogrified into a murderous orangoutang, or a toothy court jester who takes hideous revenge on his king by inundating him and his court with boiling tar, thus converting haughty whites into writhing blacks. In Southwestern humor, however, Prospero, the Self-controlled Gentleman, presents Caliban in his own blatant identity, and in a starring role. Being myth-makers, the humorists were of course careful to show the world many a fond portrait of lovable Cuffee, bowing and scraping, kicking up his heels, ki-yi-ing in falsetto laughter. Joseph B. Cobb's *Mississippi Scenes* (1851), for example, wavers nervously between defensive assertions that the sin of the slave ships was New England's, not the South's, and vignettes of "Negro Character in the South" which emphasize the loyalty and incorrigible cheerfulness of the slaves. Avoiding logical consistency with laughter, the humorists also justified the "peculiar institution" on the grounds that the Negro was a beast.

In *Georgia Scenes,* Longstreet told the grimly pointed story of a silly young bride who refuses to discipline her slaves. Her kindness is repaid in badly prepared meals, robbery, and open contempt. Unable to convince his wife that the household is falling apart, the distraught husband falls ill and finally dies. The moral of this tall tale was abundantly clear. The Negro was an animal which had to be kept in close rein. The corollary of this proposition was that it was good fun to unleash the creature on one's enemies; in many a Southwestern anecdote, Caliban appears as Prospero's secret weapon. From the point of view of a society morally on the defensive, no story of William Tappan Thompson's was quite so delicious as his variation on "The Legend of Sleepy Hollow," wherein a pernicious schoolteacher from Yankeeland is got rid of by marrying him to a beautiful Southern belle, who, raising her white veil after the ceremony, turns out to be the blackest Negress in the county. Mark Twain would also consider the white-black confidence game a fascinating subject, but if

Pudd'nhead Wilson is in some remote sense the literary descendant of Thompson's story, Twain's concern for the pathetic victims of the game contrasts sharply with Thompson's triumphant laughter at their expense.

Mean-spirited as Longstreet's and Thompson's stories were, they were nevertheless innocuously mild in comparison to the Negro anecdotes which appeared in Southwestern humor in the 1850s. In the decade of Dred Scott and bleeding Kansas, Southwestern jokes at the black man's expense reached an apotheosis of fury. George Washington Harris's Sut Lovingood delighted in humiliating and frightening slaves; while black men yelled with pain or terror, Sut stood by and snickered. But even Harris's vindictiveness was eclipsed by the ferocious humor of Henry Clay Lewis, a Louisiana physician. To Lewis, the female Negro was a carnal animal whom it was fun to torture under the guise of medical treatment. In a story called "Cupping the Sternum," he told of applying a "scarificator" to a slave woman's breasts and buttocks. "Click! click! went the scarificator, and amidst the shouts of the patient and my awful solicitude for fear I might cut out an artery, the 'deed was did.' But no blood flowed, nothing but grease, which trickled out slowly like molasses out of a worm hole." Elsewhere, Lewis delighted his readers with the story of his attempt to steal a Negro baby in order to dissect it; he also told, in a jocular tone, of obtaining the skull from an albino Negro cadaver — "It was the work of a few minutes to slice the face from the skull" — and then using it to frighten a superstitious widow; and he recounted in nightmarish detail how an ugly Negro dwarf tried to choke the life out of him in the middle of a swamp, and how the dwarf fell into a fire and died horribly, while the gasping author looked on. That Lewis's book, *The Swamp Doctor's Adventures in the South-West,* was considered a humorous work is amazing, but true. Published in 1858, it furnishes a significant insight into the psychology of the slavocracy on the eve of the Civil War.

ii

Yet even the savage grotesqueries of an H. C. Lewis could not finally convince the South, or the North, either, that the slave was not really a human being. For the animalistic image had to compete in men's minds with a far more compelling stereotype of the Negro. If this stereotype was every bit as misleading as either the Caliban or Happy Darky characterizations, it had a profounder emotional appeal than both of them put together; indeed, no other myth of the Negro has ever been so cherished by white America as the myth of the Black Christ.

Like the Happy Darky masquerade, the myth began in the self-consciousness of the slaves themselves — which meant that the myth was not without humor; and the essence of its humor was its two-facedness, its presentation of one image to the white man and of another to the black. The original medium of the myth was music.

As was true of the ribald, tambo-and-bones routines of the plantation verandas, and of the slower-rhythmed work songs of the river levees and the cotton fields, the spirituals sung by the slaves were full of double meanings. To the white outsider, these were songs of passive endurance, of helplessness and sorrow, of prayerful waiting for deliverance from this world into the promise of the next. Colonel Thomas Wentworth Higginson, whose command of black troops during the Civil War gave him an immense authority on Negro questions, put it this way: "Almost all their songs were thoroughly religious in their tone, and were in a minor key, both as to words and music. The attitude is always the same, and, as a commentary on the life of the race, is infinitely pathetic. Nothing but patience for this life — nothing but triumph in the next. Sometimes the present predominates, sometimes the future; but the combination is always implied." Inasmuch as Higginson would prove himself not very adept at fathoming the subtleties of Emily Dickinson's poems when he became her literary adviser, it is perhaps not surprising that as an interpreter of Negro spirituals he was somewhat simple-minded.

Beyond any doubt, the spirituals expressed a genuine religious emotion; to a people in bondage, the figure of the suffering servant of Christ was a tremendous consolation. But thanks to modern scholarship, especially Miles Mark Fisher's, we now know that there were other resonances in these songs as well.

First of all, the slaves were wont to make fun of their own religious seriousness with light hearted take-offs. Thus "I went down in the valley to Pray/My soul got happy an' I stayed all day" was sometimes sung with the alternative line, "I got drunk an' stayed all day." More importantly, many of the spirituals, even when sung "straight," expressed the Negro's outraged protest against his enslaved condition. By couching his protest in the imagery of Christian resignation, the Negro discovered the perfect disguise for his subversive thoughts — and activities. "Didn't My Lord Deliver Daniel?" and "Let My People Go" voiced a slave people's desire for freedom here and now, as well as for the beatitudes of Heaven. Jordan could mean Africa, as well as the hereafter, and Jerusalem often referred to the little town in which Nat Turner was jailed. "Steal Away" was sung by Turner and others as a signal for clandestine meetings. Death — the persistent theme of the spirituals — symbolized the Negro's awareness of the odds he faced if he attempted to escape to the North, along with his yearning to be joined with Christ. So irreligious in intent were certain versions of the spirituals that many devout slaves were shocked or disgusted by them.

Such facts were lost on most white men, Northerners and Southerners alike. All they heard — all it was intended they should hear — was the lament of helplessness. Consequently, white America developed the idea that Negroes were a *peculiarly* religious people, for to white America the growing popularity of the spirituals among Negroes in the pre-Civil War decades was a symbol of the black man's profound, unquestioning, untroubled Christian faith, and of nothing else. Through the failure of the whites to recognize in Negro spirituals their vein of characteristically American humor (for what is more characteristic of our joking than saying one thing and meaning another?), the spirituals became the irrefutable proof that Negroes were infinitely gentle, infinitely suffering things who spent their lives wailing in resigned helplessness to their God, calling out "How long, O Lord?" from their collective cross. In a period when the old religious certainties were being challenged on every side, the nation was somehow comforted by the thought that America was still the home of a fervently religious people, so that even the most suspicious Southerners, those who were sure that the Negro was a trickster and could never be trusted, were prone to accept the black man's faith at face value. Entering more and more fully into the national consciousness in the antebellum years, the spirituals built up a stereotype of the Negro which not even the most hateful anti-Negro jokes could pull down. In 1852, the myth received a further impetus from a fantastically best-selling novel. To the people of America, as Henry James would later observe, *Uncle Tom's Cabin* was "much less of a book than a state of vision."

iii

All through her childhood, Harriet Beecher felt neglected and forgotten, and not without cause. She was one of ten children; her mother died before she was six; her father, Lyman Beecher, the most dynamic Congregational preacher of a time filled with Unitarians and worse, was busy with other things. To give vent to self-pity in his household was unthinkable; one repressed such feelings, forced them to "burn inward," as Harriet once wrote, "till they burn the very soul, leaving only dust and ashes." To her feelings of neglect she added at sixteen an even more disturbing realization: she was unregenerate. This, too, had to be repressed. It was easier to lie in bed, "crying and groaning till midnight and wishing she could die young," than to tell her father that she was not among the elect. The death by drowning of young Professor Fisher of Yale increased her anguish. The fiancé of Catherine Beecher, Harriet's elder sister, Fisher died before his conversion, which to Lyman Beecher meant that he was doomed to eternal punishment. Catherine, after a period of torment, refused to accept this interpretation of her lover's fate. Her subsequent defection from her father's faith had a profound effect upon her younger sister. Even so, in the winter of 1844-1845, Harriet Beecher finally felt herself able to submit her will to God. "I am calm, but full — everywhere and in all things instructed," she wrote at the time, "and find I can do all things through Christ." A few years later, when her year-old son died from cholera, she still held firm in her faith, but beneath the surface powerful doubts must once more have begun to work upon her. In 1857, when her eldest son, whom she loved best of all her children, was drowned, and she was faced once more with accepting a Calvinistic judgment of his fate, she could contain her protest no longer: "No! no such slander as this shall the Devil ever fix in my mind against my Lord and my God!"

Mrs. Stowe's lifelong preoccupation, bordering on obsession, with the problem of religious faith canalized her literary talent. Taken as a whole, her fiction constitutes an anatomy of religious doubt that tells us much about the mind of American Protestantism in the nineteenth century. Charles H. Foster, an authority on Mrs. Stowe, has argued that *Uncle Tom's Cabin* does not fit this generalization. Mrs. Stowe's best-known novel, he says, was a product of religious conviction, written during a period when her commitment to Lyman Beecher's God was still firm; furthermore, Uncle Tom is the symbol of "the perfect Christian she felt she had become through conversion." The fault in this argument is that while Uncle Tom is certainly a perfect Christian, he is also an utterly unbelievable one, a cardboard character of cloying goodness. The reason for the failure of Uncle Tom as a character is precisely that he does *not* symbolize the perfect Christian the author felt she had become, but rather represented the person she devoutly wished she *could* become — but could not. As always with personal religious expression, the forcing of symbols beyond the point of what one feels to the point of what one feels one ought to feel is made perfectly apparent by the breakdown of that expression. Mrs. Stowe created in Uncle Tom a character who always and everywhere submitted to the will of her father's God, as she herself never quite could. It is her imperfect faith which Tom's incredible perfection betrays. Mrs. Stowe's fascination with the Negro was the fascination of a doubt-ridden white Christian with a race which she believed to be innately more submissive to the will of God than her own.

By the time she became acquainted with the fugitive slave, Josiah Henson — who would serve as the prototype for Uncle Tom — she was, therefore, fully prepared to believe what Henson very much wanted her to believe: that he was one of the saintliest of men. When he was a youth, both of Henson's shoulders had been broken by a flogging, crippling him for life. Other masters treated him equally badly, and Henson hated them. Then he heard the story of Jesus Christ and was converted; thereafter, he forgave his tormentors. In his autobiography, Henson describes an occasion when he was tempted to violence by a cruel master, and how his faith saved him from it:

One dark, rainy night, within a few days of New Orleans, my hour seemed to have come. I was alone on the deck; Mr. Amos and the hands were all asleep below, and I crept down noiselessly, got hold of an axe, entered the cabin, and looking by the aid of the dim light there for my victims, my eye fell upon Master Amos, who was nearest to me; my hand slid along the axe-handle, I raised it to strike the fatal blow, — when suddenly the thought came to me, "What! commit *murder!* and you a Christian!" I had not called it murder before. It was self-defence, — it was preventing others from murdering me,

— it was justifiable, it was even praiseworthy. But now, all at once, the truth burst upon me that it was a crime. . . . I shrunk back, laid down the axe, crept up on deck again, and thanked God, as I have done every day since, that I had not committed murder.

Brooding over the story of Henson's life, Mrs. Stowe became more firmly convinced than ever that "the negro race is confessedly more simple, docile, child-like and affectionate, than other races; and hence the divine graces of love and faith, when in-breathed by the Holy Spirit, find in their natural temperament a more congenial atmosphere." The fact that the slaves' spirituals did not always express submission to God, or that Henson was a self-publicizing, arrogant man who had a history of mistreating fellow slaves and whose piety was tempered always by prudence, never entered her mind. She accepted the Christian passivity of the colored man unquestioningly. If, in *Uncle Tom's Cabin,* she portrayed the efforts of the slave, George Harris, to escape to Canada, and vividly represented the "whole volcano of bitter feelings" that burned in his bosom, George Harris was a man with a good deal of white blood in his veins. He did not even speak in darky dialect. "Full glossy black" Uncle Tom, on the other hand, could not possibly have played George Harris's devious confidence game, for being truly black he obviously had no volcanic feelings to conceal. Uncle Tom, unlike the woman who created him, could even sustain final separation from his children without protest. Wanting desperately to believe in the possibility of total obedience to the ordinances of a Calvinist God, Mrs. Stowe envisioned her Negro hero as a Black Christ: "Give my love to Mas'r, and dear good Missis, and everybody in the place! . . . 'Pears like I loves 'em all! I loves every creatur', everywhar! — it's nothing *but* love! O, Mas'r George! what a thing 't is to be a Christian!"

Although an unbelievable character, Uncle Tom was also an unforgettable one, who troubled the conscience of the nation more profoundly than the animadversions of a Garrison or a Phillips ever had. For if the Negro was a Black Christ, then slavery was a daily crucifixion, and the moral acquiescence in that crucifixion by an allegedly Christian people was at least equivalent to the sin of Pilate. Against this proposition, no logical argument, no appeal to states' rights, or property rights, or the God-given superiority of the white race, could stand. The South had always feared that the Negro was a volcano, ready to burst forth at any moment in violence and revolt; ironically, it was precisely because black Tom was *not* a volcano that Mrs. Stowe's novel proved to be so explosive. The book's "eruptive effect," in Edmund Wilson's words, "as of a throbbing and breathing creation suddenly turned loose on the world," was felt by the entire nation. And when the war that Lincoln half-jokingly said Mrs. Stowe started was over, the character of Uncle Tom lingered on in the American imagination — for better and for worse. If his name became a term of scorn among Negroes for a servile and shamefully self-degrading masquerade, the Black Christ figure continued to provide a meaningful moral commentary on white America. To the future of American literature, Mrs. Stowe bequeathed a stereotype that would in time quicken into life in the characters of Uncle Remus, Nigger Jim, and Faulkner's Dilsey.

CHAPTER VI

The Volcano—Part II

As in eclipses, the sun was hidden; the air darkened; the whole dull, dismayed aspect of things, as if some neighboring volcano, belching its premonitory smoke, were about to whelm the great town, as Herculaneum and Pompeii, or the Cities of the Plain.

—MELVILLE

Believing that if only the Southern yeomanry could be aroused against the leadership of the planters the calamity of disunion could be averted, Hinton Rowan Helper published in 1857 his remarkable book, *The Impending Crisis of the South.* The chief enemies of the common man of the South, Helper wrote, were not Yankee capitalists but the "lords of the lash." The "unparalleled illiteracy and degradation" of the poor whites had been "purposely and fiendishly perpetuated" by the very aristocrats who proclaimed themselves the champions of white supremacy. Helper's message never got across. By 1857, the Southern myth had done its work. No longer did the plantation gentry have to fear that agrarian levelers would attempt to dispute their leadership. Indeed, certain Jacksonian radicals of previous decades now appeared as the most intransigent defenders of the slavocracy — and when demagogues like William L. Yancey and Barnwell Rhett raised the cry of secession, the answering rebel yell came loudest of all from the ranks of the lower-class whites.

The most moderate men in the South of the 1850s were to be found amongst the Whig planters and their professional allies, including a number of the novelists and humorists who had done so much to fix the aristocratic myth in the Southern mind, but who now shrank away from the revolutionary nationalism which the myth had engendered. Harmony, as always, was the watchword of these Whig reconciliationists; temperance, as in everything else, was their magic formula for settling the slavery question. There was no reason why the nation should be so upset, they argued; the question, if ignored, would work itself out; and there was always Liberia. Meantime, America should put its trust in gentlemen who "know no North and no South," as a Northern Whig lady phrased it, but who simply feel that "wherever the sacred Charter of Union stretches its cordon of brotherhood, and the Eagle and the Stars keep guard, is their country."

From the point of view of the Southern Whigs, the key to the success of this strategy was the continued good will of Northern conservatives. So long as the planters could count on the sympathy of the solid elements in the North, then the abolitionists would remain a lunatic fringe. With Northern extremists thus neutralized, the moderates in the South would be able to restrain the ardor of the secessionist hotheads. To maintain their traditional alliance with Northern conservatives was thus one of the chief objectives of Southern Whig propaganda. Plantation novels that conjured up soft-spoken gentlemen and lovely ladies dancing minuets in chandeliered ballrooms; genealogies that traced the bloodlines of Delta cotton farmers back to Cavalier refugees from Cromwell's England; sociologies that proved the South to be the successor to fifth-century Athens; these things were all a part of the process of keeping the moneyed classes of the North persuaded of the virtues of the slavocracy. So was Southwestern humor.

In satirizing the viciousness and ignorance of Jacksonian clowns, Longstreet and his successors had for years been tacitly reminding Northern gentlemen that when they criticized the slaveholding aristocracy they were undermining the very class that was the primary guarantee of social stability in the South, and that in so doing they were threatening their own security as well — for the triumph of the yeomanry over a weakened and demoralized aristocracy in one section of the country would inevitably lead to similar revolutions elsewhere. In this regard, the didacticism of Southwestern humor was akin to the preachments of John C. Calhoun, who ever since the early 1830s had been hoping to persuade Northern conservatives to silence the abolitionists by demonstrating how they would serve their own interest by upholding and preserving what he called the "equilibrium of the slaveholding states." "Let gentlemen then be warned," Calhoun said in 1847, "that while warring on us, they are warring on themselves." Ransy Sniffle and Simon Suggs were comic illustrations of Calhoun's somber analysis of the threat posed to all American conservatives by "the needy and corrupt," as he contemptuously termed the lower-class whites. If, as Richard Hofstadter has said, Calhoun was the "Marx of the Master Class," then one might call Porter's *Spirit of the Times* the *Krokodil* of Southern Whiggery. Like Helper's exposé of the planters, ironically enough, the strategy of Calhoun and the Southwestern humorists was to bind the Union together by throwing lifelines of class-consciousness across the widening breach between the sections.

By the end of the 1840s, it was clear to Calhoun that his plan was not working. On the floor of the Senate he now called for a united Southern party to defy the North. Inside Southern Whiggery, meanwhile, two inharmonious factions developed: the reconciliationists and the intransigents. In their frustration, large numbers of Whigs deserted the party altogether for the more aggressive Democracy. Yet the Compromise of 1850, with its ingenious resolution of sectional disagreements, gave the moderates new hope. In the swift, twilight years of the early 1850s, when gods like Clay and Webster and Calhoun were dying and the calmness

114

created by the clever Compromise was none the less heavy with storm warnings, a rear guard of reconciliationist Whig humorists appealed once more to the Northern upper classes for the sort of moral support that Calhoun had long since realized the slavocracy would never receive. Spurred on by desperation, the humorists staged the most urbane comedy in the history of the Southwestern tradition. Of all those who attempted to charm Northern readers with the fluency of his style and the elegance of his wit, none was more accomplished than Joseph G. Baldwin. Singing what would prove to be the swan song of Whig humor, Baldwin's Self-controlled Gentleman spoke with an unusual eloquence.

Baldwin had come to the Southwest from his native Virginia in the boom year of 1836. Twenty-one years old, he was full of schemes for getting rich quick. Both in De Kalb, Mississippi, where he first settled, and later in Gainesville, Alabama, he practiced law with some success. But he was always overextended financially and his income was never commensurate with his aspirations. Despondent over his failure to become the great man he had dreamed of being, he began to suffer from recurrent headaches, followed by long periods of physical exhaustion. He was further plagued by an uncontrollable temper. "An ebullition . . . of spleen comes flashing over me at such a rapid rate and at such an unexpected time," he wrote his wife in 1848, "that before I can think of putting myself on guard it is out." Baldwin's penetrating analysis of his hero John Randolph's temperament was widely thought to be a self-portrait:

> Apart from his other diseases, he was hypochondriacal, sometimes even to hysteria. Hypochondriacism is itself a dreadful disease, or, at least, the consequence of it. . . . He may be considered, too, during most of his life, an unsuccessful man. His political life was a series of failures, relieved, here and there, by an occasional success. He saw other men of less talent rising far above him in place and fortune. But the most effective cause of his unhappiness, he has given himself. It was his "ungovernable temper." His fierce passions had destroyed

the balance of his character. Vindictiveness is more of a
scourge to its possessor than to his enemy. There can be no
peace of mind — without which there can be no happiness —
where the heart is in perpetual warfare.

Political disappointments also had something to do with
Baldwin's despondency. Although his political career began
auspiciously enough with a successful campaign for the Alabama Legislature, when he ran for Congress in 1849 he was
up against a Democratic incumbent whose prestige in Alabama was high as a result of his having knocked down an
abolitionist Congressman on the floor of the House. Baldwin
himself was on record as saying that abolitionism was the
"anti-christ of southern policy." "What a little while ago were
the insane ravings of Fanaticism," Baldwin cried, "are now the
solemn enactments of a powerful State." He also deplored the
fact that the "red hot lava of crazy enthusiasm has already
hardened into LAW." Yet, as a Whig, Baldwin took a more
conciliatory line toward the North than his hardfisted opponent; his gentlemanly disapproval of the boiling lava of
abolitionist enthusiasm meant to some Alabamans that hot-
tempered Joe Baldwin disapproved of *all* volcanic eruptions,
including those by Southern patriots. When he refused to go
beyond a characteristically Whiggish endorsement of the Constitutional guarantees of states' rights, there was no longer any
doubt of the outcome of the election. The Democrat soundly
trounced the Whig.

Convinced that firebrand tactics would only end in disaster
for the South, and in particular for the plantation class (with
which he was allied by marriage), Baldwin took his political
rebuff very hard. As Longstreet had done before him, the
frustrated politician became a writer in order that he might
continue to have an influence on public affairs. In the early
1850s, Baldwin began work on a book of biographical sketches
of five American political leaders, in which he attempted
to establish a sense of a glorious American past that might
serve as a rallying point for agreement among all sections and

all classes. A sketch of Jefferson was placed side by side with an essay on Hamilton; a study of Andrew Jackson was followed by one of Clay; the fifth essay was devoted to the maverick, John Randolph. Each sketch portrayed a great man, and yet each hero was shown to have his limitations. The point of the book was that *they needed one another,* and that the greatness of America rested on the contributions of Americans of various points of view. But by the time the book was published in 1855 (under the title *Party Leaders*), the nation was too deeply embroiled in the bitterness of Kansas-Nebraska to pay much heed to Baldwin's historical allegory. The book sold well, but it was only a straw in the whirlwind — as the author himself recognized. Even before his manuscript was published, Baldwin had become so deeply pessimistic about the chances of *rapprochement* between the Union he loved and the South he adored that he had simply walked out on both of them. Just as Mark Twain would do seven years later when he found himself caught in the crossfire of a war about which he had very ambivalent feelings, Baldwin in 1854 took off for the West.

His flight was further motivated by the allure of fortune. Having failed to get rich in the Southwest, he resolved to try his luck with California gold and Nevada silver. (In 1862, Baldwin would pay a visit to Virginia City to attend to some mining investments. Mark Twain was by that time one of "the Comstock features which it was proper to see, along with the Ophir and Gould and Curry mines." Is it possible that the two humorists met?) Baldwin's investments never did make him a wealthy man — at least, not for very long — but California brought him other rewards. Setting up as a lawyer in San Francisco, he found the city threatened with vigilante rule. At the risk of his life, Baldwin and a group of other citizens insisted that the so-called "committee of thirteen" had no right to take the law in its own hands, but must submit to constituted authority. A few years later, he was made a justice of the California Supreme Court, where he was instrumental

117

in regularizing the anarchic legal procedures of the mining industry. In the final decade of his life (he died in 1864), Baldwin took pride in the belief that he had helped to bring the social chaos of the gold rush days under control. In California, the Whig gentleman from Alabama finally came into his own.

It was while he was beginning his work on *Party Leaders* that Baldwin published *The Flush Times of Alabama and Mississippi*. Like the biographical book, *Flush Times* is cast in the form of a series of sketches, and its perspective is historical. Ostensibly, the book is simply a comic account of the Southwestern frontier in the boom days of the mid-'30s, but implicit in every line are a vigorous defense of the planter aristocracy's achievement in stabilizing a lawless and violent society and a warning to all the gentlemen of America as to what sort of people would come to power in the South if outside interference should succeed in overturning the *status quo*. With sprightly grace and ingratiating humor, Baldwin dramatized an earnest message.

"Those were jolly times," Baldwin reminded his readers. "Nothing was settled. Chaos had come again, or rather, had never gone away. Order, Heaven's first law, seemed unwilling to remain where there was no other law to keep it company." "Society," he continued, "was wholly unorganized: there was no restraining public opinion: the law was well-nigh powerless — religion scarcely was heard of except as furnishing the oaths and *technics* of profanity." As for the crime rate . . .

> What country could boast more largely of its crimes? What more splendid roll of felonies! What more terrific murders! What more gorgeous bank robberies! What more magnificent operations in the land offices! Such McGregor-like levies of blackmail, individual and corporate! Such superb forays on the treasuries, State and National! Such expert transfers of balances to undiscovered bournes! Such august defalcations! Such flourishes of rhetoric on ledgers auspicious of gold which had departed forever from the vault! And in INDIAN affairs! — the

118

very mention is suggestive of the poetry of theft — the romance of a wild and weird larceny! What sublime conceptions
of super-Spartan roguery! Swindling Indians by the nation!
(*Spirit of Falstaff, rap!*) Stealing their land by the township!
(*Dick Turpin and Jonathan Wild! tip the table!*) Conducting
the nation to the Mississippi river, stripping them to the flap,
and bidding them God speed as they went howling into the
Western wilderness to the friendly agency of some sheltering
Suggs duly empowered to receive their coming annuities and
back rations! What's Hounslow heath to this? Who Carvajal?
Who Count Boulbon?

"Such," wrote Baldwin, "is a charcoal sketch of the interesting region — now inferior to none in resources, and the character of its population — during the FLUSH TIMES; a period
constituting an episode in the commercial history of the
world — the reign of humbug, and wholesale insanity, just
overthrown in time to save the whole country from ruin."

*Just overthrown in time to save the whole country from
ruin.* The corruption of judges and juries; the perjury and in-
timidation of witnesses; the hypocrisy of ministers and the
quackery of doctors; the mendacity of Simon Suggs, Jr., the
Indian agent, named by Baldwin in honor of Johnson Hooper's
Confidence Man; the whole furious carnival of printing-press
money and wildcat loans: here is what the Southwest once
was, Baldwin says. If this nightmare had been allowed to
persist, it would have spread until it had swallowed up the entire nation. Who was responsible for thus saving the United
States from the reign of humbug and wholesale insanity? Who
was it who had controlled the chaos in the Southwest, and
transformed a lawless frontier into a region "inferior to none
in resources, and the character of its population"? The answer
to these questions comes first of all from Baldwin's style.

In *Flush Times,* the vernacular is seldom allowed to muddy
a prose the incontestable gentlemanliness of which was so vital
to the argument that Baldwin was advancing. Only William
Byrd, among the writers of the Southwestern tradition,
was more chary about letting the Clowns speak out of their

own nature than was the author of *Flush Times*. Major Foreman, for example — a militia officer and a fervent, Whig-hating Democrat — is portrayed by Baldwin with extraordinary vividness: "His eyes stood out and were streaked like a boy's alley — and he wore a ruffled shirt; . . . on the whole, he was a pretty good live parody on an enormous goggle-eyed sun perch." Yet Major Foreman, except for one short speech, is a character who is seen and not heard. Simon Suggs, Jr., is given nowhere the number of lines to speak that Johnson Hooper had given his father. Ovid Bolus, the celebrated liar and Baldwin's most memorable Confidence Man, is never once permitted to speak, despite the fact that he is known for his loquacity; his fabrications are neither given to us first-hand nor reported *verbatim*, but are summarized by the narrator in his own quite different language. "Uproarious, bizarre humor," Baldwin once advised his son in a Chesterfieldian letter, "is not the style of a gentleman or a scholar." Restricting his use of the vernacular to a bare minimum, and employing an elegantly lapidary imitation of Addisonian prose as his narrative style, Baldwin made the "I" who is the historian of the *Flush Times* a strongly felt and unmistakable presence. To this Self-controlled Gentleman, the style everywhere implies, went all the credit for saving the Southwest, and by extension the nation, from anarchy.

Lest his style alone not plead the Southern moderate's case with sufficient clarity and persuasiveness, Baldwin also hung in his rogues' gallery of fictitious Confidence Men a number of portraits of real-life Whig gentlemen of the period. Here were the heroes to whom America should be eternally grateful. The "Hon. Francis Strother," as Baldwin portrays him, is the quintessence of Whig responsibility: "The blue eyes, strong yet kind, beaming out the mingled expression of intelligence and benignity, which, above all other marks, is the unmistakable, uncounterfeitable outward sign of a true gentleman." As a government official Strother was incorruptible, while his business conduct was above reproach. "System — order — punctuality" were his most striking personal traits; "the hinges of his mind moved as if oiled, in any direction." Bestowing what for Baldwin was heartfelt praise, he said of Strother that "he was never out of temper, never flurried, never excited." Appointed commissioner of the State Banks of Alabama, he was supposed to "bring order out of chaos," and "he succeeded wonderfully. He kept untarnished the honor of the State."

The didactic intent of Baldwin's comic history, then, was to present the Southern Whig aristocrat as the guarantor of a stable America. The difficulty with Baldwin's myth-making, however, was that it was violently at odds with the facts of American life. By the early '50s, "mild" Southern Whigs like Baldwin could no longer pretend to be in control of the forces of Southern society; unable to guarantee stability in the South, they hardly reinforced it in the North. As a consequence of this hard fact, we find all through *Flush Times* a despairing pessimism helplessly seeping into Baldwin's official attitude of amused optimism. This phenomenon is very much evident in the style. A certain pomposity; a tendency to overload sentences with displays of his literary erudition; an exaggerated elegance of diction; a weakness for inflated sentences which break down of their own weight — these are characteristics of Baldwin's style which betray a sense of strain — which reveal how terribly hard he was working to keep up the equable, unruffled pose of the Self-controlled Gentleman. His historical portraits of real Southerners also manifest the disjunction between myth and fact; in particular, those of the "Hon. S. S. Prentiss" and "Samuel Hele, Esq."

Seargent S. Prentiss of Mississippi was unquestionably one of the most dynamic political leaders that Southern Whiggery produced. His death at the age of forty-one was accounted in the conservative press of the nation a tragic loss. To many Americans, including Clay, Webster, and Calhoun, he was a haunting figure. That Baldwin should have elected to memorialize Prentiss in *Flush Times* is a tribute to Prentiss's enduring reputation in the antebellum South. It is also a fascinating illustration of how a writer's emotions can triumph over the dictates of his intellectual purpose. For Prentiss's career was hardly material for an exemplary Whig biography. To come upon Baldwin's sketch of Prentiss midway through a book dedicated to the triumph of self-control is about as startling as if one were to encounter Poe's "William Wilson" there. Although Baldwin's penchant for Addisonian moralism makes the disorder and breakdown of Prentiss's life read rather more like a cautionary tale than a Gothic horror story, the sketch is nevertheless the first instance in the myth-making history of Southwestern humor where a Whig gentleman is represented as fatally irresponsible and undisciplined. As Baldwin saw him, Prentiss was "a noble, whole-souled, magnanimous man: as pure of honor, as lofty in chivalric bearing as the heroes of romance." Yet this paragon of Southern knighthood was also the victim of "vices of mind and habit." He lacked, says Baldwin, "regular, self-denying, systematic application," and was ever attracted by "the faro-table, the midnight revel, the drunken carouse, the loose talk of the board laden with wine and cards." Finally, the "penalty" comes, "as it must ever come for a violation of natural and moral laws." Lamenting his wasted life, Prentiss falls ill of an "insidious disease" and dies. Prentiss, in sum, was gifted but weak, and clearly it is his weakness that fascinates Baldwin, as if he saw in the tragedy of this one Whig leader the prophetic image of a great political party's collapse and disintegration.

"Samuel Hele, Esq." is a different sort of history altogether, telling not of Byronic tragedy but of Falstaffian triumph. Unlike Strother, Prentiss, *et al.*, the subject of this sketch is a fire-eating Democrat, not a Whig. Hele's real name was Samuel Hale, but as Baldwin portrayed him in *Flush Times* his fictional name is more indicative of his character, for Hele is the Jacksonian wild man *par excellence*, to whom nothing in the Whig pantheon is sacred: "The faculty of veneration was not only wanting, but there was a hole where there ought to have been a bump. *Family* he had no idea of, except as a

122

means of procreation. . . . He had no respect for old things, and not much for old persons. Established institutions he looked into as familiarly as into a horse's mouth. . . . He would, if he could, have wiped out the Chancery system, or the whole body of the common law." Hele's ruthless irreverence is made very apparent in the central episode of the sketch, in which we see him pitted against a certain Miss Charity Woodey, an ugly, unsexed, gullible, hypocritical schoolteacher from the North. Just as Hele is the pseudonym for Hale, so Miss Charity Woodey is the fictional name of a real American. That she writes a letter, in the course of the story, to "Mrs. Harriet S——" only points up the obvious: the Yankee school-marm is a cruelly vicious caricature of Harriet Beecher Stowe. Ever since Longstreet's "The Village Editor," Southwestern humorists had been making fun of the Yankee intruder, but the savagery of Baldwin's story dramatically illustrates how deeply, after twenty years, the iron barb of the abolitionist critique had penetrated into the Southern soul, and in particular how profound an effect *Uncle Tom's Cabin*, published just the year before *Flush Times*, had already had on the emotions of all Southerners.

The pumpkinheads which frightened the Yankee out of Sleepy Hollow in Irving's story become in Baldwin's sketch gruesome, hobgoblin images of Southern cruelty to the Negro. Just as the frontiersman had once mocked the outsider with tall tales of his own brutishness, so Samuel Hele replies to Miss Woodey's questions about slavery with a burlesque rendition of Mrs. Stowe's account of life among the lowly: "They took the negro down to the rack in the plantation dungeon house," says Hele, "and, sending for the neighbors to come into the entertainment, made a Christmas frolic of the matter. They rammed a powder-horn down his throat, and lighting a slow match, went off to wait the result. When gone, Col. Gyves bet Gen. Sam Potter one hundred and fifty dollars that the blast would blow the top of the negro's head off; which it did." When Miss Woodey timorously inquires, "But, Mr. Hele,

— do tell me, — do they *now* part the young children from their mothers — poor things?" Hele replies, "Why, no, — candidly, — they do *not* very much, now. The women are so sickly, from overwork and scant feeding and clothing, that the child is worth little for the vague chance of living. But when cotton was fifteen cents a pound, and it was cheaper to take away the child than to take up the mother's time in attending to it, they used to send them to town, of a Sunday, in big hamper baskets, for sale, by the dozen. . . . There was a great feud between the planters on this side of Sanotchie, and those on the other side, growing out of the treatment of negro children. Those who sold them off charged the other siders with inhumanity, in drowning theirs like blind puppies in the creek, which was resented a good deal at the time, and the accusers denounced them as abolitionists." Absolutely terrified, Miss Charity Woodey departs for the North as fast as she can.

Apart from its extremely revealing insights into the psychology of white Southern guilt, "Samuel Hele, Esq." is significant primarily because of the role played in the sketch by the main character. Samuel Hele, a family-hating, tradition-scorning Democrat, precisely the sort of Jacksonian wild man who was the traditional object of Whig laughter, is here represented as the Brom Bones who defends the Southern Sleepy Hollow against the Yankee intruder. One of the last sketches that Baldwin wrote before his departure for the West, the story symbolizes the weakening of Whig authority in the South even more unmistakably than did his sketch of S. S. Prentiss, for it tacitly admits the increasing ability of the intransigent Democracy to speak as the voice of a united and defiant Dixie. *Flush Times* begins by celebrating the Self-controlled Gentleman; it ends with the Gentleman surrendering his hero's role to a Hele.

ii

The fall of the Self-controlled Gentleman from a powerful and commanding figure into a Southwestern version of Roderick Usher was a phenomenon that other authors besides Baldwin recognized. Mrs. Stowe was no Southerner, but neither was she the gullible Miss Charity Woodey. With her sensitivity to the vibrations of national feeling, she intuitively understood the moral paralysis that had overcome conservative Southerners of good will, and why it was that in the South of the 1850s the best seemed to lack all conviction, while the worst were full of passionate intensity. In the figure of Augustine St. Clare, the planter aristocrat of *Uncle Tom's Cabin,* she might conceivably have characterized the fieriness of an Edmund Ruffin, or the intemperateness of a Preston Brooks, or the coarseness of a Barnwell Rhett; attracted as she always would be by the agonies of conscience, she chose instead to make St. Clare a man of sensitivity and taste, who scorns the Northern businessman for his ruthlessness, and yet is himself tormented by the daily cruelties exacted from him by the slavery system. Weak-willed, voluble, a heavy drinker, St. Clare would prefer to indulge, in the manner of Roderick Usher, his "decided genius for music" and let the world go hang, but his aesthetic enjoyments are haunted by the fear that the world will end by hanging him. It is a fear which casts a long shadow in the book. For if Mrs. Stowe comes forward in the closing pages to tell the reader in her own vigorous New England way that faith and good works can yet save the nation from disaster, all through the novel the brilliant, sickly St. Clare has been setting forth another and darker vision of history. Mrs. Stowe's is the energetic voice of Jeremiah, warning America to be true to the Word of God, lest the nation incur God's awful wrath; St. Clare's is the voice of a fatalistic skepticism, doubting both God and man. Ridiculing the Liberia solution, to which Mrs. Stowe was strongly committed; envisaging the working classes of Europe as about to explode like a steamboat boiler and the United States as a volcano about to erupt; prophesying, shortly before his death, a universal and inescapable *dies irae* — Augustine St. Clare embodies the pessimism and the terrible indecisiveness that were the most conspicuous qualities of the moderate Southerner in the final decade before the Civil War.

How sensitively Mrs. Stowe had registered the thoughts and feelings of the "mild" Southern Whigs can be measured by looking at the most notable of the many "answers" to *Uncle Tom's Cabin* — *The Master's House,* by Thomas B. Thorpe, author of "The Big Bear of Arkansas." It is the story of a Southern gentleman named (in perfect accordance with Whiggery's temperate ideals) Mildmay. His life is devoted to harmony, especially harmony between the sections. He defends the North to his planter friends and *vice versa,* and he deplores the zeal of both the abolitionists and the Southern nationalists. Returning all Negroes to Africa, he believes, will be the ultimate solution to the slavery question. Meanwhile, he is simply concerned to keep the lid on what he calls "the moral volcano" of American life. Mildmay, in other words, is the Whig hero *par excellence,* holding the centrifugal forces of society together by the sheer force of his temperate personality. This man would seem indeed to be an "answer" to Mrs. Stowe, an utter refutation of Augustine St. Clare.

Yet *The Master's House* is a product of the same year that brought forth Kansas-Nebraska; by the time the novel was published, Thorpe himself had already deserted the sinking ship of Whiggery for the xenophobic assurances of Know-Nothingism. What is truly striking about Thorpe's "answer" is the extent to which the story of Mildmay confirms rather than repudiates *Uncle Tom's Cabin.* In 1841, in "The Big Bear," Thorpe had managed to surmount his sense of gathering disaster with a last-minute affirmation of the Self-controlled Gentleman's continuing mastery of affairs, but by the middle '50s Thorpe no longer believed that the forces of moderation would win, and his novel reflects that fact. When Sylvanus Toadvine, Mildmay's brutal overseer, commits a murder, the entire structure of harmonious Southern life comes tumbling down. Mildmay saves Toadvine from being lynched, because he believes in government by law — only to see a piney woods judge and jury acquit the overseer. The mob gets further out of control when a tobacco-chewing oaf, who cannot even spell his name, but who knows how to curse Negroes and Northerners, defeats Mildmay's planter friend, Moreton, for political office. At the climax of the novel, a misunderstanding between the two friends causes the embittered Moreton to challenge Mildmay to a duel. Stung by Moreton's taunts, Mildmay throws over his temperate ideals, fights the duel, and kills his friend. At the end of the book, a broken and mournful Mildmay sits in pitch-darkness in a graveyard. Vulgar parvenus and demagogic politicians have taken over the plantation houses and Mildmay has been ostracized. The world he had known and upheld has been destroyed, and he with it.

The implication of this extraordinary novel for Southwestern humor is that its traditional hero was finished. In a decade in which the metaphor of the volcano became the obsessive figure of politicians, poets, preachers, editorialists and novelists,[1] all of whom used it to express their sense that America was going out of control, it became less and less possible for conservative humorists to keep up the serenely superior manner of the *Spectator*. In a world where Mildmay sat in darkness, gentlemanly narrators could not speak with the confidence of an A. B. Longstreet about the triumph of the moral light over the moral dark. Baldwin's *Flush Times*, published the year before Kansas-Nebraska, was the last important example of the Whig manner in Southwestern humor. If imita-

[1] To take only one example out of many, consider Melville's references to the volcano in his work of the 1850s: in the chapter on "The Doubloon" in *Moby Dick*; in the description of the slave ship in *Benito Cereno*; and in the description of the city in *Israel Potter*.

tions of the manner continued to appear for the rest of the decade, even as the Whig party — broken as it was — continued to have its adherents, here and there, these imitations no longer carried the oldtime conviction.

By far the most interesting of the imitators was the young Georgia writer, Richard Malcolm Johnston, who began writing comic sketches in the latter half of the '50s. Appearing between the collapse of the Whig tradition and the advent of Mark Twain, Johnston's early work reveals the death pangs of an old hero and the struggles of a new one to be born.

A reconciliationist, Johnston continuously and outspokenly denounced the idea of Southern nationalism, until finally his courage cost him his professorship at the University of Georgia. During and after the Civil War, Johnston conducted various private schools, where he put into effect his theory that education should inculcate self-discipline. In part, his educational views were a reaction to the harsh treatment of rural schoolmasters to which he had been subjected as a boy. In part, too, his educational ideal represented a response to his fear of his own temper. Challenges to duel, angry disputes with friends over card games, unreasonable bursts of anger at his students, constituted a recurrent pattern in Johnston's life which firm resolutions could never obliterate. But most of all, Johnston's desire to teach Southern boys self-control was the product of his aversion to the hotheaded leadership of ex-Whig planters who, joining hands with the demagogues of the Democracy, had taken the antebellum South down the road to disaster. His fiction, like his educational theories, asserted his faith in the younger generation.

The title Johnston gave to his first collection of stories was *Georgia Sketches*, an indication that he thought of himself as belonging to the Longstreet tradition. But *Georgia Sketches* is a very different book from *Georgia Scenes*. The tone of Johnston's narrative, first of all, lacks the self-assurance of Longstreet's. Even more significantly, the aristocrats who appear in his stories are more often ugly-tempered brutes

than they are urbane spectators. The most consistently responsible and attractive human beings in *Georgia Sketches* —
and in Johnston's later fiction as well — are children. The
schoolboys of "The Goosepond School," who overthrow the
despotic rule of their master, and the twins in the story called
"The Expensive Treat of Colonel Moses Grice," whose peace-
able relations with one another make such a contrast to the
hotheaded Colonel Grice and his brother, are the real heroes
of Johnston's imaginative world. In after years, as Johnston's
fiction softened into sweetly sentimental recollections of the
past and self-conscious quests for the quaint, the Self-controlled Gentleman staged a comeback in Johnston's work in
the guise of that nostalgic tourist who figures so prominently
in all the "local color" fiction of the 1870s and 1880s. Yet, even
in these later stories, the Gentleman is only intermittently the
moral center of Johnston's humor. In a South that preferred to
go to war rather than to remain in the Union, a moderate ex-
professor, appalled by the irresponsibility of adults, turned
toward the child-hero as the hope of the future.

iii

For diametrically opposite reasons, the most extreme Southern nationalists also repudiated the Self-controlled Gentleman. Isolated, outnumbered, haunted by its own guilt, the
secessionist South was in no mood to hear moderation and
temperance extolled. In place of the Gentleman, there
emerged as the comic spokesman of the slavocracy a series of
red-necked, dialect-drawling louts, like Bill Arp or Mozis Ad-
dums, whose opinion of the Union was that the "Gnashnul
Dimmockracy of the North and South ar jined together like
the rooms in a jale," and who boasted that he was an "outenout
ole fashin, strait up and down, Staits rite, Jacksin, Kansis
dimmokrat, bleevin in nuthun but what the party bleeved in,
voting fur a dimmokrat aginst eny body, I don't keer hoo."

Of all this raffish crew, by far the most colorful was an illiterate, whisky-drinking youth from the Tennessee mountains. A "queer looking long legged, short bodied, small headed, white haired, hog eyed, funny sort of genius," his name was Sut Lovingood. His literary début was made in the *Spirit of the Times* for November 4, 1854, although he was destined never to appear in Porter's pages again. For the *Spirit* pursued a policy of Whiggish conciliation to the bitter end, and Sut Lovingood's yarns were a stronger brand of Southwestern humor than the magazine cared to dispense. Thenceforward, Sut Lovingood appeared in Southern newspapers, principally in the Nashville *Union and American,* a fire-eating Democratic sheet.

Sut's creator, George Washington Harris, had been born in the North, in Allegheny City, Pennsylvania, but had moved to Knoxville, Tennessee, while still a boy. Leaving school after a year or so, he had a varied career in East Tennessee as a jeweler's apprentice, steamboat captain, metal worker, surveyor, politician, postmaster, copper mine manager, glass works manager, sawmill operator, and — at the last — railroad employee. During the 1840s he was a frequent contributor to the *Spirit of the Times* of "sporting epistles" and backwoods anecdotes. He learned to manage the Addisonian style with slick facility, while his command of the vernacular showed right from the start that "rare kind of dramatic imagination that can get movement directly into words" which F. O. Matthiessen admired in his later work. To Porter's readers, Harris became a well-known author. If he and the *Spirit* editor parted company after 1854, it was not for personal reasons; their split symbolized rather the larger secession of which Harris was now becoming the fanatical exponent.

The brainchild of that fanaticism was Sut Lovingood, born in the very year that Kansas-Nebraska inflamed the slavery controversy as never before. Students of Southern nationalism who are given to buttressing their books with quotations from the fantastic sociologizing of George Fitzhugh's *Cannibals*

All!, or from the poems of Henry Timrod, or from the grandiloquent rhetoric of the "chivalry politicians," would do well to remember that birthday. For in ignoring Sut Lovingood, as they have, they not only overlook the most gifted humorist to come out of the Southwest before Mark Twain, but an author who has more to tell us than any other Southern writer of his time about the mind of a society at bay.

Many of the Sut Lovingood yarns are political satires. Consumed by hatred for the North, Harris went to extraordinary lengths to vilify Northern politicians. Following the Presidential election of 1860, he turned the full force of his invective on Abraham Lincoln, representing him as a coward and a fool, and savagely caricaturing his physical appearance. Harris's most violent humor, however, was reserved for fellow Tennesseans. For not only was Tennessee the last Southern state to leave the Union, but the eastern part of the state, particularly the region around Knoxville, was notorious for its anti-secessionist sentiments. In Knoxville itself, the eccentric Parson Brownlow, an itinerant Methodist preacher who had drifted into politics, conducted a brilliantly sarcastic campaign against disunion in the pages of the Knoxville *Whig*. The last Unionist paper in the Southeastern United States, the *Whig* was the moving spirit behind the East Tennessee "rebellion against the rebellion" in 1861. Harris, detesting Brownlow and despising Knoxville for its "treason" against the South, poured out his rage in a series of ferociously comic diatribes.

When the war came, Harris refused to live in such a contemptible city any longer and took his family away. For four years, he and his wife and their five children wandered through the South — from Chattanooga to Decatur, Alabama, to Trenton, Georgia, and beyond. No one knows exactly how they lived, or all that they did; one catches sight of Harris near Rome, Georgia, late in the war, passing through the Federal lines on muleback to procure some salt, but it is only a passing glimpse; the years of the South's agony were years of silence for Harris. He came out of the war an unreconstructed Democrat, and soon Sut Lovingood was back at work spewing out his contempt for the South's newest crop of enemies: the carpetbaggers, the Radicals, "nigger rule," and Ulysses S. Grant. But Grant's election to the Presidency in 1868 was the last straw. Too bitter even to go on fighting, Harris managed to turn out three more comic sketches and then wrote no more. A year later, he was dead, under bizarre circumstances. In December of 1869, Harris traveled up to Lynchburg, Virginia, to transact some business for his railroad employers; on the way back, he became ill and had to be taken off the train when it reached Knoxville. He died without regaining consciousness on the night of December 11. A man who had spent his life believing that the horizons of his world were ringed with deadly enemies, he went to his grave amidst rumors that he had been the victim of foul play. "In behalf of a community, who deeply deplore the death of Captain Harris," wrote the Knoxville *Press and Herald* a few days later, "and who shudder to think of his horrible, lonely ride in a railway train, without one pitying glance or gentle hand to soothe his dying moments, we ask that whatever facts in the possession of anyone, tending to explain this most mysterious death, be published, that the world may know, whether Capt. George W. Harris died by the stroke of his God, or the poisoned chalice of a wicked man." The mystery as to whether or not Harris died by poison has never been cleared up. The only certainty is that he had lived by it.

iv

As always in Southwestern humor, the best of the Sut Lovingood stories are not Harris's overtly political satires, but rather those stories which issued from a deeper level of his imagination — which turn away from the "real world" of contemporary affairs and have their being in the realm of comic fantasy.

In these fantasies, Harris retained vestiges of the traditional forms of Whig comedy. We are, for example, made aware of a Gentleman, named George, who speaks a genteel language; and his occasional introductions of the action constitute a rudimentary "frame." But the striking thing about George is how shadowy a figure he is. Harris the secessionist had nothing but contempt for Whiggery's ideals, and as a consequence the voice of temperate gentlemanliness is as severely restricted in his comedy as the vernacular Clown's had once been. At best, Harris's Gentleman is heard for as long as a short paragraph; in some stories, he does not speak at all. His role is as peripheral as that of the end-man in a minstrel show: popping in occasionally from the wings, he feeds lines to the star performer, the once-despised Clown.

To a degree, Harris's choice of a teen-aged youth as his hero reveals once again the vestigial influence of the gentlemanly tradition upon his imagination. William Byrd's *Dividing Line* had represented the North Carolina frontiersman as a childish figure, who should be seen and not heard; the Self-controlled Gentleman in "The Big Bear of Arkansas" had condescendingly referred to Jim Doggett as a child of the woods; James K. Paulding had conceived of Nimrod Wildfire as just an overgrown boy. In the Southwestern tradition, the Clown was funny precisely because he was unselfconsciously infantile, even when he was technically an adult. Whooping and hollering and jumping into the air, he behaved with childlike unrestraint in no matter what company; his vernacular speech — grotesque, drawling, ungrammatical — was a sort of babytalk. Regarded as a child in spirit, the Clown tended more and more to become a child in fact, thus establishing an image of the vernacular character which has lasted down to the present. From the boy-Quixote of "Georgia Theatrics" to Sut Lovingood, from Huck Finn to Nick Adams to Holden Caulfield, the most memorable vernacular voices in American literature have been the voices of children. However, what differentiates Harris from Longstreet and the earlier humorists, and makes him the forerunner of Mark Twain and Hemingway and Salinger, is that he negotiates the crucial transition from regarding the child with the patronizing attitude of the fond adult, who "knows better" about everything in life, to looking at the adult world through the eyes of a child and judging it by the standard of values of a child. Richard Malcolm Johnston made the child his hero in the same decade as did Harris, but Johnston nevertheless continued to view the child as Longstreet had: in detachment, and at a distance. In the Sut Lovingood yarns, the child becomes the author's persona. Although Harris christened gentlemanly George with his own name, it is more significant that Harris was known all through East Tennessee by the nickname of "Sut." On those comparatively rare occasions in the yarns when George is on stage, we view the child-hero from an external and superior vantage point, but not until *Huckleberry Finn* would an American book sustain a child's point of view more faithfully than the Sut Lovingood stories.

Paradoxically, Harris the secessionist was driven to adopt a child's point of view for the same reason that had prompted Johnston the Unionist to make children the moral center of his stories — namely, that in all societies children are to a greater or lesser degree aliens, barred by their youthfulness and inexperience from full membership in the tribe, and kept in ignorance of its mysteries. If a vernacular view of the world has so often been a child's view as well, in modern American literature, it is because both represent unofficial — or even antiofficial — ways of seeing things. Harris in the pro-Union atmosphere of Knoxville and Johnston in a university where one could not teach if one did not hate the North both felt themselves strangers in the community, and their imaginative sympathy with the children of their fiction is symptomatic of their alienation.

However, just as Harris and Johnston had nothing in common politically, so their child-heroes are different. Edmund Wilson's succinct summary of what sort of youth Sut Lovingood is makes it clear that Sut could hardly have symbolized Richard Malcolm Johnston's piously Whiggish hope that the future would bring forth a more self-controlled South: "The deadpan homicides and corpses of the early Mark Twain," Wilson has written, "are given a certain dignity by the stoicism of the pioneer, and the nihilistic butcheries of Ambrose Bierce a certain tragic force by his background of the Civil War. But Sut Lovingood is something special. He is not a pioneer contending against the wilderness; he is a peasant squatting in his own filth." An outsider in the community, Sut is further cut off from love and human connection by reason of his estrangement from his half-crazy family; like old Mr. Flood in E. A. Robinson's poem, the boy has a whisky jug for his closest friend; in all the heterogeneous company of orphans and castaways who make up the heroes of American literature, there is no one more lost or miserable than Sut Lovingood. Lonely, afraid, often half-drunk, he imagines himself surrounded by enemies, as in a bad dream. Everywhere he looks, he sees a fundamental disorder; in Sut's view, normal human arrangements have degenerated in a frenzy of superstition, lust, and hypocrisy. Nor is evil a thing of the past in Sut's world. When the youth tells, as he does in one of his yarns, about a doctor who is a grave-robber, a planter who is an adulterer, a sheriff who is a coward and a Negro parson who is a common thief, he is not reminiscing in the manner of the Self-controlled Gentleman about former unpleasantnesses, he is describing society *as it now is*. The triumph of the moral light over the moral dark, and all the other Whig reassurances as well, have quite faded away in Sut's yarns, along with the virtual disappearance of the gentlemanly style. The vernacular narration of this outcast is not intended to instruct the reader in the virtues of the temperate life — indeed, just the reverse. For Sut's humor blocks critical awareness in order to release a tremendous burst of emotion; he is concerned not to reprove society, but to revenge himself upon it. Although Sut never comes to explicit revolt, his sadistic practical jokes — on women, on his parents, on Yankees and Negroes, on Methodist preachers who resemble Parson Brownlow, on anyone who has had an education or who smacks of a genteel upbringing — constitute his war against the world. While his despised victims scream, knowing Sut laughs in enjoyment. His one hero is Wirt Staples, a mountain bully-boy who is everything that this weak, ugly youth wishes he could be:

> His britches wer buttoned tite roun his loins, an' stuffed 'bout half intu his boots, his shut bagg'd out abuv, an' wer es white es milk, his sleeves wer rolled up tu his armpits, an' his collar wer es wide open es a gate, the mussils on his arms moved about like rabbits onder the skin, an' ontu his hips an' thighs they play'd like the swell on the river, his skin wer clear red an' white, an' his eyes a deep, sparklin', wickid blue, while a smile fluttered like a hummin bird roun his mouf all the while.

Whenever Wirt is kicking a sheriff, or booting a Negro through a window, or riding horseback through a courtroom, Sut is there to cheer him on with laughter.

Yet no matter how hard Sut laughs, he can never get rid of his harrowing guilt-complex and his implacable self-contempt. No matter how well he succeeds in humiliating his enemies, he always comes back to the characterization of himself as a coward and a "durn'd fool," and to the terrible assertion that he was born without a human soul and would be glad to be dead, except that he is afraid of dying. No other detail about the boy's life is more important than this. For if there can be little doubt that Harris's depiction of Sut is a ghastly caricature of his own furious, inner life — that the youth's antisocial pranks were Harris's symbolic way of getting even with contemptible Knoxville — the fact of Sut's corrosive sense of guilt rounds out an even more significant correspondence. Sut Lovingood's haunted imagination reflects like a cracked mirror the frantic state of mind of the secessionist South. Perhaps the first juvenile delinquent in American literature, Sut Lovingood is a rebel without a cause; but his guilty contempt for himself, and his paranoid hatred of the enemies whom he sees all about him, tell us much about those rebels of the Lost Cause whom the Southern intellectual, George Tucker, described in 1861 as "crazed in the fancies of imaginary evils, and of their strange remedies." More intensely than any other figure in American literature, Harris's hero embodies the worst aspects of the slavocracy, even as the name "Sut" is an ugly contraction of "South."

The youth also represents, however — and it is this complexity which makes him such a fascinating character — a prototypical Huck Finn, whose youthful refusal to submit to orthodoxy compels our sympathy as well as our despair. Sut's ingratiating qualities were what Faulkner was thinking of in 1956 when he responded to a question about his favorite characters in literature:

> My favorite characters are Sarah Gamp. . . . Mrs. Harris, Falstaff, Prince Hal, Don Quixote and Sancho, of course. Lady Macbeth I always admire. And Bottom, Ophelia and Mercutio. . . . Huck Finn, of course, and Jim. Tom Sawyer I never liked much — an awful prig. And then I like Sut Lovingood from a book written by George Harris about 1840 or '50 in the Tennessee mountains. He had no illusions about himself, did the best he could; at certain times he was a coward and knew it and wasn't ashamed; he never blamed his misfortunes on anyone and never cursed God for them.

Sut is an appealing character, in other words, because unlike the adult society in which he lives he has no pretensions. His realism is oftentimes unpleasant, but it is always candid, and he infallibly sees himself for who he is. The romantic notions of what their life was like which beguiled so many Southerners of the period seem particularly preposterous by comparison with Sut's vernacular honesty. Thus in a post-Civil War story called — with grotesque humor — "Well! Dad's Dead," Sut turns an account of the death of his father into an appeal to the South to give up its absurd illusions that the dead past could somehow be recaptured. The appeal is entirely typical of Sut's imagination. Huck and Sut are very different children in many respects (for example, Sut has a sex life, Huck does not), but they are very much alike in their mutual refusal to take any stock in dead people. As in *The Adventures of Huckleberry Finn,* the tension between myth-minded adults and literal-minded Sut is a source of comic delight.

In the Sut Lovingood stories, too, the style is the man — or rather, the youth — and there is a wonderful, lifesaving freshness to Sut's language which almost always redeems his adventures from sordidness. In the teeth of a frightful world, his spontaneous metaphors and original images generate laughter and renewed hope. Sut's admiration for Wirt Staples may be a deplorable sign of his nihilism, but the passage in which he describes his feelings toward Wirt's wife is an affirmation of life. As F. O. Matthiessen has said, the description is a hymn to fertility — a hymn, it must be added, with an ache in its music, for Sut affirms a life which is beyond his youthful grasp. At the very heart of his vernacular style is the wistfulness, and the awed attention to details, of a lost and lonely boy:

> Wirt's wife got yearly supper, a rale suckit-rider's supper, whar the 'oman ove the hous' wer a rich b'lever. Thar were chickens cut up, an' fried in butter, brown, white, flaky, light, hot biskit, made wif cream, scrambil'd aigs, yaller butter, fried ham, in slices es big as yure han, pickil'd beets, an' cowcumbers, roas'in ears, shaved down an' fried, sweet taters, baked, a stack ove buckwheat cakes, as full ove holes es a sifter, an' a bowl of strained honey, tu fill the holes. . . . Fur drinks, she hed coffee, hot, clar an' brown, an' sweet milk es cold es a rich man's heart. Ontu the dresser sot a sorter lookin potbellied bottil, half full ove peach brandy, watchin a tumbler, a spoon, an' a sugar bowl. Oh! massy, massy, George! . . . . I gets dorg hongry every time I sees Wirt's wife, ur even her side-saddil, ur her frocks a-hangin on the closeline.
> Es we sot down, the las' glimmers ove the sun crep thru the

histed winder, an' flutter'd on the white tabilcloth an' play'd
a silver shine on her smoof black har, es she sot at the head ove
the tabil, a-pourin out the coffee, wif her sleeves push'd tight
back on her white roun' arm, her full throbbin neck wer bar to
the swell of her shoulders, an' the steam ove the coffee made a
movin vail afore her face, es she slowly brush'd hit away wif
her lef han', a-smilin an' a-flashin hur talkin eyes lovinly at her
hansum husbun. I thot ef I were a picter-maker, I cud jis' take
that ar supper an' that ar 'oman down on clean white paper,
an' make more men hongry, an' hot tu marry, a-lookin at hit in
one week, nor ever ole Whitfield converted in his hole life;
back-sliders, hippercrits, an' all, I don't keer a durn.

v

Two years before his death, Harris collected the best of
the Sut Lovingood stories and brought them out as a book.
Generally ignored by the reviewers, the collection received
its most interesting notice in a West Coast publication called
the *Alta California*. Written by a young author whose mind
was crammed with impressions of life, but who still had not
figured out exactly what to do with them, the review responded
enthusiastically to the vernacular humor of the yarns. Whether
Harris was gratified — or even aware — that the author of
"The Celebrated Jumping Frog of Calaveras County" had
liked his stories is unrecorded. As for the reviewer, he may be
pardoned if he did not give much thought to Harris's book,
for after all, he was about to sail for Europe for the first
time. Nevertheless, the time would come when Mark Twain
would have occasion to remember Sut Lovingood.

CHAPTER VII

An American Image

It's a complex fate, being an American.

— HENRY JAMES

FROM HIS FATHER Mark Twain inherited, along with "a sump-tuous legacy of pride in his fine Virginia stock," a firm loyalty to Whig principles. Thus one of his earliest pieces for the Hannibal *Journal*, a Whig newspaper briefly controlled by his older brother, Orion, was a satire on "Democratic rascality," while a travel letter of the mid-1850s, recounting Twain's experiences in Washington, D.C., featured a description of Thomas Hart Benton which endeavored to cut the giant of the Missouri Democracy down to size (an endeavor that would be reflected twenty years later in Tom Sawyer's disillusioning discovery that "the greatest man in the world (as Tom supposed), Mr. Benton, an actual United States Senator, . . . was not twenty-five feet high, nor even anywhere in the neighborhood of it"). When the Whig party began to break up, Twain flirted for a time with Know-Nothingism; in the fateful election of 1860, faced with the Devil-and-deep-blue-sea alternatives of Lincoln and Douglas, he supported Bell, who voiced the old slogans of the Whig planters.

His taste in humor reflected his politics. Twain's unpublished notebooks reveal that such books as *Georgia Scenes, Flush Times, Simon Suggs,* and *Major Jones's Courtship* were personally familiar to him, but even if this evidence were

140

lacking, the apprentice humor of Sam Clemens demonstrates forcibly enough that the Whig humorists of the Southwestern tradition were the authors to whom he went to school. The structure, diction, and narrative tone of "The Dandy Frightening the Squatter," Twain's first comic sketch, show him imitating the Longstreet manner, while the Thomas Jefferson Snodgrass letters, which Twain began writing for the Keokuk, Iowa, *Post* in 1856, are supposedly the work of a shrewd and callous yokel remarkably like Simon Suggs.

When war came, and Whig slogans faded irrevocably away, Twain became a Confederate, although not without mixed feelings. With his prestige as a steamboat pilot, he was easily elected lieutenant of the Marion Rangers and was soon in the field with his men. Like Henry James, however, who was rendered *hors de combat* when he suffered an "obscure hurt" to his back while helping the volunteers of the Newport Fire Department to put out a blaze, Mark Twain was destined to miss the Civil War partly because of a fiery accident. Not long after his enlistment, a hayloft in which he and some of his soldiers were sleeping caught fire, and Lieutenant Clemens was forced to jump for the barnyard below. In the fall, he painfully sprained his ankle and had to be put to bed. By the time he was up and about, he had had enough of fighting for a cause he only half-believed in, so that when his brother Orion, now a fervent Lincoln Republican, was appointed Territorial Secretary of Nevada, Twain leaped at the chance to secede from the Secession and go along as secretary to the Secretary. In the American manner of Huck Finn, Henry Fleming and Frederic Henry, Mark Twain in 1861 chose to make a separate peace — only to find, as the heroes of our literature have so often discovered, that in fleeing responsibilties he was only catching up with them.

For although far beyond the battle, Virginia City was torn apart by partisan loyalties. Quite consciously, Mark Twain cultivated friends among both the Northern and Southern groups in the Territory, and in his writings for the *Enterprise* he tried to steer clear of national political issues and of what he euphemistically called "eastern news." Yet Twain was an arrogant young man with a sharp tongue in his head. When he described himself, in a letter to his mother and sister, as "the most conceited ass in the Territory," he echoed a widely held opinion in Nevada. In consequence, his ego tended to get involved in his wit-combats with other journalists, and when it did, Washoe journalism was apt to break out into facsimile civil war. The decisive battle, as far as Mark Twain was concerned, came in the spring of 1864. Wishing to make fun of a fancy dress ball that had been held in Carson City for the benefit of the Sanitary Fund (the Civil War equivalent of the Red Cross), Twain reached for the immemorial smear bucket of Southern polemics: in the *Enterprise* he editorially suggested that the funds raised at the ball were actually destined "to aid a Miscegenation Society somewhere in the East." An exchange of insults between the *Enterprise* and its Virginia City rival, the *Union,* at once ensued, and within a week — as Mark Twain ruefully confessed in a letter to Orion and Mollie Clemens — he was open to challenges to duel from three men and was awaiting the outcome of a challenge sent to a fourth. The moment ranks as one of the significant crises of his life, and Twain met it unflinchingly. Once again, he ran away. In all likelihood, he did so not because he was afraid, nor because, as he later claimed, dueling was a penitentiary offense in Nevada, but because he was wrong, and he knew it. The affair had gone too far for him to back out without being made the laughingstock of Virginia City; yet to take to the field of honor to settle a dispute he regretted seemed equally ridiculous; and so he threw away his gun once more, symbolically speaking, and fled over the mountains to California. "In Missouri," Twain would write in *Pudd'nhead Wilson,* "the highest duty in life" for a gentleman was to protect his honor by obeying the "unwritten laws" of his caste. "Those laws were his chart; his course was marked out on it; if he swerved from it by so much as half a point of the compass it meant shipwreck to his honor; that is to say, degradation from his rank as a gentleman." To refuse to fight a duel was "infamy." A Missouri Whig and the proud son of Virginia slaveholding stock, Mark Twain knew precisely what he was doing to himself when he took off for California. That he fled, nevertheless, is a sign of how profoundly the West had altered his view of life and his conception of himself.

As his friend Howells knew, Mark Twain was first and always a Southerner; Southern traits were as fundamental to his personality as Whitman had noted they were to Lincoln's; a sense of the past and a sense of place emerge as strongly from Twain's fiction as from Faulkner's. However, Twain became the "Lincoln of our literature," in Howells's beautiful phrase, only by transcending the limitations of a sectional outlook without betraying its strengths. His achievement as a literary artist was predicated on his becoming what Howells described as a "de-Southernized" Southerner. Like Lincoln, Twain reached greatness by growing beyond provinciality to a truly national stature — by becoming, in a word, an American. The process of Twain's emergence from his provincial chrysalis was a long and complicated one, but the crucial period in the transformation was his wartime sojourn in the West. For even though Twain's boyhood home of Hannibal had been a "little democracy . . . full of liberty, equality, and the Fourth of July," the town had also been marked by what Twain came to call an "aristocratic taint." "The class lines were quite clearly drawn," he remembered in his *Autobiography*, "due to the circumstance that the town's population had come from slave states and still had the institution of slavery with them in their new home." Not until he reached the free air of the Nevada Territory did Twain come in contact with an unalloyed democracy. The effect wrought upon him by his Western experience can be traced in Twain's changing attitude toward the Civil War, as he expressed himself on the subject in a series of letters to William H. Claggett, his old mining partner. In February, 1862, we find Twain writing, "Well, Billy, tell Tom Smith they've gone and done it. Old Curtis, you know. He has thrashed our Missourians like everything. But by the Lord, they didn't do it on the Sacred Soil, my boy. They had to chase 'em clear down into Arkansas. . . ." [1] The point of view, as betrayed by the use of "they" and "our," is clearly Confederate. A letter of the following month reveals a Yankee-hating intransigency: "I have heard from several reliable sources that Sewall will be here shortly, and has sworn to whip me on sight. Now what would you advise a fellow to do? — take a thrashing from the son-of-a-bitch or bind him over to keep the peace? I don't see why he should dislike *me*. He is a Yankee, — and I naturally love a Yankee." [2] By the end of the following summer, however, he was writing worriedly to Claggett that "it appears to me that the very *existence* of the United States is threatened, just now I am afraid we have been playing the game of brag about as recklessly as I have ever seen it played, even on an Arkansas steamboat." [3] Not only does the "we" here refer to the Union forces, but he is disturbed that "we" have been displaying a reckless Southern pride! His disturbance foreshadowed the man of 1864 who would not be too proud to run away from the gentlemanly requirements of the code duello. Twain in the West retained Whiggish misgivings about popular government, as his reporting of Nevada politics makes clear, but in these years he shucked off forever the outlook of the slave-holding aristocrat.

ii

In search of new forms to express a new idea of himself, Twain experimented in his Western period with a variety

[1] Copyright 1959 by the Mark Twain Company.
[2] Copyright 1959 by the Mark Twain Company.
[3] Copyright 1959 by the Mark Twain Company.

of humorous devices. Caricatures, puns, burlesques, hoaxes, and editorial badinage were the stock-in-trade of Washoe journalism at the time, and Mark Twain of the *Enterprise* tried them all. In one of his most significant experiments, he produced a sort of literary ventriloquist's act, wherein the writer debated various questions with an uninhibited *alter ego* named "the Unreliable." By putting words in the mouth of this stooge, Twain was able to float out newly-thought-up opinions like so many trial balloons, without being held responsible for them. The fascination of a lifetime with the literary possibilities of twins may be said to date from these early pieces. (A couple of years later, in a series of travel letters to the *Alta California,* "the Unreliable" reappeared as Mark Twain's fictitious traveling companion, the antisocial Mr. Brown. Although these letters, with their distasteful joking about the fragrance of Negroes, reveal that on some social questions the young Missourian still had a lot to learn, the name Brown seems a curiously apt one for a character whom one Twain critic has likened to Caliban. Mr. Brown would have been outraged to know it, but he nevertheless foreshadows Twain's later use of a Negro *alter ego* as a way of commenting upon white society.)

Twain's most interesting literary experiment was "The Celebrated Jumping Frog of Calaveras County," written the year after the author left Nevada. Possibly a Negro tale to begin with — the slyness with which the defeat of the champion is managed would seem to be the distinguishing mark of the slave upon it — the frog story was taken over by the rough-and tumble society of the mining camps and incorporated in its democratic myth. Various versions of the story had been published in Western newspapers before Mark Twain ever reached California. In appropriating the story for his own purposes, he made numerous changes. First and foremost, he embellished the anecdote with a "frame," in which we are introduced to the narrator, "Mark Twain," who in turn tells us of his encounter with Simon Wheeler in the barroom at Angel's Camp.

The narrator's casual reference to an Eastern friend, and his indulgently superior description of the "winning gentleness and simplicity" of Simon Wheeler's countenance, establish his affinity with the Self-controlled Gentleman of the Southwestern tradition, albeit the style of the prose in the "frame" is more informal than that of the Longstreet model. The similarities of structure and dramatic situation, however, are sufficient to make us expect the familiar puppet show. The story upsets all our calculations — and the narrator's as well. "Mark Twain," as things turn out, is not as clever as he thinks he is. Assuming himself to be more sophisticated than the man he meets, the encounter teaches him just the reverse — it is he, not Simon, who is simple. The innocence of Simon Wheeler's expression is in fact a mask, cunningly assumed to deceive the outsider by seeming to fulfill all his pre-conceived notions of Western simple-mindedness. Simon Wheeler's little joke, of course, is simply a California variation on the ancient con game of the trans-Allegheny frontiersman, but in literary terms the "Jumping Frog" marks a historic reversal. The narrator, it turns out, is telling a joke on himself, not on the Clown. In the "Jumping Frog," it is the vernacular, not the polite style, which "teaches the lesson." The Southwestern tradition, in other words, has been stood on its head.

The "frame" is a drama of upset expectations, and so is the story proper. Simon launches his vernacular monologue about Jim Smiley (after having been asked for information concerning the Reverend Leonidas W. Smiley) with an anecdote about Jim Smiley's bulldog, who could whip any other dog by fastening his teeth on his opponent's hind leg and hanging on "till they throwed up the sponge, if it was a year," but who was finally defeated by a dog "that didn't have no hind legs, because they'd been sawed off in a circular saw. . . ." Doubtless Twain's Whig upbringing had something to do with the fact that the name of Smiley's bulldog is Andrew Jackson, for in making a dog of that name look ridiculous Twain in effect ridiculed a politician who he never ceased to believe

Virginian as Gentleman:
Colonel Wiliam Byrd II.

The cover of a
well-known Crockett almanac.

Western Pastoral: *Jolly Flatboatmen,* by the genre painter
and sometime Whig politician George Caleb Bingham.

Western Violence: *A Regular Row in the Backwoods.*
From a Davy Crockett almanac.

Simon Suggs, as depicted by F. H. Darley in *Some Adventures of Captain Simon Suggs* (1845).

...t Lovingood. The drawing shows Sut enjoying his ...ther's painful encounter ...ith a swarm of hornets. ...rom the 1867 edition of ...e *Yarns*.

The cover illustration from
the first edition of Mark Twain's
The Celebrated Jumping Frog (1867).

Tom Sawyer. From the first edition of
The Adventures of Tom Sawyer.

E·W·Kemble

·1884·

Huck Finn. E. W. Kemble's famous illustration for the
first edition of *The Adventures of Huckleberry Finn*.

Mark Twain in the West. The photograph was made in San Francisco sometime between 1864 and 1866. One of the earliest likenesses of Twain showing him with a mustache.

Mark Twain's residence at Nook Farm.

From Volume 35 of *The Works of Mark Twain*, Harper & Brothers

Mark Twain and George Washington Cable. The photograph was taken during the same winter, 1884-1885, that *Huckleberry Finn* was published.

From Volume 37 of *The Works of Mark Twain*, Harper & Bro

The last photograph for which Mark Twain sat, taken a few
months before his death in 1910.

had been a disastrous President. Simon Wheeler's ironic praise of the dog — "a good pup, was that Andrew Jackson, and would have made a name for hisself if he'd lived, for the stuff was in him and he had genius — I know it, because he hadn't no opportunities to speak of, and it don't stand to reason that a dog could make such a fight as he could under them circumstances if he hadn't no talent" — would certainly have appealed to the Whiggish sense of humor of the earlier Southwestern writers. When we learn, however, as we do very shortly, that Jim Smiley's frog is named Daniel Webster, in honor of Whiggery's arch-hero, we begin to realize that this story is not playing political favorites in the old way at all, but is in fact saying a plague on both houses of a tragic era. Simon Wheeler's tall tale does not take sides on past history, it rejects the past altogether, and turns toward the West and the future. It also endorses democracy by making fun of superior feelings, as the "frame" had done. Gazing at Daniel Webster, the stranger says, in one of the most famous remarks in the history of American humor, "I don't see no p'ints about that frog that's any better'n any other frog." The subsequent triumph of the anonymous underfrog over the vaunted Daniel Webster comically vindicates the stranger's radical democracy. As the author of the "Jumping Frog" had lately discovered, it didn't pay to be too proud in the West.

Catching the upturn of the national mood at the close of the Civil War, the "Jumping Frog" was an instantaneous success, James Russell Lowell hailing it as "the finest piece of humorous literature yet produced in America." If the story had any flaws, they resided in the character of the narrator. It was not quite certain who "Mark Twain" was. He seemed a more colloquial figure than the Self-controlled Gentleman, yet he continued to play the Gentleman's role, vis-à-vis the Clown. In the period following the publication of the "Jumping Frog," Twain's major imaginative effort was devoted to solving the problem of his narrative persona.

Returning, in 1866, from Hawaii to San Francisco, Twain

was offered the chance to give a public lecture; the performance was such a success that a tour was quickly arranged. By
the time the tour was over, Twain had found himself, artis-
tically speaking. A member of the audience at one of these
lectures has left a description of the platform personality that
Twain had developed, recalling in particular "his slow deliberate drawl, the anxious and perturbed expression of his vis-
age, the apparently painful effort with which he framed his
sentences, and, above all, the surprise that spread over his
face when the audience roared with delight or rapturously
applauded the finer passages. . . ." The solution to the problem of finding a new persona for a new era was to fuse the
Gentleman and the Clown of the Southwestern tradition into
a single character. In the new dispensation, the vernacular
figure became the narrator, and the stories he told were not at
the expense of other people, à la Longstreet, but on himself.
This persona Mark Twain would someday describe as an "inspired idiot," but he was more complex than that. For this
was a character whose "preternatural shrewdness," as an
English commentator on Twain's lectures put it, was "thinly
veiled under the assumption of simplicity." His innocence, in
sum, was a mask, and the audience's awareness of the fact
was a part of the joke. In "How to Tell a Story," Twain gen-
erously acknowledged that he was neither the first nor the
only comic lecturer of his time to work up such a character.
Artemus Ward and Dan Setchell had played the innocent
years before Twain ever set foot on a platform, and Bill Nye
and James Whitcomb Riley were equally at home in the role.
What distinguished Twain from his fellow lecturers was his
ability to translate his immensely engaging dramatic personality into a literary character without any sacrifice of vitality.
Deprived of the theatricality of the stage, the humorous self-
characterizations of Ward and Nye and Riley lost a good deal
of their luster. As a stage mask, Twain's "inspired idiot" had
half a dozen peers; as a literary character he was unrivaled.

iii

It is in the travel letters he wrote for the *Alta California* chronicling his 1867 voyage to Europe and the Holy Land — which he then collected, revised, and published two years later as *The Innocents Abroad* — that Twain's new comic character enters American literature. The butt of the narrator's humor is no longer Mr. Brown or "the Unreliable," it is himself. And just as the Gentleman and the Clown have been fused, so have the contrasting styles with which they were identified. In *The Innocents*, the style seems to ramble on most casually, yet is concrete, particular, and to the point; combining an air of bewilderment with shrewdness and factuality, the narrative is never more slyly humorous than when apparently most unaware; innocence and sophistication have here been made one. The name the author bestowed on his new hero was "Mark Twain." If this persona quickly became one of the most compelling figures in all of American literature, it was because he seemed to incarnate, like Natty Bumppo and Uncle Tom, a national myth. As Twain himself observed, no American book since *Uncle Tom's Cabin* had sold as many copies as did *The Innocents Abroad*. Perhaps Twain's travel book was not read in quite the same way that Mrs. Stowe's novel had been — by the American people *as a people* — but it was far more than just another best-seller. *The Innocents* was a book which answered a deeply-felt national need.

Having triumphantly survived the severest crisis in its history, the United States in the late 1860s was ready for a new comic image of itself. For as Bergson has written, "The comic comes into being just when society and the individual, freed from the worry of self-preservation, begin to regard themselves as works of art." Constance Rourke has argued from that quotation that American society began to breathe easily about 1815, and that the embellished self-portraits of Yankees and backwoodsmen which emerged from the period following the Revolution were comic attempts to establish the identity of the American, Crèvecœur's famous "new man." But the Civil War had to be fought and won before our sense of national identity became fully secure. The wave of relief, of jubilation, of mounting patriotic enthusiasm, that swept over the country after Appomattox signified that now, unmistakably, the magical moment of seeing itself as a work of art had at last arrived for American society. To William Dean Howells, America was "better than the whole world," at once "manlier" and "purer." The victory had proved to the Old World once and for all, announced James Russell Lowell, "the amazing strength and no less amazing steadiness of democratic institutions." George William Curtis liked to conclude "The Good Fight," one of his most popular speeches, with the prophetic words, "For our America shall be the Sinai of the nations, and from the terrible thunders and lightnings of its great struggle shall proceed the divine law of liberty that shall subdue and harmonize the world." In its first issue, published with selfconscious deliberateness on the Fourth of July, 1865, a new magazine that called itself, exuberantly, the *Nation,* declared, "We utter no idle boast when we say that if the conflict of ages, the great strife between the few and the many, between privilege and equality, between law and power, between opinion and the sword, was not closed on the day on which Lee threw down his arms, the issue was placed beyond doubt." Clearly, the nation was eager to gaze into the mirror of art and find reflected there neither a Northerner nor a Southerner, neither an aristocrat nor a backwoods grotesque, but a democratic American. In the literary persona that Mark Twain created for himself in *The Innocents Abroad* a reunited people saw its own comic image — and laughed in affectionate recognition. Like the high-spirited American girls whom James and Howells would shortly begin to create, and whose intellectual grace and moral spontaneity would make Hawthorne's Hilda and Priscilla seem woefully provincial and pallid — like the symbolically-named Christopher Newman, the superbly energetic hero of the novel that James entitled with succinct perfection *The American* — Mark Twain's proud, conscious innocent testified to the nation's thrilling sense of its new identity as the heir of all the ages. In *The Innocents Abroad* there appeared for the first time a character with whom the whole world was destined to become familiar — sometimes painfully so: the American, newborn, not yet come of age, but nevertheless prepared to take over the age and judge all the nations of the earth by his own.

The comic hero of *The Innocents* is deplored by many modern readers for his smartiness and his cheap wisecracks, and certainly these qualities cannot be denied. "The information the ancients didn't have was very voluminous." "They spell it Vinci and pronounce it Vinchy; foreigners always spell better than they pronounce." "*Who* is this Renaissance? Where did he come from? Who gave him permission to cram the Republic with his execrable daubs?" Philistinism, however, was not what made "Mark Twain" a vitally fresh literary personality. Wisecracks about the monuments of the Old World, after all, had been the familiar stock-in-trade of American travel books for a long time. J. Ross Browne's *Yusef* (1853) was full of such jokes, as were the English travel letters of Major Jones, the backwoods militia officer; in *The Marble Faun* Hawthorne remarked with heavy humor that "the next best artist to Cimabue or Giotto or Ghirlandaio or Pinturricchio will be he that shall reverently cover their ruined masterpieces with whitewash!"

What distinguished *The Innocents* from previous travel books was, first of all, its fidelity to the thoughts and feelings of the narrator. Too often the American traveler abroad had been unwilling to say what he really felt, or admit what he had in fact seen. Full, at the outset, of chip-on-the-shoulder patriotism; determined — as Hawthorne had been — not to be "bamboozled" by Europe; the old-fashioned American traveler had ended by repeating, along with the author of *The*

Marble Faun, the hackneyed, romantic formulas of the guide-books as if they were his very own. The Civil War, however, produced a vast impatience with rhetorics that bore no relation to experience, and with that impatience came a new emphasis on realism. As Henry James remarked, the post-Civil War American was neither a skeptic nor a cynic — he was too optimistic to be either — but he had nevertheless "eaten of the tree of knowledge." To the emergent heroes of a new American literature, the challenge that life presented was how to break free of prefabricated romantic attitudes in order that they might see for themselves what the world was like. Thus one of the principal themes in Howells's early work is the absurdity of modeling one's life on the illusory clichés of sentimental novels. The tragedy of James's Madame de Mauves and Isabel Archer, as of Laura in Twain and Warner's *The Gilded Age,* is their discovery that what they have read about life in romantic books has terribly misled them. For all the writers of the postwar generation, the problem of seeing clearly was central, which is why they habitually talked of their craft in visual metaphors — why James talked of "recognition scenes," and why Mark Twain, in a celebrated passage in "Old Times on the Mississippi," chose to dramatize his personal discovery of the disparity between fact and fancy as an adventure in seeing:

> I still kept in mind a certain wonderful sunset which I witnessed when steamboating was new to me. A broad expanse of the river was turned to blood; in the middle distance the red hue brightened into gold, through which a solitary log came floating, black and conspicuous; in one place a long, slanting mark lay sparkling upon the water; in another the surface was broken by boiling, tumbling rings, that were as many-tinted as an opal; where the ruddy flush was faintest, was a smooth spot that was covered with graceful circles and radiating lines, ever so delicately traced; the shore on our left was densely wooded, and the somber shadow that fell from this forest was broken in one place by a long, ruffled trail that shone like silver; and high above the forest wall a clean-stemmed dead tree waved a

single leafy bough that glowed like a flame in the unobstructed splendor that was flowing from the sun. There were graceful curves, reflected images, woody heights, soft distances; and over the whole scene, far and near, the dissolving lights drifted steadily, enriching it every passing moment with new marvels of coloring.

I stood like one bewitched. I drank it in, in a speechless rapture. The world was new to me, and I had never seen anything like this at home. But . . . a day came when I began to cease from noting the glories and the charms which the moon and the sun and the twilight wrought upon the river's face; another day came when I ceased altogether to note them. Then, if that sunset scene had been repeated, I should have looked upon it without rapture, and should have commented upon it, inwardly, after this fashion: "This sun means that we are going to have wind tomorrow; that floating log means that the river is rising, small thanks to it; that slanting mark on the water refers to a bluff reef which is going to kill somebody's steamboat one of these nights, if it keeps on stretching out like that; those tumbling 'boils' show a dissolving bar and a changing channel there; the lines and circles in the slick water over yonder are a warning that that troublesome place is shoaling up dangerously; that silver streak in the shadow of the forest is the 'break' from a new snag, and he has located himself in the very best place he could have found to fish for steamboats; that tall dead tree, with a single living branch, is not going to last long, and then how is a body ever going to get through this blind place at night without the friendly old landmark?"

No, the romance and the beauty were all gone from the river. All the value any feature of it had for me now was the amount of usefulness it could furnish toward compassing the safe piloting of a steamboat. Since those days, I have pitied doctors from my heart. What does the lovely flush in a beauty's cheek mean to a doctor but a "break" that ripples above some deadly disease? Are not all her visible charms sown thick with what are to him the signs and symbols of hidden decay? Does he ever see her beauty at all, or doesn't he simply view her professionally, and comment upon her unwholesome condition all to himself? And doesn't he sometimes wonder whether he has gained most or lost most by learning his trade?

The problem of how to find beauty again in a world shorn of romantic illusion, of how to let himself go in a deep emotional response, was one that Twain would not solve very easily or very soon. In the words of G. K. Chesterton, those who are never "taken in" must inevitably be always "shut out," and Twain was determined above all else not to be "taken in." The utter failure of the author of *The Innocents Abroad* to see something more than faded colors and abject attitudes in the paintings of the Old Masters reveals how much that determination cost him. The pageant of Europe that moved James's Hyacinth Robinson so profoundly — "the monuments and treasures of art, the great palaces and properties, the conquests of learning and taste, the general fabric of civilization as we know it, based if you will upon all the despotisms, the cruelties, the exclusions, the monopolies and the rapacities of the past, but thanks to which, all the same, the world is less of a 'bloody sell' and life more of a lark" — is completely lost on Twain's democratic consciousness.

Yet if there were bad blind spots in the vision of this innocent abroad, with his Western freedom from convention he saw many unconventional things. The mind that saw through the romantic lie of the river's surface also saw through the spurious raptures of the tourists who spoke of the comely people of the Holy Land, because that was how the Bible described them, and never noted the flies clustering on the eyes of the diseased children. Furthermore, *The Innocents Abroad* rises above the imaginative sterility of defining the topics appropriate to a guidebook exclusively in terms of a museum catalogue. As a presentation of what life was actually like in Europe and the Holy Land toward the close of the 1860s — or at least, of what life looked like and smelled like, what sort of clothes people wore, how efficient the train service was, the quality of hair cuts and tobacco, and the exact height of famous buildings — *The Innocents* deserves the praise lavished upon it by Thomas Sergeant Perry, that great "lumberjack of libraries," as his friend Henry James called him, who felled volumes and sets of volumes as if they were trees in a forest, absorbing whole literatures at a time, and who was certainly one of the most sophisticated American readers of his day. *The Innocents*, Perry wrote in a letter to Howells, was "the only true book of travels ever written." "Really good rank outright Americanism," said Perry, "is a superb thing in its genuineness and earnest effort to see things for itself and I love it."

But the most important achievement of *The Innocents* arose out of Twain's willingness to acknowledge the tensions between tourists and natives, and to explore, however tentatively, the psychological problem of being an American abroad. It is this achievement which marks the book as the true beginning of modern American writing. The old-fashioned American traveler had "an air," as James remarked of Hawthorne, "of being remotely outside of everything he describes." Just as the humorists of the Southwestern tradition represented themselves as Self-controlled Gentlemen who were outside and above the backwoods world they described, so the pre-Civil War American traveler in Europe depicted himself as a shopper who gazed into store windows but who never went inside. To quote James on Hawthorne once again, this traveler was a "mere spectator." *The Innocents Abroad,* by contrast, chronicles the journey of an American who is by no means a remote and disinterested spectator. There is no "frame" in *The Innocents;* no stylistic hauteur; no superior point of view. The distance between the narrator and his subject which the Southwestern tradition emphasized so strongly has been utterly wiped out. Twain's narrator is emotionally involved in Europe, albeit the emotional range is narrow: Europe makes him nervous. He feels as uncomfortable in the palace of the Czars as he would in Abraham's bosom; when he cannot make himself understood in a restaurant, he begins shouting; he cannot remember the currency exchange rates; there is the constant, nerve-racking fear that he is being cheated — and in a glove store in Gibraltar his worst suspicion is confirmed. Translating the comedy of the confidence game from a frontier locale to the great stage of Europe, and viewing the comedy not from an amused outsider's standpoint, but from the potential victim's, Twain wrote the first act of an international drama that would be Henry James's greatest theme. Behind the supreme achievement of Lambert Strether in *The Ambassadors,* desperately uncertain as to whether the glittering surfaces of Paris are but the screen of a dark abyss, stands the nervous hero of *The Innocents Abroad.*

Running along beneath the nervousness of Twain's comedy is a more somber emotion, which he only fitfully hints at and never explains, but which is nevertheless always there. Thus at the outset of the voyage the narrator suggests, in a manner reminiscent of Melville's Ishmael, that he has taken to the ship in order to relieve his spirit of certain dark feelings: "The next morning, we weighed anchor and went to sea. It was a great happiness to get away. . . . All my malicious instincts were dead within me; and as America faded out of sight a spirit of charity rose up in their place that was as boundless, for the time being, as the broad ocean." The spirit does not last. "Damaging premonitions" that the pleasure trip on board the *Quaker City* might turn out to be "pleasuring with a vengeance" are amply confirmed. "A long sea voyage," the narrator finds, "not only brings out all the mean traits one has, and exaggerates them, but raises up others which he has never suspected he possessed." Although he insists that he has made several staunch friends while on board, the statement is not confirmed dramatically by the narrative. Beyond a superficial camaraderie with jolly fellows, his relationship with his fellow passengers does not go: Twain's Ishmael never finds his Queequeg. In Europe, he seems as eager for experience as James's Christopher Newman, but instead of meeting Claire de Cintré he only encounters the professional friendliness of people who are trying to sell him something. In terms of the future direction of Twain's art, it is certainly significant that the most sympathetic guide he encounters in his travels is a Negro from South Carolina, but in terms of *The Innocents* it is not: the relationship with this offspring of slaves never gets beyond a commercial basis. Twain's American is a lonely man, and his jesting description of himself as a "helpless orphan" has the overtone of a confession.

Nor is this the only joke that has its unfunny side. Again and again, the gaiety and lightheartedness of the humor reveal a surprising strain of morbidity. That this lonely tourist chooses to inspect holy relics and miraculous liquefactions whenever and wherever he can seems at first to be entirely explainable as the desire of an anti-Catholic to ridicule the Church, just as his careful attention to all the foul smells and dirt of Europe seems motivated by his pride in American hygiene. But when he includes on his sightseeing tour of Paris a visit to the city morgue we begin to sense the existence of a deeper urgency in his soul:

> Next we went to visit the Morgue, that horrible receptacle for the dead who die mysteriously and leave the manner of their taking off a dismal secret. We stood before a grating and looked through into a room which was hung all about with the clothing of dead men; coarse blouses, watersoaked; the delicate garments of women and children; patrician vestments, flecked and stabbed and stained with red; a hat that was crushed and bloody. On a slanting stone lay a drowned man, naked, swollen, purple; clasping the fragment of a broken bush with a grip which death had so petrified that human strength could not unloose it — mute witness of the last despairing effort to save the life that was doomed beyond all help. A stream of water trickled ceaselessly over the hideous face.

Wherever he goes, this American, he seeks out the horrors of violence and death, and the contemplation of each new spectacle is apt to set off a chain reaction of morbid memories stretching far back into his childhood. Take, for example, his visit to the Cathedral in Milan. The account begins with a description of the Cathedral's lofty spires and its central steeple, towering against the sky. Ascending to the roof, the narrator gazes down on the city below. Clambering down again, he now enters the church, where almost at once he confronts the statue by Phidias of the man without a skin. "It was a hideous thing," he says, "and yet there was a fascination about it." Then with the words, "It is hard to forget repulsive things," he enters upon a long recollection of the nightmarish time, long ago, when he had discovered a dead man lying in the darkness of his father's office with a "ghastly stab" in his bare breast. With the conclusion of this reminiscence, the narrator descends into the crypt of the Cathedral, where he is shown the rock-crystal coffin of St. Charles Borromeo. "The decaying head was black with age," he tells us, "the dry skin was drawn tight to the bones, the eyes were gone. . . ." The movement of the entire sequence in Milan Cathedral has been downward and inward: from the vertiginous heights of the roof, the narrator has proceeded past ghastly statues and ghastlier reminiscences toward the face of death buried deep in the bowels of the church. *The Innocents Abroad* tells of a horizontal voyage from New York to the Holy Land and back, but the Milan Cathedral episode reminds us that the official purpose of the *Quaker City* expedition was to make a vertical descent into a tomb, and that Twain's narrator has been moving toward the Holy Sepulchre via an extraordinary number of cemeteries, grottoes, caves, prisons.

Of all these gruesome sights on his itinerary, prisons, particularly solitary confinement cells, attract him most powerfully. The fantasy of being locked up and forgotten seems to stir this tourist as deeply as the idea of being buried alive does the heroes of Poe. In Marseilles, for example, he hires a sailboat and a guide and makes a special excursion to the Chateau d'If:

This ancient fortress has a melancholy history. It has been used as a prison for political offenders for two or three hundred years, and its dungeon walls are scarred with the rudely-carved names of many and many a captive who fretted his life away here, and left no record of himself but these sad epitaphs wrought with his own hands. . . . We loitered through dungeon after dungeon, away down into the living rock below the

level of the sea, it seemed. Names everywhere! — some plebeian, some noble, some even princely. Plebeian, prince, and
noble, had one solicitude in common — they would not be forgotten! They could bear solitude, inactivity, and the horrors of
a silence that no sound ever disturbed; but they could not bear
the thought of being utterly forgotten by the world.

In Venice, he crosses the Bridge of Sighs and descends:

> Down below the level of the water, by the light of smoking
> torches, we were shown the damp, thick-walled cells where
> many a proud patrician's life was eaten away by the long-
> drawn miseries of solitary imprisonment — without light, air,
> books; naked, unshaven, uncombed, covered with vermin; his
> useless tongue forgetting its office, with none to speak to; the
> days and nights of his life no longer marked, but merged into
> one eternal eventless night; far away from all cheerful sounds,
> buried in the silence of a tomb; forgotten by his helpless
> friends, and his fate a dark mystery to them forever; losing his
> own memory at last, and knowing no more who he was or how
> he came there; . . . ceasing to scratch vain prayers and com-
> plainings on walls where none, not even himself, could see
> them, and resigning himself to hopeless apathy, driveling
> childishness, lunacy!

Thus, on across the rest of Europe and through the Near
East, the pilgrim wends his underground way toward the
tomb of Christ. "To go abroad," Twain once observed in his
notebook, "has something of the same sense that death
brings." [4] Although we are not told enough about him to know
why, clearly the narrator of The Innocents has gone voyaging
in search of that sensation. The Quaker City expedition has
indeed been, as he says, "a funeral excursion without a corpse."

The expedition ends where it began, in New York Harbor.
The spiritual progress of the narrator has similarly gone nowhere. The pilgrimage has not essentially changed this man;
it has not resolved the inner contradictions of his personality;
nor has he been initiated into the manners and nature of a new

[4] Copyright 1959 by the Mark Twain Company.

life; he remains, in the end, what he was in the beginning, a lonely wanderer, nervous as ever. He has seen Europe only to reject it: in effect, his final opinion of the Old World is that he has "been there before." When all is said and done, the grandest sight the voyage has offered to his gaze was a ship off the Spanish Coast:

> A stately ship, with canvas piled on canvas till she was one towering mass of bellying sail! She came speeding over the sea like a great bird. Africa and Spain were forgotten. All homage was for the beautiful stranger. While everybody gazed, she swept superbly by and flung the Stars and Stripes to the breeze! Quicker than thought, hats and handkerchiefs flashed in the air, and a cheer went up! She was beautiful before — she was radiant now. Many a one on our decks knew then for the first time how tame a sight this country's flag is at home compared to what it is in a foreign land. To see it is to see a vision of home itself and all its idols, and feel a thrill that would stir a very river of sluggish blood!

Unquestionably, America, "the beautiful stranger," is better than famous old Europe, and Twain's narrator — who also calls himself a stranger — comes home to his own with a glad heart. Yet his narrative concludes without offering any hint as to what sort of place in American society he will occupy, or who his friends are, or where, having traveled many thousands of miles, he intends to settle. Like Christopher Newman, whom James would leave standing irresolutely in the Street of Hell in Paris, he does not seem to know what to do next. Moving with the tide of an uncertain destiny, Twain's lonely American walks down the gangplank at the end of the book into a blizzard of waving handkerchiefs which conceals a featureless beyond. "The long, strange cruise was over," he says, adding as a comic afterthought his benediction: "Amen."

iv

Roughing It, the author's prefatory note announces, is a "personal narrative." The adjective is to be understood in an etymological sense. For the narrator who tells us in the first chapter of the book that he is about to go West as the secretary to the Secretary of Nevada Territory is "young and ignorant," and "never had been away from home," a description which hardly fits the seasoned steamboat pilot and erstwhile Confederate Army officer who, not quite twenty-six years old, made his separate peace in the summer of 1861. The character called "Mark Twain" who is the narrator of *Roughing It* is a persona, as the "Mark Twain" of *The Innocents* had been. The narrators of the two travel books are, in fact, the same literary character, and *Roughing It* represents a continuation of this innocent's adventures, albeit the continuation has taken us backward in time. In the second installment of Mark Twain's imaginative projection of himself, his hero — significantly enough — has grown younger.

Exactly how old he now is cannot be determined with any precision. During an audience that his brother, the Secretary, has been granted with Brigham Young, the narrator tells how the Mormon chief "put his hand on my head, beamed down on me in an admiring way and said to my brother: 'Ah — your child, I presume? Boy or girl?'" This, however, would seem to be what Huck Finn would call a "stretcher," not only because Orion Clemens never met Brigham Young in his life, but because throughout most of the book the narrator clearly behaves like an adult. That he is a younger man than either the narrator of *The Innocents* or the actual Mark Twain who went West in 1861 is nevertheless unmistakably established, and it is done so primarily by the style. For if the prose in *Roughing It* has a disciplined fluidity and an incisiveness that mark how much more accomplished a writer Twain now was as compared to when he wrote *The Innocents,* the literary sophistication of the style is slyly masked by a tone of youthful naïveté:

> I envied my brother. I coveted distinction and his financial splendor, but particularly and especially the long, strange journey he was going to make, and the curious new world he was going to explore. . . . Pretty soon he would be hundreds and hundreds of miles away on the great plains and deserts, and among the mountains of the Far West, and would see buffaloes and Indians, and prairie dogs, and antelopes, and have all kinds of adventures, and maybe get hanged or scalped, and have ever such a fine time.

These are, indeed, the accents of a tenderfoot who has never been away from home before. In *Roughing It,* Twain has not yet fully responded to the magnetic pull of childhood, but he has clearly felt the tug.

Entering, in the second installment of his hero's adventures, the realm of memories now a decade old, Twain evokes at the outset of *Roughing It* an almost pastoral vision of the West. The trip to Nevada represents for his narrator an escape from all the cares and obligations of the contemporary world:

> By eight o'clock everything was ready, and we were on the other side of the river. We jumped into the stage, the driver cracked his whip, and we bowled away and left "the States" behind us. It was a superb summer morning, and all the landscape was brilliant with sunshine. There was a freshness and breeziness, too, and an exhilarating sense of emancipation from . . . the years we had spent in the close, hot city, toiling and slaving.

That Mark Twain in 1861 had not been toiling and slaving in a close, hot city only points up the deliberate effort of this passage to contrast the workaday reality of American society to the fabulous play-world of the Western frontier. To a people publicly committed to the frantic hustle of the American Way of Life, the idea of quitting work, of simply walking out, suddenly and without explanation, on all responsibilities, has been a haunting one; in American literature, the idea can be traced from "Rip Van Winkle" to *Walden,* from Walt Whitman to Sherwood Anderson. Of all American writers, however, Mark Twain is the principal celebrant of the escape dream. There was, of course, the Mark Twain who was a go-getter, who liked the friendship of millionaires and schemed to become one himself, who could write enthusiastic letters to the unsuccessful Orion in praise of energy and single-minded purpose, even as Lincoln had once written to his shiftless stepbrother, John D. Johnston. On the other hand, there was a side of Lincoln's personality that was drawn very strongly toward the slower, easier rhythms of drifting along and taking things easy, and this was also true of Mark Twain. Laziness to William Byrd was a horrid and appalling temptation; but to the heroes of Mark Twain, thoroughly unconcerned with keeping up a gentlemanly front, loafing is very Heaven. Thus as the trip West gets under way, the narrator of *Roughing It* tells us that the stagecoach in which he and his brother are traveling is loaded with mail sacks; when rearranged, the sacks fill up the seats to make a wonderful "lazy bed." And so they go bowling westward, lying down, luxuriously stripped to their underclothing, over a land that is as level as a calm sea. The resemblance of this stagecoach to a raft is unmistakable.

Set aside for a time — for the opening chapters of *Roughing It* compose a kind of overture in which many themes are introduced — the laziness theme is reintroduced and given its fullest development in the narrator's account of his journey to Lake Tahoe with his friend Johnny. If Hannibal had not existed, Tahoe would have been the great good place of Twain's imagination. Whenever Europe was pressing his patriotism hard, the narrator of *The Innocents* had only to think of Tahoe to be reassured of America's superiority. In *Roughing It,* the lake and its surrounding countryside come to us in the terminology of Paradise: Tahoe's air "is the same the angels breathe." In the "delicious solitude," Johnny and the narrator loll in the sand, smoke their pipes, and sleep. But "we seldom talked. It interrupted the Sabbath stillness, and marred the dreams the luxurious rest and indolence brought." Mocking the world they have left behind, they act out a parody version of the American success myth. They will get rich, they decide, by developing a certain forested area which is theirs for the asking if only they will fence the property and build a house on it. After an enthusiastic start, however, the work proves troublesome and they abandon it to return to the "business" of drifting around the lake in a boat, soaking in impressions. The decision looks forward to the narrator's comic career as a miner who dreams of making a fortune without doing any physical labor, and who lets a fabulous property slip through his fingers when he goes off in pursuit of some other interest and fails to develop the claim in time. Like the narrator of *Walden*, the hero of *Roughing It* finds the work involved in getting rich too expensive an outlay of time and energy. Quite obviously, he prefers his own drifting rhythm to the hustle of the money-getters a fact which makes the Parrington-Van Wyck Brooks criticism that the values of *Roughing It* are vulgarly materialistic seem somewhat mysterious. Twain's young man has come to the West for "adventures," of which the possibility of getting rich quick is only one.

As was true of his European trip, the narrator is determined to see the frontier clearly, and not in the manner ascribed by Twain to Fenimore Cooper — "through a glass eye, darkly." In *Roughing It*, however, this determination confronted Twain with a serious artistic problem. Reporting the facts of life in Virginia City, where the first twenty-six graves contained the corpses of murdered men, was a rather different proposition from simply refusing to blink at the existence of poverty in the Holy Land. William T. Porter's humorists had faced up with brutal frankness to the violence of the frontier, but the *Spirit of the Times* had been a magazine for gentlemen only. As both William Dean Howells and H. H. Boyesen testified, women in post-Civil War America came to compose an enormous bloc of the reading population to whom book publishers and magazines of national circulation appealed. How was it possible to talk about eyeball-gougers to *this* audience? And if it was not possible to do so, how could one be honest about the West?

Bret Harte got around this problem via the redemption formula. The first author to deal with the Western mining camps, Harte described a life which, as the *Atlantic* put it, was "vulgar and vicious"; in the words of a *Century* critic, Harte's stories had a "kind of devil's humor suited to the diabolism of the surroundings." What made such fiction go down with a Victorian and quasi-female audience was Harte's inevitable revelation that beneath the rough exterior of the miners of Roaring Camp or the outcasts of Poker Flat there existed what *Putnam's* sobbingly described as "the purest and loveliest feelings and influence that can touch a human heart." By glossing over the disturbing truths of his Western materials, Harte — and his imitators — pandered to a readership that wished to be titillated by roughness and then reassured by goodness.

Mark Twain, a good hater in any event, despised Bret Harte with special enthusiasm, both as a man and as an artist. To Twain, Harte's stories were as phony as the broken twigs and "scholarly savages" of the Leatherstocking Series. In *Roughing It*, the narrator makes it clear that the Goshoot Indians, "treacherous, filthy, and repulsive," have nothing in common with Uncas and Chingachgook. Nor does he minimize the depravity of white badmen in the manner of Harte. Remembering his fascination with Old World symbols of death, one might even say that Twain's narrator seems eager to talk of these harsh things, that the violence of the frontier has been deliberately sought out by this young man. (Had he not, after all, gone West because he envied his brother's opportunity to get hanged or scalped and then write home and tell about the experience?) Meeting the desperado Slade makes him "the proudest stripling that ever traveled to see strange lands and wonderful people," and the thrill of the encounter consists precisely in the nonredemptive viciousness of the man: "Here, right by my side, was the actual ogre who, in fights and brawls and various ways, *had taken the lives of twenty-six human beings,* or all men lied about him!" To this thrill-seeker, the existence of precious metals under the earth of the Western hills was not the only reason for going underground. Having once descended into the vault of the Capuchin Convent in Rome and stood enthralled ("Here was a spectacle for sensitive nerves!") at the sight of the human skulls and bones that decorated the walls, Twain's wandering sight-seer now steps onto a small platform and goes shooting like a dart down a mineshaft:

> It is like tumbling down through an empty steeple, feet first. When you reach the bottom, you take a candle and tramp through drifts and tunnels; . . . you admire the world of skeleton timbering; you reflect frequently that you are buried under a mountain, a thousand feet below daylight. . . . when your legs fail you at last, you lie down in a small box-car in a cramped "incline" like a half up-ended sewer and are dragged up to daylight feeling as if you are crawling through a coffin that has no end to it.

Proceeding from the imagery of death (skeleton timbering and coffinlike tunnels) to the actuality, he concludes his account of this underground adventure with the remark, "Of course these mines cave in, in places, occasionally, and then it is worth one's while to take the risk of descending into them and observing the crushing power exerted by the pressing weight of a settling mountain." *Worth one's while.* In some deep and inscrutable place in the personality of this lighthearted innocent, there would seem to be a terrible pessimism which feeds and grows on gruesome sights.

What made Twain's unflinching honesty — one might say compulsive honesty — about the hardness of life on the Western frontier acceptable to a national audience was the fact that his comic spotlight was focused not so much on the violence and the dangers of the West as on his narrator's reactions to these things. In Byrd's *Dividing Line,* and in the humor of Longstreet and his successors, the spotlight had never been fixed on the narrator. In the work of all these men, the hell of being laughed at was reserved for other people: the comic hazards of life left Self-controlled Gentlemen untouched. Viewing violence from a safe distance, the humor of the Southwestern tradition was consequently extremely callous; if Howells's indictment of it as monkeyishly cruel is an overstatement, at least one can say that it was predicated on a suspension of sympathy for the sufferer. In *Roughing It,* on the other hand, the frontier is not a cockpit which is viewed with haughty disdain from a back bench; it is a life into which the narrator is plunged, head over heels. "Mark Twain" is the character who is made to look ridiculous by being gulled into buying a worthless horse, a humiliation that in Longstreet's "The Horse-Swap" had been reserved for some distantly seen social inferior. By thus focusing on a scared and gullible young man's comic reactions to the confidence men, killers and corpses of the West, rather than on what causes him to react, Twain drew attention away from the disgusting details of frontier violence in which the humorists of the Southwestern tradition had reveled, while at the same time acknowledging their existence. In so doing, he accommodated his humor to the new national audience without cheating on the tough realities of his subject.

By substituting a victim's humor for a spectatorial humor, Twain transformed the comic treatment of the American frontier. Not only was his laughter more compassionate and humane, but the attitude of his narrator toward the West was psychologically more complex than that of the Self-controlled Gentleman. The Gentleman's attitude had always remained the same; the stability of his personality was the whole point about him. Plunged into the life of Virginia City, Twain's narrator grows up, or at least changes his mind about lots of things. His experience in Nevada is an initiation, as Henry Nash Smith has observed, into a new and different society; and the jokes he tells on himself compose a progression by which a tenderfoot from the city is slowly transformed into a member of the Western tribe. A recent critic of Twain's work, Paul Schmidt, has said that the values of life which the West opens up to Twain's innocent might be summed up under the headings of color, brotherhood, and freedom: the vibrant possibilities of a various experience; the democratic companionship of "bright-eyed, quick-moving, strong-handed men"; and the moral spontaneity of a society uncoerced by the inhibitions and cautious restraints of a more established America. To dramatize the contrast between the pale life he has left behind with the new vigor that has inspired him in Virginia City, the narrator tells the anecdote of Scotty Briggs and the parson. Scotty, whose customary suit is "a fire helmet, flaming red flannel shirt, patent leather belt with a spanner and revolver attached, coat hung over arm, and pants stuffed into boot tops," speaks in the vernacular of the Nevada miner — "the richest and most infinitely varied and copious [slang] that had ever existed anywhere in the world." The parson, a "fragile, gentle, spirituel new fledgling from an Eastern theological seminary," speaks in the language of the genteel tradition in its final stages of desiccation. The conflict between two radically different styles is the enduring drama of American humor, representing as it does a conflict between two utterly different concepts of what American life should be. The ludicrous failure of Scotty Briggs and the parson to communicate to one another signifies a more far-reaching incompatibility, and the anecdote makes it quite clear that as between the two Americas thus symbolized the narrator prefers Scotty Briggs's. "Virginia City," the narrator says flatly, "afforded me the most vigorous enjoyment of life I had ever experienced."

The tribute is unqualified; ironically, it is also a valedictory. Sounding like the statement of a man who has spiritually come home, the tribute in fact announces his departure from Virginia City. Twain's narrator has been involved in the frontier community; he has learned many things from it, including a new dissatisfaction with his former life; but in the end he rejects it, even as he had rejected Europe. "I began to get tired of staying in one place so long," he says, trying to define the itch that drives him on. "I wanted to see San Francisco. I wanted to go somewhere. I wanted — I did not know *what* I wanted." Trying once more to put his feelings into words, he says simply, "I wanted a change." Restlessness, as Tocqueville noted, is one of the most striking characteristics of the American; certainly the quality shows up repeatedly in American writing — in Melville, in Dreiser, in Sinclair Lewis (himself a man so restless he could not bear to sit still in a room, or even live in the same house on the same continent for very long: the "Minnesota tumbleweed," his first wife called him), among many others. In the second half of *Roughing It*, restlessness emerges as the dominant trait in the narrator's personality. For the move to San Francisco is no solution. Soon Twain's American is running before the wind again: into the mountain country of the California mining camps; back to San Francisco; across the Pacific to Hawaii; to San Francisco again; back to Nevada; back to San Francisco once more — where "I projected a pleasure journey to Japan and thence westward around the world." Changing his mind, he sails for New York, where he signs on for an excursion, that will take him, he says, to Europe and the Holy Land. Uncommitted, unsure of himself, with no secure base anywhere, the narrator sets off at the end, as he had at the beginning of the book, in pursuit of adventures — perhaps seeking in the very process of change itself the solidity he cannot find in permanence.

v

"That word 'travel' had a seductive charm for me," Twain's persona had announced at the outset of *Roughing It;* in "Old Times on the Mississippi," the third installment of his adventures, he exclaims, "I was a traveler! A word never had tasted so good in my mouth before." Once again, an innocent voyager launches himself out into a strange and exotic world. And this time he is even younger than he had been in *Roughing It*. He is also considerably younger than Mark Twain was at the point in his career which "Old Times" purports to record. Albert Bigelow Paine, Mark Twain's official biographer, has observed that "in the Mississippi book the author conveys the impression of being a boy of perhaps seventeen. . . . He was in reality considerably more than twenty-one years old. . . ." Paine's additional comment that "Old Times" records incidents that were "more or less inventions" is further proof — if further proof is still needed — that "Mark Twain" is a literary, not a historical, character.

The book, or rather the seven papers which appeared in the *Atlantic* between January and August, 1875, tells the story of the youth's education as a steamboat pilot. After eighteen months of training, the real-life Mark Twain had become a fully licensed pilot, but throughout the two-and-a-half-year time span of "Old Times" the hero remains a cub who is learning his trade. His education begins with his departure from Hannibal, Missouri. Twain had mentioned Hannibal from time to time in newspaper articles during his Nevada and California days. In the period following the publication of *Roughing It*, he returned to the subject of his old home town when he began to work on a novel about his persona's boyhood. Unable, seemingly, to negotiate with ease the long, backward jump in time that the transition from *Roughing It* to *Tom Sawyer* entailed, Twain found that the novel advanced only by fits and starts. By the late fall of 1874, however, his "tank," as he called the source of his inspiration, had filled up again and he was writing furiously — only not on *Tom Sawyer*. In ten days' time, he wrote three papers of the "Old Times" series and began a fourth. Apparently what had happened was that as soon as Twain had decided to take his hero backward toward childhood at a more even rate of speed, the writing came with wondrous ease. When "Old Times" had filled in the gap of intervening years in the imaginative pattern of his persona's career, Twain immediately went back to the uncompleted novel and finished it in a few months.

Hannibal, as presented in "Old Times," is a drowsy village from whose uneventful life every boy hopes to escape. To join a minstrel show or a circus, to become a pirate or a steamboat pilot, are the dreams that kindle the imagination of the youthful narrator. "So, by and by, I ran away." A Mississippi steamboat is his Yale College and his Harvard, and the hero appropriately describes his experiences as a cub pilot in the terminology of the classroom. "He agreed to teach me the Mississippi River from New Orleans to St. Louis for five hundred dollars, payable out of the first wages I should receive after graduating. I entered upon the small enterprise of 'learning' twelve or thirteen hundred miles of the great Mississippi River with the easy confidence of my time of life." In Twain's most extended educational metaphor, the face of the water is compared to a book,

> a wonderful book . . . that was a dead language to the uneducated passenger, but which told its mind to me without reserve. . . . And it was not a book to be read once and thrown aside, for it had a new story to tell every day. Throughout the long twelve hundred miles there was never a page that was void of interest, never one that you could leave unread without loss, never one that you would want to skip, thinking you could find higher enjoyment in some other thing. There was never so wonderful a book written by man; . . . when I had mastered the language of this water, and had come to know every trifling feature that bordered the great river as familiarly as I know the letters of the alphabet, I had made a valuable acquisition.

Repeatedly, the narrator contrasts his callow youthfulness and naïveté with the schoolmasterly exasperation of Mr. Bixby, his teacher, to the point where almost every comic situation revolves about some sort of examination, which the narrator usually flunks or does badly in, although the progress of his education is steady.

The mysteries into which Mr. Bixby initiates him are designed to give the cub pilot and the tremendous machine that he directs complete dominance of the mighty Mississippi. The student's ambition to learn his lessons well is a familiar one in Mark Twain's work. From Beriah Sellers of *The Gilded Age*, who is constantly tinkering with perpetual motion machines and other gadgets, to the Connecticut Yankee who brings the Industrial Revolution to Arthurian England, Twain's characters dream of mastering their environment by means of the latest technology. The cub pilot's awed respect for Mr. Bixby, the "lightning pilot," whose audacity and know-how have conquered the mighty river, anticipates Thorstein Veblen's celebration of the engineer as the real hero of American society. Indeed, so unqualified is the cub's admiration for Mr. Bixby that it raises the question: Has the questing "Mark Twain" at last found the identity — the image of himself — with which he can be content? Having traveled so far and so long, has this restless spirit finally discovered who it is he really wants to be? Unlike *The Innocents* and *Roughing It*, "Old Times" does not end with the narrator fleeing toward a featureless beyond; neither does the ending answer the questions raised. For the narrative of "Old Times" actually has no ending at all. It simply breaks off. That his conclusion was unsatisfactory Twain himself recognized, and when he worked up the *Atlantic* papers into book form some years later, he added a few chapters to round out the cub pilot's career. The additions completely destroy the optimistic queries evoked by the earlier part of the narrative.

In its completed form, the cub pilot's story terminates with a scene of disaster, made the more terrible and shocking by its being so unexpected. Henry Adams's *Education* would reach its climactic moment in a chapter called "Chaos"; the cub pilot's lessons terminate in "A Catastrophe." If the machine can control the river, the pilot's tragedy is that he cannot always control the machine. The boilers of the steamboat *Pennsylvania*, on which the narrator's brother, Henry, is serving as clerk, explode without warning, reducing the boat and most of her passengers and crew to a "mountain of riddled and chaotic rubbish." As the cub recreates the horrible scene in his imagination, the fantasy of being locked up and forgotten, of being hopelessly cut off from all human contact, towers up once again in his mind. The fate of the young fellow trapped in the boiler room of the burning steamboat is even more hideous than that of the doomed prisoners in the Chateau d'If: "He said he was not injured, but could not free himself, and when he saw that the fire was likely to drive away the workers he begged that some one would shoot him, and thus save him from the more dreadful death. The fire did drive the axemen away, and they had to listen, helpless, to this poor fellow's supplications till the flames ended his miseries." As for the narrator's brother, "his hour had struck; we bore him to the death-room, poor boy." These are the last words of the narrative.

At the end of his cubhood, the adult world which he has been preparing himself to enter literally blows up in the youth's face. Once the news of the *Pennsylvania* has reached him, no further mention is made of his ambitions to become a pilot, nor is Mr. Bixby's talismanic name any longer invoked. The tragedy falls athwart the youth's career like a tree across his path, as if in warning of the deadly dangers that lie ahead for anyone leaving the sacred precincts of childhood. His lighthearted escape from Hannibal has only brought the runaway to grief. A backtrailer in time since we first met him, Twain's restless persona would continue his search for a haven by fleeing even further into the past.

CHAPTER VIII

The Happy Valley

Remembrance is like direct feeling; its object is suffused
with a warmth and intimacy to which no object of mere
conception ever attains.

— WILLIAM JAMES

MARK TWAIN, unlike the rootless wanderer who was his literary self, came home from Europe in 1867, married Olivia Langdon in 1870, and settled down, first in a substantial home in Buffalo, New York, and then not quite two years later in Nook Farm, one of the best residential areas of the wealthiest per capita city in the nation, Hartford, Connecticut. As Twain said, Hartford was "the best built and handsomest town" he had ever seen, and he had seen a good many, from Honolulu to Constantinople. Living in suburban ease (the modified Gothic mansion the Clemenses moved into in 1874 had nineteen large rooms and five baths, cost seventy thousand dollars to build, plus thirty-one thousand for five acres of land, and twenty-one thousand to furnish); surrounded by an adoring wife and growing children; with congenial and distinguished neighbors (including Harriet Beecher Stowe and her husband Calvin; the novelist and newspaper editor Charles Dudley Warner; John Hooker, outstanding Hartford lawyer, descendant of the famous Thomas, and husband of Isabella Beecher Hooker, a daughter, like Harriet, of Lyman Beecher,

174

and a well-known suffragist in her own right; and Joseph R. Hawley, organizer of the Republican party in Connecticut, sometime Governor of the State, and eventually Senator); Mark Twain truly seemed to fit his own gently ironic description of himself as "an immovable fixture among the other rocks of New England."

However, as Kenneth R. Andrews has demonstrated in his excellent study of Nook Farm, the intellectual turmoil of the inhabitants belied the impressive solidity and serenity of the community's external appearance. After the exhilarating excitement produced by the Union victory in the Civil War had subsided, the residents of Nook Farm became aware of new and troubling problems. Mark Twain and Charles Dudley Warner summed up their neighbors' disturbed sense of titanic change in a passage in The Gilded Age: "The eight years in America from 1860 to 1868," they wrote, "uprooted institutions that were centuries old, changed the politics of a people, transformed the social life of half the country, and wrought so profoundly upon the entire national character that the influence cannot be measured short of two or three generations." As Professor Andrews has shown, it was the problem of religious belief that bedeviled the postwar life of many of Nook Farm's citizens. What bothered Mark Twain, however, and Warner, too, was "the politics of a people."

Although Twain in the West had ceased to believe in the hierarchic social distinctions on which Southern Whiggery had pinned its hopes for a stable America, his response to the vigorous egalitarianism of Nevada had not been unmixed with doubts. His reporting of Territory politics for the Enterprise was tinged with cynicism of the sort that later found its way into Roughing It, wherein the narrator attacks democratic juries as a system that gives the responsibility for maintaining law and order to "fools and rascals," instead of to "honest men and men of brains." The "prominent banker," the "merchant of high character," and the "quartz mill owner," whom the narrator cites as the sort of man who should be called for jury duty, indicate the conservatism of Twain's thinking.[1] A brief tour of duty following his return from the Holy Land as the private secretary of Senator William M. Stewart of Nevada gave Twain a firsthand acquaintance with the social pretentiousness and the official corruption of postwar Washington. Young Henry Adams, getting an eye- and an earful of this brave new world at about the same time, wrote up his disillusionment in some of the most brilliant pieces of analytical reportage in the history of American journalism. Mark Twain preferred to convert his outrage into satire. In "The Facts in the Case of the Great Beef Contract," "The Facts in the Case of George Fisher, Deceased," and "My Late Senatorial Secretaryship," he warmed up for the major satirical task of *The Gilded Age*, which he and Warner undertook in the months following Grant's re-election to the Presidency in the fall of 1872.

Ever since his Nevada days, Twain had made a personal cult of Grant. His admiration for him as a general and as a man extended without qualification to his opinion of him as President. He voted for him twice and would have done so a third time, if he had had the opportunity. The corruption of the national administration was in no wise to be blamed on the military hero in the White House, in Twain's opinion. The responsibility lay first of all with Grant's White House staff, with the Federal bureaucracy, and with the Congress. Ultimately, however, the fact that bribe-takers were in office was the fault of the system — of the political system, not the economic one, for both Twain and Warner believed in unrestricted free enterprise. The nation's trouble — they were sure of this — was universal suffrage, which delivered power into the hands of an unscrupulous few. In an unsigned piece for the *Atlantic*, entitled "The Curious Republic of Gondour," Twain sketched

[1] Twain and Warner's description of the jury that sits in judgment on Laura in *The Gilded Age* is in the same vein: "Low foreheads and heavy faces they all had; some had a look of animal cunning. . . . The entire panel formed that boasted heritage commonly described as the 'bulwark' of our liberties."

out his idea of a political Utopia. Gondour reconciles Twain's fervent belief in American democracy with his dismay at the ignorance of the electorate and the folly of its decisions: "Every citizen, however poor or ignorant, possessed one vote, so universal suffrage still reigned; but if a man possessed a good common-school education and had no money he had two votes, a high-school education gave him four; if he had property, likewise, to the value of three thousand *sacos* he wielded one more vote; for every fifty thousand *sacos* a man added to his property he was entitled to another vote; a university education entitled a man to nine votes, even though he owned no property." Warner's political writings displayed similar reservations about the Declaration of Independence. In *The Gilded Age*, the authors of these opinions sought out the comic possibilities of a rampant democracy.

The conservative standard of values implicit in the novel is not that of pre-Civil War Southern Whiggery, but of enlightened, egghead Republicanism — of Nook Farm, in brief. An episode at the beginning of the second volume makes this very clear. Laura, riding high on her beauty and Senator Dilworthy's bankroll, becomes the reigning belle of Washington. In her new role, she discovers that the city contains "three distinct aristocracies." The first two, called "the Antiques" and "the Parvenus," are mercilessly caricatured. The conversation of the Antique ladies is as vapid and inane as it is haughty; the contrast with Laura's vigorous and informal speech recalls the episode of Scotty Briggs and the parson — and makes the same value judgment in favor of the colloquial style. As the ladies depart in "Elizabethan stateliness," Laura speaks for Twain and Warner when she says, "I think I could always enjoy icebergs — as scenery — but not as company." The Parvenus are a different kettle of fish. Miss Breezhay Oreillé, formerly Miss Bridget O'Reilly, and her father, the Hon. Patrique Oreillé, "the wealthy Frenchman from Cork" who has parlayed a hod carrier's job into a saloon, a saloon into political power, and political power into a fortune as a contractor (he "furnished shingle nails to the new court-house at three thousand dollars a keg"), are indeed the "other extremity" of social Washington. Between the two extremes stands the third aristocracy, called "the Middle Ground." In describing this group, Twain and Warner endowed it with all the virtues that had attracted them both to the Nook Farm community:

> It was made up of the families of public men from nearly every state in the Union. . . . These gentlemen and their households were unostentatious people; they were educated and refined. . . . They had no troublesome appearances to keep up, no rivalries which they cared to distress themselves about, no jealousies to fret over. . . . They were people who were beyond reproach, and that was sufficient.

From the standpoint of Nook Farm, Twain and Warner portrayed a great nation being despoiled by a band of smooth-talking fakers: lobbyists, Congressmen, and promoters; slick operators like Colonel Selby, who with his fine Virginia manners tricks Laura into loving him; frauds like Senator Dilworthy, who covers his corruption with a loud allegiance to the temperance movement, Bible classes, and Negro rights; and the age's type-symbol, Colonel Beriah Sellers. Although *The Gilded Age* was very much a collaborative enterprise, the character of Sellers was exclusively Twain's invention. Obviously bespeaking Twain's long acquaintance with the Confidence Man of the Southwestern tradition, Sellers re-enacts on a national stage Simon Suggs's back-country imitation of a well-heeled *homme d'affaires,* while his visionary description of a scheme for widening a tiny Missouri creek into the finest river in the West carries the loose-mouthed promotionalism of Joseph G. Baldwin's Ovid Bolus and "Blowing" Cave to new heights of floridity. ("That's the way I block it out, sir," Sellers exclaims, "— and it's as clear as day — clear as the rosy morn!") Yet Sellers is also very different from his clownish predecessors. With his usual imaginative sympathy for the feelings of a fool, Twain saw more deeply into Sellers's personality than any of the conservative humorists of antebellum days could possibly have done. He saw, for example, that in a world which glorified the conspicuous consumer and made a hero of the fast-buck operator Sellers was as much the victim as the victimizer. Not content simply to caricature Sellers's absurd pretentiousness, Twain caught the pathos behind his mask, the anguish and shame that Sellers felt at being poor, the constant effort he had to make to avoid confronting the truth about himself. Caught in the act of heating his stove with a candle, or feeding his family on turnips, Twain's con man pauses in awful silence for a moment, before the words come to him that will mercifully shroud reality in illusion. As Sellers grows older in the course of the novel, the deception that is his life becomes harder and harder for him to pull off; toward the end of the book, when Washington Hawkins inadvertently calls him a "nameless man," Sellers has no comeback to make, only a pathetic appeal: "I have always been a friend of your family, Washington, and . . . I don't think there has ever been anything in my conduct that should make you feel justified in saying a thing like that." Raised in a family whose social pretensions outran its economic position, Mark Twain had learned early — as had Melville, Emerson, Hawthorne and Thoreau before him, all of whom had grown up in good families which had suffered a loss of status — how remorselessly American society drives the shabby-genteel pretender into a corner. As we first meet him, Sellers seems to be just another clownish pretender of the sort that the Southwestern tradition had once made fun of — and that would be revived a century later in a series of magnificent characterizations by W. C. Fields; but as we come to know him better, we understand him in the way we do Willy Loman. With Beriah Sellers, Twain went beyond the requirements of conservative satire to create one of the truly memorable characters in American literature.

ii

Outraged as Twain was by the looting operations of political spoilsmen, he was even more disturbed, in the early 1870s, by the exposure of corruption in another quarter. When he wrote to Orion that *"Politics* are not going to cure moral ulcers like these nor the decaying body they fester on," [2] the principal "moral ulcer" he had in mind was the sensational accusation that had been leveled against the Reverend Henry Ward Beecher.

As Howells later recalled, Twain was "tremendously worked up" by the Beecher affair, and this was understandable, for Twain's life had been peculiarly intertwined with the Beecher family. The expedition to the Holy Land that Twain made famous had been organized by members of Henry Ward Beecher's Brooklyn parish, Plymouth Church, and Beecher himself had toyed for a time with the idea of going along. When the *Quaker City* returned to New York, Beecher entertained Mark Twain at dinner, where he was introduced to Henry Ward's celebrated sister, Harriet. On that occasion Twain also renewed his acquaintance with Isabella Beecher Hooker, whom he had previously met through the Langdon family of Elmira, New York, Twain having come to know the Langdons through young Charley Langdon, who had been one of the innocents abroad. When Twain and Charley's sister, Olivia, were married, it seemed only natural that Thomas K. Beecher, another son of Lyman and pastor of the First Congregational Church of Elmira, should officiate at the ceremony. The fact that two Beecher sisters were in residence at Nook Farm undoubtedly influenced the Clemenses' decision to move there from Buffalo.

In the very year of their arrival, 1871, stories began to be heard in and around New York that Henry Ward Beecher, the most influential American preacher of his generation, had en-

[2] Copyright 1959 by the Mark Twain Company.

tered into an adulterous relationship with the wife of Theodore Tilton, a member of the Plymouth Church Congregation.
The gossip burst out into the open in the fall of 1872, when the
beautiful and eccentric Victoria Woodhull, a militant defender
of the American woman's right to vote in elections and to
sleep in any bed she pleased, and who had been denounced
by Beecher on the latter score, proclaimed to a convention of spiritualists in Boston — for Victoria was as interested
in the mysteries of the other world as in the pleasures of
this — that although the pastor of Plymouth Church might ex-
coriate free love from the pulpit, he was not practicing what
he preached. Two months later, she repeated the story in
Woodhull and Claflin's Weekly, a magazine with a national
circulation. Plymouth Church Congregation, seeing its duty
clearly, dropped Theodore Tilton from its list of parishioners.
But this forthright action failed to close the case. For Tilton,
succumbing finally to the pressure of publicity, sued Beecher
for alienation of affections. Although the trial lasted all through
the first half of 1875 and generated a thousand headlines —
the trial being beyond doubt the greatest scandal of the American nineteenth century — the results were inconclusive. Ignoring the fact that Elizabeth Tilton, some three and a half
years before, had confessed her guilt to Susan B. Anthony and
Elizabeth Cady Stanton, and apparently unable to fathom
Beecher's ambiguously worded letter of apology to Tilton for
having wronged him in some unnamed way, the jury voted
nine to three for acquittal. An advisory council of Congregational ministers, including Nook Farm's pastor and Mark
Twain's dearest friend, the Reverend Joseph H. Twichell, now
descended on Brooklyn to investigate the charges. Nothing
could be more illustrative of the mood of the '70s — a decade
in which most Americans wished to believe that everything
was fundamentally all right with their society, while at the
same time they had a foreboding sense that corrupt forces were
at work in it — than the ministers' decision. They completely
exonerated Beecher from all guilt, while criticizing him for

his " 'inexpressible folly' in falling so easy a prey to his enemies." Just who these "enemies" were, the council did not say. As for Mark Twain, he at first refused to believe the story that *Woodhull and Claflin's Weekly* had printed. Along with the rest of the Nook Farm community, he was outraged when Isabella Beecher Hooker announced that in her opinion her brother was guilty, and he actively approved the community's decision to cut Isabella dead until she had purged herself of heresy. Yet by the time of the trial Twain was sufficiently unsure of who was lying and who was telling the truth that he felt it necessary to attend several sessions. Twichell's conclusive judgment, rendered during the course of the ministerial investigation, that Beecher *"seemed* like a good man, and I know that many delegates as they listened to him and watched him were conscious of ceasing to doubt his integrity," undoubtedly expressed an opinion of the affair that Twain would have dearly loved to share. But like millions of his countrymen, he found that his formerly high opinion of Beecher had been forever damaged.

Out of the moral confusion of the '70s, which the Beecher case symbolized, came a yearning — nationwide in scope — for a return to innocence. If only America could find once again the moral certainties of childhood, then everything would be all right, for to be a child was to be safe from the adult temptations of a Beecher, or a Beriah Sellers. In the mind of 1870 America, to be a child was a wonderful thing. Therefore, when he sought to praise his pastor in the highest possible terms, a member of Joseph H. Twichell's congregation lauded neither his mind nor his spirituality, but his youthfulness: "To thousands he is still 'Joe' Twichell; he is as approachable as one boy is to another." And when another of Twichell's parishioners — it was Mark Twain — was invited to give one of the toasts at the 1879 "Reunion of the Great Commanders," held in honor of General Grant, he turned down the opportunity to deliver the toast to "The Ladies" in order to toast "The Babies" — for reasons which are worth exploring.

The fifteenth and last speaker of the evening, Twain stood up in the packed banquet hall in Chicago at two o'clock in the morning. "We have not all had the good fortune to be ladies," he began. "We have not all been generals, or poets, or statesmen; but when the toast works down to the babies, we stand on common ground." Ringing the changes on his theme, he came to the climax of his speech, turning to face the guest of honor as he reached the end:

> Among the three or four million cradles now rocking in the land are some which this nation would preserve for ages as sacred things, if we could know which ones they are. In one of these cradles the unconscious Farragut of the future is at this moment teething — think of it! . . . In another the future renowned astronomer is blinking at the shining Milky Way with but a languid interest — poor little chap! — and wondering what has become of that other one they call the wet-nurse. . . . And in still one more cradle, somewhere under the flag, the future illustrious commander-in-chief of the American armies is so little burdened with his approaching grandeurs and responsibilities as to be giving his whole strategic mind at this moment to trying to find out some way to get his big toe into his mouth — an achievement which, meaning no disrespect, the illustrious guest of this evening turned *his* entire attention to some fifty-six years ago; and if the child is but a prophecy of the man, there are mighty few who will doubt that he *succeeded.*

Returning to his hotel room at five in the morning, Twain could not go to bed until he had written to his wife, telling her all about the "night of my life":

> They let my first sentence go in silence, till I paused and added "we stand on common ground" — then they burst forth like a hurricane and I saw that I *had* them! From that time on, I stopped at the end of each sentence, and let the tornado of applause and laughter sweep around me — and when I closed with "And if the child is but the prophecy of the man, there are mighty few who will doubt that he succeeded," . . . the house came down with a crash. For two hours and a half, now, I've been shaking hands and listening to congratulations. Gen.

Sherman said, "Lord bless you, my boy, I don't know how you do it — it's a secret that's beyond me — but it was great — give me your hand again." . . . Lots and lots of people — hundreds I might say — told me my speech was the triumph of the evening. . . . Ladies, Tom, Dick and Harry — even the policemen — captured me in the halls and shook hands, and scores of army officers said, "We shall always be grateful to you for coming." General Pope came to hunt me up. . . . Gen. Schofield, and other historic men, paid their compliments. . . . Gen. Augur — well, I've talked with them *all*, received invitations from them all — from people living everywhere — and as I said before, it's a memorable night. I wouldn't have missed it for anything in the world.

What was it about envisioning General Grant as a baby that called forth such an extraordinary response? Was it simply the comic incongruity of the idea? Or was it that the idea was somehow joyously reassuring? Wishing to honor the man who was not only their old commander, but the symbol of the Union itself, did not the men present respond so enthusiastically because in one unforgettable image Twain had testified that in his own true and fundamental self Grant was a child — a child who could not possibly have been guilty of the misdeeds that had besmirched his Presidency? On the most memorable night of his life, Twain gave Grant back to his old lieutenants in a guise that they adored: symbolizing determination and innocence, Twain's reincarnation of Grant transcended the moral ambiguities of the Gilded Age. Truly there was an immense reassurance, a wonderful sense of moral refuge, in harking back to the "common ground" of childhood.

But post-Civil War Americans sought more than safety in going back to childhood. They also sought to recapture a Wordsworthian freshness of experience, to taste again the delicious newness of first impressions. Joel Chandler Harris expressed the yearning of a whole generation when he had Uncle Remus say, "Folks aint half as smart when they grow up as they is when they're little children. They shet their eyes to one whole side of life. Kin you fling your mind back to the time when your heart was soft, an' your eyes sharp enough for to see what grown people never seed?" To a civilization that was shifting rapidly from a rural to an industrial basis, it seemed that the lustrous magic and mystery of nature was simply being blotted out of the world. As an editorial writer for Henry Grady's Atlanta *Constitution,* the principal spokesman in the New South for industrialism and an end to the old ways, Joel Harris was thoroughly committed to the business ideals of the age. At the same time, he could not help feeling that the self-help ethic was the deadly enemy of the imagination. The dreams of the businessman, he once said, "remained so persistently on the hither side of concrete things, he was so completely invested with the cold and critical views that were the result of his education, that his mind never ventured much beyond his material interests, and he never tried to peep around the many corners that life presents. . . ." To rediscover enchantment in modern America, one had to become a child again. In the Uncle Remus stories, Harris's persona is not a gentleman of the press, but a little boy.

The same hunger that drew Harris to identify himself with a child attracted Henry Adams to the Middle Ages. Adams, to be sure, did not use the persona of the child on his journey into the medieval past — he preferred the mask of a somewhat exhausted avuncular figure. Nevertheless, as he wrote in *Mont-Saint-Michel and Chartres,* "the man who wanders into the twelfth century is lost, unless he can grow prematurely young." For what aging uncles hoped to encounter in the twelfth century was a world as keenly alive, and every bit as fantastic, as Uncle Remus's puerile imaginings:

> The twelfth century had the child's love of sweets and spices and preserved fruits, and drinks sweetened or spiced, whether they were taken for supper or for poetry; the true knight's palate was fresh and his appetite excellent either for sweets or verses or love; the world was young then; Robin Hoods lived in every forest, and Richard Coeur-de-Lion was not yet twenty years old. The pleasant adventures of Robin Hood were real, as you can read in the stories of a dozen outlaws, and men troubled themselves about pain and death much

as healthy bears did, in the mountains. Life had miseries enough, but few shadows deeper than those of the imaginative lover, or the terrors of ghosts at night. Men's imaginations ran riot, but did not keep them awake; at least, neither the preserved fruits nor the mulberry wine nor the clear syrup nor the gingerbread nor the Holy Graal kept Perceval awake, but he slept the sound and healthy sleep of youth, and when he woke the next morning, he felt only a mild surprise to find that his host and household had disappeared, leaving him to ride away without farewell, breakfast, or Graal.

Shot through with color and light, a haven of refuge against the corruptions of the new era, the childhood condition was exalted by Americans of the 1870s and 1880s as never before. One of the most striking examples of this fact is the number of post-Civil War authors who turned to writing about children. On the subliterary level, the age witnessed a flood of Sunday School books; the Alger stories sold copies in the millions; dime novel Westerns which had once celebrated Kit Carson and Calamity Jane now recounted the exploits of boy and girl heroes as well. A middlebrow audience found the "bad" boys of Thomas Bailey Aldrich and George Wilbur Peck and the "little women" of Louisa May Alcott enormously appealing. William Dean Howells reminisced in more than one volume about his Ohio boyhood, and in *Being a Boy* Charles Dudley Warner recalled his youth in the Berkshires. Mrs. Stowe's *The Pearl of Orr's Island* told of the brief, doomed life of the child, Mara, and of her love for a baby named Moses who had been found in a basket on the shore of the sea; and in both *Oldtown Folks* and *Poganuc People* she wrote about young people growing up; attempting to explain her fascination with what she termed "the pleasant valley of childhood," she once said: "Looking back on it from the extreme end of life, it seems to my weary eyes so fresh and beautiful, the dew of the morning lies on it; — that dew which no coming day will restore."

One has only to think of Steinbeck's early work, of Hemingway's Michigan stories, of the novels of Sherwood Anderson and John P. Marquand, to realize that "the pleasant valley of childhood," that Happy Valley of unspoiled youth and crystal-clear impressions which so captured the imagination of the post-Civil War generation, has had a continuing appeal for modern America. But no American writer, past or present, has ever surpassed the extraordinary vividness of Mark Twain's evocations of the Happy Valley of his childhood. Twain's achievement rests primarily on two things, the power of his literary style and the shrewdness of his psychological insight into the minds of children. But style and insight were in turn the outgrowths of love, a love of amazing intensity for the Hannibal, Missouri, of his youth.

To think of Hannibal, Twain once wrote, was like "bathing in the Fountain of Youth," and almost any memento of the past could bring forth the life-giving waters. Four days after his marriage, he received a letter from his boyhood friend, Will Bowen. It "stirred me to the bottom," he wrote Bowen, "and I have rained reminiscences for four and twenty hours." Similarly, the poems of James Whitcomb Riley made "my mouth water for an Elder Time, and a big toe with a rag around it." Mark Twain, as the "Jumping Frog" testifies, repudiated the antebellum past, and in *The Innocents* he said in effect that all history was a bucket of ashes. If he was nostalgic about Hannibal, it was not because the town had been part of a better America of long ago, but because Hannibal represented the world of his childhood. Like the Garden of Eden, the Hannibal of Twain's memory stood outside of time altogether, insulated from the taint and the tragedy of history by the magic circle of youth.

iii

Viewed as a continuous history, Twain's early travel books show a lonely American backtrailing in time toward that magic circle. In *The Adventures of Tom Sawyer,* the long voyage home is over; Twain's persona is now a boy in Paradise.

The choice of a fictional name for heavenly Hannibal was perhaps inevitable: St. Peters-burg. Just why he settled on a third-person narrative, instead of the first-person style that had previously served him well, is not, however, so easily understandable, and there is reason to believe that he ultimately regretted his decision. (In the sequel he would write to *Tom Sawyer* he would not repeat the mistake.) Deciding, too, that his persona had become too fictitious a character to be called "Mark Twain" any longer, he hit upon Tom Sawyer as an appropriate substitute, a name that would be echoed in "Villagers of 1840-3," an unpublished autobiographical reminiscence of Hannibal written during the '90s, in which Twain gave the Clemens family the pseudonym of Carpenter.

Despite the changes in name and point of view, the child in the Happy Valley is nevertheless the same lonesome character whom we have met before. If the narrator of *The Innocents* jokingly described himself as a "helpless orphan," Tom Sawyer is precisely that. And not only is Tom being brought up by a woman who is not his mother, but he believes that Aunt Polly loves his half-brother Sid more than she does him. Tom feels himself further disaffected, not only from Aunt Polly but from the whole community, by his youthful high spirits. Whereas Sid and Mary are fond of going to church, Tom hates it "with his whole heart." There is a "restraint about whole clothes and cleanliness that galled him"; and he envies lawless Huck Finn because the river waif does not have to go to school or call any human being master. Phrases like "away off" and "far off" recur frequently in the novel, signifying the boy's wish to escape to the drifting river, or to the "soft green sides" of Cardiff Hill, to go somewhere, in fine, far beyond "the reach of capture and punishment." Throughout the novel, we are presented with two realities — the prosaic reality of the town, and the fantastic reality of Tom Sawyer's imagination — and the boy continually strives to escape from the former to the latter, with the result that the movement from realistic confinement to romantic freedom utterly dominates the action. Thus the voice of restrictive authority, as symbolized by Aunt Polly, is heard in the very first word of the book — "Tom!" — and in the ensuing chapter Tom twice makes a bolt for freedom. The first time he does, Aunt Polly seizes him as he bolts from a dark hiding-place toward the light and freedom of outdoors, but he scares her and gets away. A page or so later, he flees the supper table to escape her wrath at his having played hooky and gone swimming. The chapter culminates, however, as it had begun, with the reassertion of the confinement idea, as Aunt Polly decides to turn the boy's Saturday holiday into "captivity at hard labor."

But in St. Petersburg, inside the magic circle of childhood, familiar feelings of disaffection and fears of confinement have been turned into child's play in a garden. Tom is only half-serious about his rebellion, just as Aunt Polly is merely half-hearted about her punishment of the boy. To put it another way, an indulgent St. Petersburg permits a boy to "run away" without his ever having to leave home — which is why the place is so heavenly. Rebellion, alienation, and flight are muted and contained in *Tom Sawyer* within a larger framework of acceptance and connection. Partaking in many ways of the quality of a dream, *Tom Sawyer* is a story of wish-fulfillments, in which the hero's most fantastic imaginings are made flesh and the pleasure principle reigns triumphant.

In the first of the notable wish-fulfillments of the novel, the "hard labor" of whitewashing the fence is transmuted into a glorious game; by a dreamlike inversion of the maxims of Poor Richard, laziness becomes the way to wealth. One need go no further than Twain's essay, "The Late Benjamin Franklin," to realize how much the author of *Tom Sawyer* cherished that inversion. Poor Richard's maxims were full of animosity toward boys, in Twain's opinion, and in making that statement he had in mind certain private memories as well as public observations. For Mark Twain not only shared Joel Chandler Harris's general misgivings about the narrowness and imaginative sterility of a business civilization, he had seen what Poor

Richard's philosophy had done to his brother Orion, that hapless incompetent who made his life miserable by following Franklin's dietary and timesaving rules in the belief that proper habits would make him rich, and who had once operated a thoroughly unsuccessful printing establishment named, with pathetic optimism, the Ben Franklin Print Shop. If Twain was himself given to writing self-help letters to his brother, he was also capable of taking off Orion's devotion to *The Way to Wealth* in an essay called "Advice to Youth," in which he advised young men to get up with the lark, and then train the lark to get up at half-past nine, etc. Similarly, in "Autobiography of a Damned Fool" he told of how he had once modeled himself on the rigorous regimen described in Franklin's *Autobiography* by taking a cold swim every morning, until one day a thief stole his clothes while he was in the water and he nearly died of exposure. Perhaps his most succinct opinion of Franklin was rendered in "3000 Years Among the Microbes," where he introduced the pride of Philadelphia in the guise of a yellow fever germ. The whitewashing episode in *Tom Sawyer*, however, is Twain's most prodigious piece of anti-Franklinism. In its portrayal of a gloriously relaxed Tom allowing his friends to pay him for the privilege of painting the fence for him, the scene comically illustrates the thesis that neither work nor the appearance of work is necessary for success. In *Roughing It*, Twain's hero had aspired to easy wealth, but failed to attain it; in the wish-fulfillment-world of *Tom Sawyer*, he succeeds.

Following this triumphant scene, the metronomic rhythm of the novel, with its movement from confinement to freedom and back again, begins to describe more drastic arcs. Slapped sprawling to the floor by Aunt Polly for a crime he has not committed, Tom flees to the river's edge where, in a manner reminiscent of the death-fascinated narrators of *The Innocents* and *Roughing It*, he sits contemplating the "dreary vastness of the stream, wishing, the while, that he could only be drowned, all at once and unconsciously, without undergoing the uncomfortable routine devised by nature." Like all other wishes, Tom's death-wish is soon granted to him, but again the grimness of adult reality is transmuted into child's play. Tom desires to "die *temporarily*," and the sojourn on Jackson's Island with Huck Finn and Joe Harper, culminating in the boys' dramatic appearance at their own funeral, fully meets the morbid requirements of his puerile imagination. As in the scene of the beautiful sunrise on Jackson's Island that follows upon the terrific, nocturnal thunderstorm which has all but torn the island apart, the sun is always shining the next morning in Tom Sawyer's world. Nothing serious has really happened; indeed, nothing at all seems to have happened, for time in *Tom Sawyer* appears to stand perfectly still. The beautiful woods and fields, the magnificent river, the pretty, white-painted town, sleep peacefully in the eternal Missouri summer. The action of the novel takes place some time in the 1840s, but the booming of the guns along the Rio Grande is not heard in the Happy Valley; when Senator Benton comes to town to speak, no report is given of what he said; in hermetic St. Petersburg there is not the least hint of the slavery crisis, or of an oncoming civil war. When Tom acts out in private an imaginary version of a fight with a schoolmate, his vengeance has no cruelty in it of the sort that Longstreet's Gentleman described in "Georgia Theatrics"; the schoolmaster, Dobbins, resorts to the whisky bottle and the birch cane as often as do the vicious teachers in Richard Malcolm Johnston's stories, but the whisky merely makes him harmlessly "fuddled" and his whippings never seem to hurt. Memory, so runs a phrase in *The Innocents Abroad*, filters out the disagreeable: the image of Hannibal, viewed across the years from the gilded '70s, summoned up by Twain amidst the hog-swilling of the spoilsmen and the degrading comedy of the Beecher affair, is not at all disagreeable. St. Petersburg is a morally immaculate society, and *Tom Sawyer* is "simply a hymn," as Mark Twain said, "put into prose form to give it a worldly air" — a hymn sung in honor and glory of the possibility of American innocence.

Evil appears in St. Petersburg only in the person of a social outcast who is both a criminal and a colored man: Injun Joe. When, having played Robin Hood in the woods with Joe Harper, Tom trudges off home, "grieving that there were no outlaws any more, and wondering what modern civilization could claim to have done to compensate for their loss," events are as usual conspiring to satisfy his wishes in the very next chapter. In the graveyard in the dead of night, Tom and Huck come upon, as Sut Lovingood once had done, a respected doctor of the town stealing a body from a grave. The sight terrifies the boys, but it produces no further reaction. Unlike Sut Lovingood, Tom Sawyer is not disillusioned or made cynical by what he has seen. Terror does not lead him on to any disturbing speculations about Dr. Robinson, or about doctors in general, or about the possibility of moral hypocrisy in respectable St. Petersburg. Huck is equally unwilling to consider the possibility of corruption in Eden; as is true of his discovery later in the book that the Temperance tavern in the town is a coverup for a whisky hell, he passes off the revelation of Dr. Robinson's true character without a comment. Tom and Huck's attention in the graveyard is not fixed on Dr. Robinson, the respectable authority-figure, but on the vicious outcast who murders him. The dangers of social disillusionment are thus bypassed, and the nightmare has no significance beyond its own enthralling horror. Far from puncturing Tom Sawyer's dream-world, grim reality has simply enlivened it. Tom Sawyer in the graveyard has merely had another marvelous good time, flirting with death and getting away with it.

Throughout the novel Tom also flirts with Becky Thatcher, his schoolgirl sweetheart. At the end of the novel, the two flirtations — with love and with death — come together in the episode of the cave. It is the first underground adventure in Twain's work in which the significance of the experience of going under the earth, the effect of it on the hero's life, is made dramatically plain. As in Forster's *A Passage to India,* the cave in *Tom Sawyer* is a source of transforming experience, except that instead of upsetting things it resolves them, once and for all, and brings the novel's alternating movement between confinement and escape to an end.

In staging the climax of his novel, Mark Twain drew directly on his personal experience, for he himself had played in caves all through his childhood. As any boy who has grown up in limestone country knows, caves can provide endless enchantment to a youthful imagination. Joseph G. Baldwin, exploring the Virginia countryside in his youth, came to know a certain cave near Staunton, where, according to legend, a bag of bones had been found shortly after an Englishman living in the neighborhood had mysteriously disappeared. A doctor in the town had fallen under suspicion for a time, but he swore that the bones were the remains of a Negro corpse which he had dissected, and nothing more was done about the case. A doctor in Hannibal also contributed to the dark magic of the caves that young Sam Clemens knew. Dr. McDowell, a surgeon, rumored to be a body-snatcher like the Dr. Robinson of *Tom Sawyer*, had stored arms in one of the caves outside the town in hopeful preparation for an invasion of Mexico. Even more bizarrely, McDowell had also buried his dead daughter in a cave, placing the corpse of the fourteen-year-old girl in a copper cylinder filled with alcohol, and submerging the cylinder in a subterranean spring. The top of the cylinder being removable, young bucks of the town were given to hauling it up to the surface of the water and unscrewing the top for a look at the face of death. A further source of enchantment was the widely held belief that the Murrell gang had buried a chest of gold in one of the caves near Hannibal. Is it any wonder that Mark Twain should have confided to his notebook that in dreams "everything is more deep and strong and sharp and real than is ever its pale imitation in the unreal life which is ours when we go about awake and clotted with our artificial selves," and that when he dreamed he was apt to go wandering into caves?

In the cave episode in *Tom Sawyer*, elements of Twain's

personal experience are combined and outlandishly rear-ranged, as if by a trick of faulty memory, or as in a dream. Injun Joe, the murderer of the body-snatcher, has buried guns and gold in McDougal's (not McDowell's) cave; in its sub-terranean depths, death comes in search of the young girl, Becky Thatcher, and of Tom as well.

To this fantastic place Tom Sawyer has come in hope, as al-ways, of adventure. In company with Becky, he breaks away from his fellow picnickers to look for the romance and free-dom of the unknown; passing through "The Drawing-Room," "The Cathedral," and "Aladdin's Palace," he and Becky wan-der down into the cave's nameless and "secret depths." Once, much earlier in the book, Tom had persuaded Becky to kiss him; later they had quarreled when he discovered her looking at a naked figure in the schoolmaster's anatomy book; now, however, holding hands as they walk along, and awed by the sights of an underground anatomy book — by "shining stalac-tites of the length and circumference of a man's leg," and by "a subterranean lake . . . which stretched its dim length away until its shape was lost in the shadows" — they draw more intimately together than ever before. When awe gives way to fear of the cave's bottomless mystery, Tom puts his arm around her and she buries her face in his bosom. When they eat a piece of cake saved from the picnic, Becky says, "It's our wedding-cake, Tom."

All the while that they are descending, they are also grow-ing more fatigued. As drowsiness overtakes them, they fall asleep for long periods. When they go on again, it is as if they are walking in their sleep. The entire experience becomes more and more like a dream, so that when Tom encounters Injun Joe far down in the bowels of the cave, the boy does not logically question why or how the outlaw should be there, or if he is mistaking an illusion for reality. He accepts the In-dian's incongruous appearance with all the conviction that one accepts incongruities in dreams. In *Tom Sawyer*, as in the fiction of Twain's literary idol, Cervantes, the cave is the dwell-

ing-place of fantastically unreal creatures who yet compel belief. Pancracio, the deceived husband in one of Cervantes'
Interludes, is frightened by devils who supposedly live in the
caves of Salamanca, while Don Quixote in the cave of Monte-
sinos thinks he sees the sleeping heroes of a golden past. Tom
Sawyer's romantic imagination is equally willing to accept the
impossible, but the joke in Tom's case reverses the typical
Cervantean situation in that the dream-apparition turns out to
be real. Covered with black mud, Tom had once masqueraded
as an Indian; had boasted of taking a thousand white scalps.
Now, far down in McDougal's cave, he finds himself involved
in a far grimmer game with an Indian nightmarishly disguised
as a white man. For once in his life, Tom has strayed beyond
— or below — the bounds of Heaven; he has stepped across
the limits of safety into a subterranean vault where death
threatens to become more than a temporary condition. Terrified, the boy turns and runs — and the direction in which he
flees is back where he came from.

Having descended into the cave, Tom and Becky spend
there a Biblical total of three days and nights. At the end of
that time, they crawl up a long tunnel toward the light and
are "reborn," after having been given up for dead. From the
moment that he reappears, Tom is a changed person. He was
not the Model Boy of the village when he went into the cave,
nor is he when he comes out. He still is, and remains so
throughout *Huckleberry Finn,* a prankster. But he is no longer
even half-serious about running away. At the end of the novel,
it is Huck who speaks of "cussed smothery houses," not Tom,
while the ingenious plans for playing pirate and Indian games
with which Tom had once persuaded Huck and Joe Harper to
prolong their escapade on Jackson's Island are now employed
by Tom as a bribe to tempt Huck into living at the Widow
Douglas's and becoming respectable. To be a member of the
outlaw gang Tom now forms does not mean that one is at war
with the community; indeed, it means just the reverse. Plead-
ing to join on his own terms, Huck says, "Now Tom, hain't you

always ben friendly to me? You wouldn't shet me out, would you, Tom? You wouldn't do that, now, *would* you, Tom?" But Tom is adamant: "Huck, I wouldn't want to, and I don't want to — but what would people say? Why, they'd say, 'Mph! Tom Sawyer's Gang! pretty low characters in it!' They'd mean you, Huck." The seemingly unconnected events of the long Missouri summer have conformed, we see now, to a ritualistic pattern; the semi-rebellion of Tom Sawyer has in fact been the means of initiating him into the tribe, and his symbolic death in the cave, occurring as it does at the end of his probation, effectively concludes the ceremony of induction. With his re-birth, Tom's life becomes more definite. The money he has discovered in the cave is put out for him at a tidy six per cent return; so settled is the fact that Becky is Tom's girl that one might almost suppose they had reached a definite under-standing; when Judge Thatcher tells Tom he has high hopes of his becoming a great lawyer or a great soldier someday we cannot doubt the Judge's judgment. If the book does not fol-low Tom into manhood — for if it did, Twain said, then his hero would become a liar just like all the other "one-horse men in literature" — Tom nevertheless accepts the adult universe more fully than ever before. In embracing St. Petersburg and its values, he draws the magic circle of childhood about the en-tire society, thus reaffirming the incorruptible innocence of the heavenly town that Twain remembered from his youth. Of all Twain's major fictions, *Tom Sawyer* is the only one in which an initiation ends neither in flight nor in catastrophe, but in serene and joyous acceptance.

Such is the firmness of Tom's commitment to St. Petersburg that when in the course of time Huck Finn would grow dissatis-fied with respectability he would not even ask his old friend to run away with him. To keep from being lonesome, Huck would have to look elsewhere for a traveling companion. Does *The Adventures of Tom Sawyer* give some hint of where the hero of *Huckleberry Finn* would find his fellow Ishmaelite? One fact in the earlier novel seems significant in this regard.

With the memory seared into his brain of a family life in which "Pap and my mother . . . used to fight all the time," Huck has tried to stay clear of all family-style relationships, but occasionally, as he confesses to Tom, he has eaten meals with "a mighty good nigger," named Uncle Jake. "But you needn't tell that," he hastens to add. "A body's got to do things when he's awful hungry he wouldn't want to do as a steady thing." Armed with this insight into Huck's loneliness, and into the conflict that already is going on inside him between his need for love and his ignorant prejudice, we can find toward the end of *Tom Sawyer* an even broader hint of the identity of Huck's future friend. Like Tom Sawyer, Injun Joe had sought out the cave as an avenue to freedom, and had found it instead to be a prison. Unlike Tom, he does not escape. When the townspeople open up the entrance which they have sealed off against further excursions, they find the Indian's body, surrounded by the bones of bats and the gnawed stumps of candles, the dead face pressed close to the crack in the door, "as if his longing eyes had been fixed, to the latest moment, upon the light and cheer of the free world outside." In this final, brief glimpse of the outcast colored man, longing with his last breath to escape from the jail in which St. Petersburg has unwittingly locked him up, Nigger Jim is hauntingly foretold.

CHAPTER IX

You Can't Go Home Again

Papapa [sic] said the other day, "I am a mugwump and a mugwump is pure from the marrow out." (Papa knows that I am writing this biography of him, and he said this for it.)[1]

— Susy Clemens's biography of her father

"Do I know you? I know you clear through. I was born and raised in the South, and I've lived in the North. . . ."

— Colonel Sherburn to the mob

ALL THROUGH the month of August, 1876, Mark Twain was nervous and irritable; at the least annoyance he was apt to fly off the handle. He was tense, for one thing, about reports that the Democrat Tilden might defeat the Republican Hayes in the coming Presidential election; as he wrote to Howells on the ninth, Twain believed that "if Tilden is elected I think the entire country will go pretty straight to — Mrs. Howells's bad place." But nervousness about the possibility of a Democrat in the White House could hardly have been the inner dissatisfaction that prompted him, a few weeks later, to denounce his old friend from Hannibal days, Will Bowen. Bowen had written to Twain concerning the demise of his fire insurance agency. The letter was defensive; it reviewed with pride Bowen's past career as an insurance agent; its evocation of the good old days was a trifle self-pitying. On the other hand, the

---

[1] Copyright 1959 by the Mark Twain Company.

letter certainly did not warrant the scorching response Twain hurled at Bowen on August 31: "As to the past, there is but one good thing about it, & that is, that it *is* the past — we don't have to see it again. There is nothing in it worth pickling for present or future use. Each day that is added to the past is but an old boot added to a pile of rubbish — I have no tears for my pile, no respect, no reverence, no pleasure in taking a rag-picker's hook & exploring it." Reminiscences of the sort that six years before had stirred Twain "to the bottom" were now denounced as "mental & moral masturbation." Behind these furious and shocking words there surely lay a titanic frustration. When one casts about for reasons that made Mark Twain so terribly bitter about the past during that particular month of 1876, one soon comes upon the fact that all summer long he had been trying to write another novel about St. Petersburg, and that in August he finally had given up on it.

Twain had resisted, in *Tom Sawyer*, "the strong temptation to put Huck's life at the Widow's into detail," deciding instead simply to generalize about it, in a paragraph. As he wrote to Howells, "Something told me that . . . [*Tom Sawyer*] was done when I got to that point." However, in the summer of 1876, with *Tom Sawyer* finished and the hillside study of his summer home at Elmira beckoning, Twain began a novel which took up where his earlier book about St. Petersburg had left off — with the efforts of the Widow Douglas to "sivilize" Huck Finn. Sherwood Anderson, thinking of Twain sitting on that high hilltop in upstate New York writing his masterpiece, imagined him "a splendid playboy, playing with rivers and men"; and for a time, apparently, Twain did turn out pages as easily and effortlessly as if he were playing a game, or making up a story for his own children. Then, without warning, his inspiration failed him completely. No matter how hard he tried, the words refused to come. To Howells on August ninth, Twain joked lightly about whether he should pigeonhole the uncompleted manuscript or burn it forthwith. But to Will Bowen he showed his true feelings. When his unsuspecting friend brought up their favorite topic of time past, Twain turned on him like a tiger. In his new novel, Twain had been writing about things that were very important to him; that the Happy Valley had failed him, for some reason, made thoughts of Hannibal intolerable.

ii

Among other things, what Twain had wanted to express in his Huck Finn manuscript was his changing attitude toward the society in which he lived. The years after the publication of *Tom Sawyer* were years of reappraisal for Mark Twain; the extent to which his ideas had altered became fully clear only in the mid-1880s, but the process of change had begun well before then.

Politics, always one of his chief interests, concerned him more and more; beginning with the Hayes-Tilden campaign, Twain started to play an active political role. The armchair satirist of *The Gilded Age* became, by degrees, a public man. A speech on civil service reform, enthusiastically endorsing Hayes and denouncing the patronage system as the child of "General Jackson and the democratic party," brought Twain wide publicity. Howells, who had written the campaign biography of Hayes, told Twain, "You are the only Republican orator quoted without distinction of party by all the newspapers."

Although Hayes's victory in November, 1876, was as dubious as it was narrow, the outcome of the election was greeted as a moral triumph by Twain, for with Hayes in the White House, conservative intellectuals seemed to acquire a new influence in the national government. To clean up the Interior Department, the new President turned to Carl Schurz; he appointed Bayard Taylor and James Russell Lowell to ambassadorships, and Bret Harte to a consulship. John Hay also joined the new Administration. The plum of Minister to Switzerland would surely have gone to Howells — Mark Twain was one of those who strongly urged the appointment — if the *Atlantic* editor had not indicated that he would not accept the post (lest the Administration be accused of undue favoritism toward Hayes's biographer). Delighted by these appointments,[2] and by Hayes's reforms in the civil system, Twain wrote to Howells on July 4, 1877, that he was reading "everything about the President's doings with exultation. He looms up grand and fine, like the oldtime national benefactors of history. Well, it's a long time since we've had anybody to feel proud of & have confidence in. I mean to take my fill now while the meal's hot & the appetite ravenous." [3]

Twain's new enthusiasm for the Republican party was destined to be short-lived. As a result of his public denunciations of patronage abuses, Twain became friendly with George William Curtis and other Mugwumpish Republicans, who helped him to see that Hayes's reforms had by no means cleaned up either the party or the government. The Hayes Administration also did nothing about the wage cuts, the bitter strikes, and the shocking rise in unemployment to a total of more than four million men that were the result of the financial depression of the late '70s. Faced with the spectacle of human suffering, Mark Twain began openly to sympathize with the most militant labor groups in the nation, to the chagrin of his conservative friends. The 1880 campaign found Twain hewing the orthodox Republican line once again — "Garfield suits me thoroughly and exactly," [4] he said — but his disgust with party hacks like Roscoe Conkling and James G. Blaine was mounting. When Blaine — "the filthy Blaine," as Twain called him — was named to head the G.O.P. ticket in 1884, Twain took the momentous step of announcing that he would vote Democratic in November. Despite the clear evidence of Blaine's dishonesty, neither Howells nor the Republi-

---

[2] Except, of course, the Harte appointment, which outraged Twain.
[3] Copyright 1959 by the Mark Twain Company.
[4] Copyright 1959 by the Mark Twain Company.

cans of Nook Farm could quite bring themselves to renounce the party of Lincoln, national victory, and big business. When it was disclosed that there was a woman in Grover Cleveland's past, Howells seized on the disclosure as an excuse for not voting for him. "I shall vote for Blaine," Howells wrote to Twain . . .

> I do not believe he is guilty of the things they accuse him of; and I know they are not proved against him. As for Cleveland, his private life may be no worse than that of most men, but as an enemy of that contemptible, hypocritical, lopsided morality which says a woman shall suffer all the shame of unchastity and a man none, I want to see him destroyed politically by his past. . . . Besides, I don't like his hangman-face. It looks dull and brutal.

Understandably, Howells's tone was lame, for only a few days before he had received a letter from Twain which made no secret of Twain's contempt for such reasoning:

> To see grown men, apparently in their right mind, seriously arguing against a bachelor's fitness for President because he has had private intercourse with a consenting widow! These grown men [know] what the bachelor's other alternative was & tacitly they seem to prefer that to the widow. *Isn't* human nature the most consummate sham and lie that was ever invented? Isn't man a creature to be ashamed of in pretty much all his aspects? Is he really fit for anything but to be stood up on a street corner as a convenience for dogs? [5]

All through the fall of 1884 Twain worked with the Mugwumps, chairing their rallies and beseeching his Nook Farm neighbors to rise above their orthodoxy. In the end, however, not even Joseph Hopkins Twichell, Twain's closest friend and himself an outspoken critic of Blaine, found it possible to vote for a Democrat for President. Twichell compromised instead on the Prohibition candidate. Standing by his guns to the last, Mark Twain cast his ballot for Grover Cleveland.

[5] Copyright 1959 by the Mark Twain Company.

Rumblings of Twain's coming revolt against the conservative opinions of his friends and neighbors could be heard in his humor as early as January, 1876. For on the evening of the twenty-fourth of that month, while entertaining in his Nook Farm home the genial and distinguished lawyers, ministers, and editors who made up the Monday Evening Club of Hartford, Twain read to his guests his latest fantasy, which he later called "The Facts Concerning the Recent Carnival of Crime in Connecticut." The narrator of the story — "Mark Twain" — recalls the time when he had been psychologically persecuted by a tiny creature who looked like a caricature of himself and who was in fact his conscience, a term which to Twain meant something vaguely like what we would call the superego. ("Conscience," Twain once explained in his notebooks, "is . . . moral, not physical. . . . It is merely a *thing;* the creature of *training;* it is whatever one's mother and Bible and comrades and laws and system of government and habitat and heredities have made it. . . . Inborn nature is Character, by itself in the brutes — the tiger, the dove, the fox, etc. Inborn nature *and* the modifying Conscience, working together make Character in man." [6]) A dream story involving a conflict between will and conscience, "Carnival" markedly resembles Poe's "William Wilson," although instead of concluding in a nightmare of guilt and suicidal retribution it ends with "Mark Twain" triumphantly murdering his tiny oppressor. "In an instant I had my lifelong foe by the throat. After so many years of waiting and longing, he was mine at last. I tore him to shreds and fragments. I rent the fragments to bits. . . . At last, and forever, my Conscience was dead!" Freed from the pressure to conform to the conventions of society — with mother, Bible, comrades, laws, and government all slain in one fell swoop — the narrator forthwith sets out to murder various people in Connecticut whom he has hated for years. "I settled all my old outstanding scores," he says, "and began the world anew."

[6] Copyright 1959 by the Mark Twain Company.

How, one wonders, did Twain's listeners respond to this story? Did any of them take seriously the hatred for Connecticut that it proclaimed? Did the distinguished members of the Monday Evening Club have any sense that this was a momentous occasion in the developing pattern of Twain's art? For it *was* a momentous occasion. With "Carnival," Mark Twain began to pit himself in imaginative opposition to the respectable community whose mores he had so eagerly adopted at the beginning of the '70s and whose approval he had so anxiously cultivated. Not quite two years after "Carnival," he desecrated New England's holiest poets — in the so-called "Whittier Dinner Speech," delivered in the Brunswick Hotel in Boston before the most famous company ever gathered together in America — by characterizing Ralph Waldo Emerson, Oliver Wendell Holmes, and Henry Wadsworth Longfellow as three deadbeats from the West. And in his major works of fiction that came after "Carnival," in *Huckleberry Finn* and *A Connecticut Yankee*, in *Pudd'nhead Wilson* and *The Mysterious Stranger*, Twain's very different heroes are all conscience-killers who would liberate not only themselves but others from the coercions of social convention.

In the course of embarrassing "Mark Twain" with a review of his past transgressions, the "Conscience" of "Carnival" adds insult to injury by informing him that henceforth he intends to address him in "your o-w-n s-n-i-v-e-l-i-n-g d-r-a-w-l — baby!" — an epithet which by early 1876 had already taken on considerable resonance in Twain's writing and was destined to acquire more. For while the "Mark Twain" of "Carnival" merely talks like a baby, the liberators in many of Twain's subsequent works are children in fact, like the little girl in "The Death Disk," who persuades Oliver Cromwell to release her father from a death sentence, and the boy detective in *Tom Sawyer, Detective* who is the indispensable agent of social justice. If, as Twain said, his books are "sermons," then their favorite text may be said to be the one which bored Tom

Sawyer into releasing the chinch-bug in church — "And a little child should lead them."

Thus the book on which Twain lavished the most care, and the one he liked best of all, was *Personal Recollections of Joan of Arc*, the story of "the only person," so the epigraph from Kossuth reads, "who has ever held supreme command of the military forces of a nation *at the age of seventeen.*" Not only is the heroine a child, but her saga, so Twain implies, can be truly understood only by those who possess the audacious imagination of children — for the old man who is the narrator of the book explicitly addresses the story of Joan to his "great-great-grandnephews and nieces." A few years later, Henry Adams would say that his *Mont-Saint-Michel and Chartres* was "written for nieces." For Twain and Adams both went back to the Middle Ages in order to become young again in imagination. The world was fresh then, and alive. That Twain, again like Adams, used this bygone world of youth as a symbolic means of talking about modern, adult America is emphasized by the fact that the old man tells his story of Joan in the year that Columbus discovered the New World. When, in other words, he describes Joan calling medieval France to arms, the narrator is actually presenting to his childish audience the quintessential image of the Twainian child-liberator who sees American society as a trap from which timid but basically good people must be freed in order that they might begin the world anew:

> The contrast between her and her century is the contrast between day and night. She was truthful when lying was the common speech of men; she was honest when honesty was become a lost virtue; she was a keeper of promises when the keeping of a promise was expected of no one; she gave her great mind to great thoughts and purposes when other great minds wasted themselves upon pretty fancies or upon poor ambitions; she was modest, and fine, and delicate, when to be loud and coarse might be said to be universal; . . . she was steadfast when stability was unknown, and honorable in an age

which had forgotten what honor was; . . . she was unfailingly true in an age that was false to the core; . . . she was spotlessly pure in mind and body when society in the highest places was foul in both. . . .

In the light of this passage, it becomes evident that Mark Twain spent a large part of the last three decades of his writing life telling the story of Joan of Arc over and over again in various forms and guises. And the ultimate reason for his extraordinary fascination with the Maid is that Twain identified with her — as he himself hinted in his anecdote of how he became a writer. Stooping in the dust of a Hannibal street, Twain recalled, the youthful Sam Clemens picked up a page that had been torn from a book, read it, and — comprehending for the first time what a power there was in words — resolved on a literary career. On the page was written a description of Joan of Arc. The story is quite possibly apocryphal, for Twain was as much of a self-mythologizer as Benjamin Franklin or Edgar Allan Poe or Ernest Hemingway. However, what is significant about it finally is not its veracity, but its association of Joan of Arc with the idea of power inherent in the written word. If Twain spent his life writing about liberators, it was because he believed that the writer in America might himself play a liberating role — that the humorist, more precisely, might serve as the modern world's equivalent of Joan of Arc. Henry James considered that only primitive persons could be interested in Mark Twain,[7] but James's belief in the supremacy of the artist and the glory of art has a worthy counterpart in Twain's conception of humor. The nihilistic vision of *The Mysterious Stranger* is perhaps a strange place

[7] Twain returned James's scorn with interest by remarking that he would rather be "damned to John Bunyan's heaven" than read *The Bostonians*, yet in the end he was more generous to his contemporary than James ever would be to him. In a letter of 1900 to T. Douglas Murray, thanking him for a collection of documents relating to the trial of Joan of Arc, Twain speculated how the evidence might have been worked up by a "master" like Henry James. The association of a writer's masterliness with Joan is also significant.

to look for affirmations, but that book was for Twain what *The Tempest* was for Shakespeare, a valedictory; and the Stranger — for all his cosmic despair — is as bold as Prospero in asserting the glory of his creator's life. The human race, says the Stranger, for all its grotesqueries and absurdities and shams, has one really effective weapon: laughter. "Power, money, persuasion, supplication, persecution — these can lift at a colossal humbug — push it a little — weaken it a little, century by century; but only laughter can blow it to rags and atoms at a blast. Against the assault of laughter nothing can stand." Over and over again in his writings, Twain played with fantasies of power that expressed the scope of his ambition. The hero of *A Connecticut Yankee* does not amount to much in nineteenth century America, but in the world of King Arthur he is "the Boss." The pauper from Offal Court becomes the heir to the English throne. In *The Innocents Abroad,* Twain's narrator is overcome with admiration for Napoleon III's dazzling rise to power. Richard Watson Gilder might assure the readers of the *Century* that Mark Twain was not a "giber at religion or morality"; Howells might hail him as "a humorist who never makes you blush to have enjoyed his joke . . . [and] whose fun is never at the cost of anything high or good"; Nook Farm, the Monday Evening Club, all America, might regard him as a funny man and nothing more; but Twain had other ideas about the uses of his art. Like Joan, Twain wished to call a complacent age to greatness.

Given the fact that America persisted in regarding him as a jokesmith who was not to be taken seriously, it is no wonder that the most memorable of Twain's fantasies of power are also prophecies of tragedy and defeat, and that the description of Joan of Arc which determined him to become a writer was, so he said, an account of her last miserable days in the cage at Rouen, locked up and forgotten by the nation she saved. Images of cages — and of tombs and dungeons and prisons and caves — had tantalized Twain's mind for a long time. But as he moved, in the middle '70s, toward full possession of his creative talent, the nightmare of being locked up and forgotten began to haunt him as never before.

iii

In *Huckleberry Finn*, begun six or seven months after the reading of "Carnival" to the Monday Evening Club, Twain proposed to develop for the first time on a major scale the conflict adumbrated in the story. The novel was to be told in the first person, and the action was to be essentially psychological: in his own words, the boy would tell of being caught in the crossfire between his environment-trained conscience and his "Voices," as Twain's Joan would say, and of his agonizing struggle to decide whether or not to become a liberator. The main difference between Huck Finn and the baby-talking narrator of "Carnival" would consist in Huck's gentleness. Unlike "Mark Twain," the boy-hero of *Huckleberry Finn* would never be a vengeance seeker or a murderer.

The liberation theme is announced in the title of the novel's very first chapter: "I Discover Moses and the Bulrushers." For although Huck soon loses all interest in the Moses story, "because I don't take no stock in dead people," the humorous introduction of the Biblical saga at the very start of the book effectively ushers in the majestic theme of slavery and freedom, and inextricably associates Huck — a native of the river valley which its most famous citizen, Abraham Lincoln, called the "Egypt of the West" — with the little Jewish child who, abandoned in a great, continental river, grew up to lead an enslaved people to freedom. In the early chapters the liberation theme is developed *a verso* in terms of the idea of confinement, for these describe Huck's life at the Widow's which Twain had been tempted to include in *Tom Sawyer* and then had decided not to on the grounds that they were not a part of Tom's story. Once again the tribe is attempting to administer the ephebic rites to a free-spirited boy, with comic results.

When Huck is sworn into Tom Sawyer's gang and introduced to Miss Watson's and the Widow Douglas's piety, he is in both cases being shown how a respectable St. Petersburg boy is expected to behave, and in both initiations he resists the mysteries. Sancho Panza to Tom's Quixote, Huck sees only turnips and Sunday school picnickers where Tom imagines "julery" and "rich A-rabs." For his down-to-earth honesty, Tom calls him a "numskull," a judgment which is echoed by Miss Watson when she discovers that he has called on God for fishhooks as a result of her having told him that he would receive whatever he prayed for. But revealing as these incidents are, the most telling indication of Huck's spiritual difference from the rest of the community, as well as a premonition of the stirring drama of liberation that lies ahead, is his refusal to help Tom Sawyer tie up Nigger Jim "for fun."

Restless in his confinement to respectability, Huck echoes the narrator of *Roughing It* in his confession that "All I wanted was to go somewheres; all I wanted was a change." Yet in these early chapters, his rebellion does not seem much more serious, finally, than Tom's had been. His occasional forays into the freedom of his cast-off rags and his hogsheads are short-lived; by the time that winter comes we find him admitting that whereas he still prefers his old ways, "I was getting so I liked the new ones, too, a little bit." When his outcast Pap reappears and takes him off to the woods, Huck at first thinks he has regained his lost freedom, only to find that freedom means being locked up in a lonely cabin for days on end — means being a captive audience for his Pap's tirades about "free niggers"; and that for all the delights of shoelessness and pipe-smoking, he has in fact exchanged the discomforts and restrictions of respectability for a disreputable prison.

In writing the episode of Huck and Pap in their cabin home, Twain in all likelihood was drawing on the memory of his relationship with his own father. Although Twain's mother was warmhearted, the family atmosphere in the Clemens household was dominated by the personality of his father, John

Marshall Clemens. Thanks to this strange, austere, loveless man, the Clemenses were reserved and formal with one another to an almost unbelievable degree; at night, they shook hands before going to bed — a warmer gesture would have been unthinkable. Indeed, in later years Twain could remember only one time when a kiss was ever exchanged between members of the Clemens family. The story that Mrs. Clemens was disappointed in love and married her husband out of spite has never been satisfactorily verified, but there is no doubt as to the nature of the relationship between the father and his son Sam. As Twain recalled, "My father and I were always on the most distant terms when I was a boy — a sort of armed neutrality, so to speak." In such an atmosphere, Twain must have suffered almost daily from rejection, but the instance that seemed to him to epitomize all his experiences of parental neglect was the time when his family, moving from Florida, Missouri, to a new home in Hannibal, drove off without him. Writing an article in later years for the *North American Review,* Twain could still remember the "grisly deep silence" that fell upon the locked house after his family had gone, and the nameless terrors that gripped him as the afternoon waned into evening. The story is engrossing, but as Dixon Wecter has pointed out, untrue, for Twain was here describing as a personal experience something that in fact happened to his brother, Orion. So acute, apparently, was Twain's sense of rejection that in looking back on his early life he was convinced that it was surely he who had suffered the agony of being locked up and forgotten.

Huck's lonesome vigil in the locked-up cabin is the equivalent of the experience that Twain believed had happened to him. And Huck's outlaw Pap is a nightmare version of Twain's hardhearted father: "He was most fifty, and he looked it. His hair was long and tangled and greasy, and hung down, and you could see his eyes shining through like he was behind vines. . . . There warn't no color in his face, where his face showed; it was white to make a body's flesh crawl — a tree-toad white, a fish-belly white." Between this terrible father and his son armed neutrality is but the prelude to open war. The day after Pap tries to kill Huck with a clasp-knife, Huck manages to escape from the cabin by committing symbolic suicide and murder. So that his Pap will not pursue him, Huck simulates his own death by killing a wild pig and distributing its blood around the cabin; but this act has a double meaning, which emerges only when we recall Pap Finn's notorious habit of lying drunk amongst the hogs in the tanyard, as well as the drunkard's slobberingly self-pitying identification of himself with his sleeping companions: "There's the hand that was the hand of a hog." Huck's slaughter of the pig not only symbolizes his desire to end his own miserable life, but to slay his father and the sordid animality of his ways.

Bursting clear of the locked-up cabin, Huck is simply running away from his past, rather than toward any definable future. On the one hand, he is not prepared to go back and be "cramped up and sivilized" at the Widow's, while on the other — as his symbolic murder of his Pap makes clear — he has also rejected the life of a social outcast. He has neither embraced St. Petersburg nor turned his back on it. Slipping into the river, an officially dead Huck is "reborn." Yet he has no ideas about a new life and a new identity for himself. Irresolute and uncertain, Huck instinctively turns toward a familiar goal: Jackson's Island, Tom Sawyer's halfway-house of rebellion where all irrevocable decisions are magically held in abeyance.

The means by which Huck will find out who he now is is illustrated by a parable in Chapter XVI. The parable is a part of an episode which did not appear in the novel when it was finally completed, because Twain had already thrown it — the verb is his — into *Life on the Mississippi.* Unsure as to when, if ever, he would finish *Huckleberry Finn,* and wishing to flesh out his history of the river with a dramatization of "keelboat talk and manners" as they had existed in the 1840s, Twain improved a good book at the cost of looting his masterpiece of an episode of extraordinary richness, of great beauty and humor, which takes us to the heart of the novel.

The episode begins immediately after Huck and Jim's terrifying experience of getting lost in the fog. Drifting down an unfamiliar and "monstrous big river," the boy and the Negro decide that Huck should find out where they are by swimming over to a huge raft they have seen in the distance and gathering the information by eavesdropping. Under cover of darkness, Huck reaches the raft, climbs on board without being noticed, and settles down to listen to the talk of the raftsmen — to their colossal boasting, their roaring songs, and above all, to the fantastic tall tale about a man named Dick Allbright and the mysterious barrel that followed him on the river wherever he went rafting, bringing terror and death to his companions. Nothing, the teller of the tale assures his audience, could keep the barrel off Dick Allbright's trail, or mitigate its inexorable fatality, until finally a raft captain swam out to the barrel and hauled it aboard. Inside its wooden walls, the captain and his men found a stark naked baby —

> . . . Dick Allbright's baby; he owned up and said so. "Yes," he says, a-leaning over it, "yes, it is my own lamented darling, my poor lost Charles William Allbright deceased," says he — for he could curl his tongue around the bulliest words in the language when he was a mind to. . . . Yes, he said he used to live up at the head of this bend, and one night he choked his child, which was crying, not intending to kill it — which was prob'ly a lie — and then he was scared, and buried it in a bar'l, before his wife got home, and off he went, and struck the northern trail and went to rafting; and this was the third year that the bar'l had chased him.

Crouched in the darkness, naked and afraid, Huck seems utterly apart from these coarse, rough men. Nevertheless, the fantasy of violence and terror which the raftsman has spun for the scoffing delight of his fellows vitally involves the runaway boy, an involvement which Huck himself acknowledges. For when he is suddenly seized from his hiding-place and surrounded by strange men demanding to know his name, he jokingly replies, "Charles William Allbright, sir." Always in Twain the best jokes reveal the profoundest connections, and with the release of laughter triggered by this superbly timed response we are made aware that we have been eavesdropping on a parable about Huck Finn's life. The entire incident magnificently exemplifies how Mark Twain could exploit for the purposes of high art the tradition of Southwestern humor — and shows, too, what very different effects he achieved. The ignorant river waif who has replaced the Self-controlled Gentleman as auditor is deeply and personally involved in the story he hears, rather than amusedly aloof from it. Charles William Allbright afloat in his barrel mirrors the situation of Huck on the raft: having died, both boys have come alive again in the flowing waters of the great Mississippi. Charles William Allbright in his barrel also calls up once again the infant Moses hidden in the ark of bulrushes in the Nile, and in so doing associates the drama of liberating an enslaved people with the ideas of freedom and renewal of life that the river connotes. At the very heart of the parable there is an even more breath-taking illumination. Charles William Allbright, having lost his father, has taken to the river to go in search of him. In telling us that, the parable tells us things about Huck Finn that Huck himself cannot possibly communicate. Drifting down the river toward a goal he can neither define nor scarcely imagine, Huck is in fact looking for another father to replace the one he has lost. And this quest is also a quest for himself, because once Huck has found his new father he will know at last who he himself really is. Upon that recognition, in turn, rests the resolution of the struggle between Huck's conscience and the impulse of his generous heart as to what to do about Jim. The novel's grand theme, then, the Mosaic drama of liberation, depends ultimately upon the outcome of Huck's search for a father.

The parenthood problem is officially introduced in the fifth chapter of the novel, when Judge Thatcher and the Widow

Douglas go to court to get permission to take Huck away from his Pap. Who should be his parents, the respectable aristocrats who are no blood relation to him, or his violent, drunken father? Nothing less than a human life is at stake; the decision would seem to call for the wisdom of Solomon. Echoing Huck's judgment of Moses, Nigger Jim "doan' take no stock" in the wisdom of Solomon, yet in Chapter XIV — entitled "Was Solomon Wise?" — our laughter at Jim's stupidity carries with it the realization that the parenthood problem, like the liberation theme, has been given a deeper moral seriousness through a Biblical association. Jim regards it as utter foolishness that Solomon should have attempted to settle the parenthood dispute by offering to cut the child in two and give half to each mother — "De 'spute warn't 'bout half a chile, de 'spute was 'bout a whole chile; en de man dat think he kin settle a 'spute 'bout a whole chile wid a half a chile doan' know enough to come in out'n de rain." Twain himself was very fond of this chapter and delighted in reading it aloud in public lectures. But if it can be successfully taken out of context, the scene is also a vital element in the moral pattern of the novel. For Huck, like Solomon, is listening for the voice of truth and the accents of love as a means of identifying the true parent he seeks. Neither side in the legal contest so identifies itself, and therefore Huck retreats from both respectability and hoggishness to the way station of Jackson's Island. In doing so he is certainly not acting self-consciously: he is simply drifting with the tide — quite literally — and not even wondering what will happen to him next. All that this ignorant and inexperienced child is able to tell us directly about himself is that it is awful to be so "dreadful lonesome." Encountering the outcast colored man in hiding on the island, Huck is at first merely amused and exasperated by the black man's stupidity, but part of the drama of their relationship is Huck's gathering awareness that Jim is "most always right" about things that really matter, about how certain movements of the birds mean a storm is coming, about the dangers of messing with snakes, and the meaning of dreams. But while Jim's relationship to Huck is fatherly in the sense that he constantly is correcting and admonishing the boy, forever telling him some new truth about the world, he is identified even more unmistakably as Huck's father by the love that he gives him. As Huck is searching for a father, so Jim is attempting to rejoin his family, and he lavishes on the love-starved boy all of his parental affection. Jim's ludicrous horror at Solomon's apparent willingness to split a child in two is seen in retrospect to be a humorous statement of his loving care for the integrity of his white child.

As it gradually dawns on Huck — and the gradualness of his realization is very delicately controlled by Twain — that Jim loves him, the psychological battle within Huck's mind intensifies accordingly. "Remorse! remorse!" the narrator of "Carnival" had cried. "It seemed to me that it would eat the very heart out of me!" In Chapter XVI of *Huckleberry Finn,* an environment-trained conscience punishes Huck for his subversive association with the runaway slave with an even greater ferocity:

> Jim said it made him all over trembly and feverish to be so close to freedom. Well, I can tell you it made me all over trembly and feverish, too, to hear him, because I begun to get it through my head that he *was* most free — and who was to blame for it? Why, *me.* I couldn't get that out of my conscience, no how nor no way. It got to troubling me so I couldn't rest; I couldn't stay still in one place. It hadn't ever come home to me before, what this thing was that I was doing. But now it did; and it stayed with me, and scorched me more and more. I tried to make out to myself that *I* warn't to blame, because *I* didn't run Jim off from his rightful owner; but it warn't no use, conscience up and says, every time, "But you knowed he was running for his freedom, and you could a paddled ashore and told somebody." That was so — I couldn't get around that noway. That was where it pinched. Conscience says to me, 'What had poor Miss Watson done to you that you could see her nigger go off right under your eyes and never say one single word? What did that poor woman do to you that you could treat her so mean? Why, she tried to

learn you your book, she tried to learn you your manners, she tried to be good to you every way she knowed how. *That's* what she done."

I got to feeling so mean and so miserable I most wished I was dead.

With these words, the first of the novel's really notable representations of moral doubt, Huck at last comes to understand the dilemma confronting him. The battle in his mind is at this point fully joined.

And at this point, Twain could go no further. Having brought a rich and various novel to a moment of psychological crisis; having managed all the complexities of the action with superb facility; Twain abandoned *Huckleberry Finn* at the end of Chapter XVI and threatened to burn the manuscript. The author did not, probably could not, analyze why he was unable to go on. To Twain — accustomed as he was to writing by fits and starts — the failure of his inspiration may not even have bothered him as much as his bitter letter to Will Bowen might suggest. At least, not at first. For Twain was also accustomed to having his "tank" fill up again in a reasonable period of time. In this case, seven long years would pass before he would find himself able to finish the novel. Renewed efforts to get the book moving again during this Biblical period of barrenness resulted in a few additional chapters, but nothing more. Clearly, Twain in August of 1876 had run into unprecedented difficulties which his usual remedy for a recalcitrant manuscript of pigeonholing it for a time could not overcome.

The question — the fascinating question — is: What was the nature of those difficulties? What was the problem that arose in Chapter XVI and that so stubbornly resisted solution? Some of Twain's most knowledgeable critics, including Bernard DeVoto and Henry Nash Smith, have pointed to the fact that in Chapter XVI Huck and Jim discover they have drifted past Cairo in the fog, and that therefore Jim's plan of taking a steamboat up the Ohio toward a free state could no longer be used by Twain as an excuse for moving Huck and Jim downstream on the Mississippi. Now, Twain obviously wanted to have the two runaways continue their voyage southward, if only because it was the Mississippi Valley, not the Ohio, that he knew so well from his piloting days; yet to have a slave seek for freedom by heading deeper and deeper into the heart of the slave country was quite incredible. Baffled as to how to resolve this problem — so Professor Smith has argued — Twain abandoned the novel at the end of Chapter XVI; picked it up in the winter of 1879–1880 long enough to add Chapters XVII and XVIII; but was unable really to get rolling again until he struck upon the idea of introducing the King and the Duke. For once the King and the Duke come aboard the raft in Chapter XIX, they master it, and the desire of Nigger Jim to head for a free state perforce gives way to the plan of the two confidence men to proceed downstream in search of sucker money. Thus did Twain logically account for the continued southward progress of Huck and Jim. Once he had done this, he was able to go on with the book.

The flaw in this argument is that the introduction of the King and the Duke emphatically did not enable Twain to proceed very far or very fast. Thanks to the ingenious detective work of Walter Blair, we know that Chapter XIX — in which the two con men first appear — was probably written in the summer of 1880, as in all likelihood was Chapter XX. But having written these chapters, Twain's inspiration once again failed him, for on the basis of the evidence he has assembled Professor Blair suspects that Chapter XXI was not written until the spring of 1883, almost three years later. Therefore, the invention of the King and the Duke can hardly be said to have released Twain's pent-up imagination, and in view of that fact it does not seem very likely that whatever was stymieing him had much to do with the question of how to account for Huck and Jim's continuing to move south. (When one recalls the unexplained illogicalities and improbabilities with which his books are replete, it seems even less likely that a little detail like the direction of a slave's escape route would have delayed as resourceful a writer as Mark Twain for very long.) Yet what other explanation is there? The text of Chapter XVI itself supplies the clue to an alternative theory.

The chapter, to repeat, shows Huck for the first time fully acknowledging his moral dilemma. Perhaps in some way the boy's dilemma was the author's as well; perhaps Mark Twain no more than Huck Finn could decide what Huck should do about Nigger Jim. To a de-Southernized Twain, it was of course unthinkable that the boy should return the Negro to slavery. On the other hand, once Huck committed the "sin" of helping Jim to freedom he would place himself forever beyond the pale of heavenly St. Petersburg; he would be carrying his irresolute rebellion against the Happy Valley to the point of no return; he would be electing to become an outcast and a renegade, like his vile Pap. As *The Adventures of Tom Sawyer* unforgettably shows, the vision of an unfallen American Eden meant an enormous amount to Twain. And that vision was validated and defined by the thought of innocent boys playing there, in a dreaming and eternal summertime. That Huck should be cast out of St. Petersburg was thus equally unthinkable to Twain. Tom Sawyer's rebellion against this magic place had been simply child's play, ending in reconciliation and acceptance. But Huck Finn's rebellion had turned into a far more drastic business. It was as if Joan of Arc had been called on to save France by flouting Heaven's decrees. Unlike the hero of "Carnival," Huck did not bear a vindictive grudge against respectable society; for antebellum Missouri, unlike post-Civil War Connecticut, was seen by Twain at long distance in both space and time, a perspective which reduced all motives for hatred, all social coercions, to delightful jokes. Without a single exception, the respectable inhabitants of the Happy Valley whom Huck encounters in the first sixteen chapters of the novel — the Widow Douglas, Judge Thatcher, Tom Sawyer, Miss Watson, Judith Loftus, the night watchman, even Mr. Parker, the slavehunter — are fundamentally decent people. What, indeed, had they done to Huck that he should treat them so mean? Twain in 1876 could present Huck's dilemma — brilliantly present it, because it sprang directly out of a deep conflict in his own feelings — but he was completely unable to resolve it.

iv

In giving up on *Huckleberry Finn*, Twain not only relinquished a majestic theme and an engaging hero, but a style which "at the period," as T. S. Eliot has observed, "whether in America or in England, was an innovation, a new discovery in the English language." For in his masterpiece Twain abandoned the easy and colloquial narrative style which was the trademark of "Mark Twain" for the untutored vernacular of a ragged and ignorant boy. "Other authors," says Eliot, had achieved "natural speech in relation to particular characters — Scott with characters talking Lowland Scots, Dickens with cockneys: but no one else had kept it up through the whole of a book." Even in the Sut Lovingood yarns there had been occasional interpolations of gentlemanly "George's" genteel voice, and in any event Harris's book was a collection of disparate tales, not a unified story. Between 1830 and the Civil War, the vernacular material of the Southwestern tradition had gradually overwhelmed the gentlemanly style; but it was Mark Twain who completed the revolution. Carrying the vernacular tendency of the Southwestern tradition to an unprecedented extreme, the author of *Huckleberry Finn* established the once-despised voice of the Clowns as the narrative style of an entire novel, thereby altering the whole future course of American literature.

What is most immediately striking about Huck's narrative style is its freshness. Like Sut Lovingood, Huck looks at the world with a childish awe; he tells about things he sees in careful detail, as if no one had ever noticed them before. Describing how Tom Sawyer whispered an instruction to him, Huck says, "Tom he made a sign to me — kind of a little noise with his mouth — and we went creeping away on our hands and knees." Of the victuals at the Widow Douglas's he remarks, "There warn't really anything the matter with them, — that is, nothing only everything was cooked by itself. In a barrel of odds and ends it is different; things get mixed up, and the juice kind of swaps around, and the things go better." Another of the qualities of Huck's imagination is his literal-mindedness. For the vernacular, as always in the Southwestern tradition, is the language of realism; from Huck's point of view, turnips are neither a culinary delight, as Beriah Sellers claims, nor "julery," as Tom Sawyer quixotically asserts: they are turnips, and nothing else. Yet Huck is also a poet, for all his literalness, and the essence of his poetry is his "great sense," as Lionel Trilling has put it, "of the sadness of human life." The Clowns of the Southwestern tradition had taken a brutal joy in acknowledging the hardness of frontier life; in *Huckleberry Finn*, the acknowledgement is still there, but the joy has been muted into sorrow, as in this long, descriptive sentence in Chapter II: "Well when Tom and me got to the edge of the hilltop we looked away down into the village and could see three or four lights twinkling, where there was sick folks, maybe; and the stars over us was sparkling ever so fine; and down by the village was the river, a whole mile broad, and awful still and grand." The vernacular had revealed a strain of tenderness before, in "The Big Bear of Arkansas," and again in the Sut Lovingood stories, but not until *Huckleberry Finn* did any author realize its full poetic possibilities. Speaking through the mask of an "irresponsible" boy, Twain was somehow able to "let himself go," as he had never been able to do before, with the result that Huck is the one Twain hero who is not shut out from the pageantry of life by his fear of being taken in by it. Huck knows the treacheries of the Mississippi as well as the cub pilot does; yet he also can accept its simple, almost pastoral, pleasures in a way that "Mark Twain" never could. Only a few hours after making his escape from the cabin, and knowing that his murderous Pap has already discovered his absence, Huck can still take time to notice, even as he is fleeing, that "The river looked miles and miles across. The moon was so bright I could a counted the drift logs that went a-slipping along, black and still, hundreds of yards out from shore. Everything was dead quiet, and it looked late, and *smelt* late. You know what I mean — I don't know the words to put it in." And along with the emotional freedom that his masquerade as Huck afforded him, Twain gained another kind of freedom: the freedom to express his response to beauty in an unorthodox way. From certain hints in Poe's *Marginalia*, Baudelaire had developed his revolutionary poetic doctrine of the interpenetration of the senses; by playing the part of an ignorant boy who doesn't know any better way to talk than to say he smells the lateness and watches the lonesomeness, Twain brought Poe's experiments back to America and prepared the way for the tragically lovely effects that Faulkner would create in the Benjy section of *The Sound and the Fury.*

Such, then, was the stylistic achievement of the book that Twain threatened to burn as an abortive mess.

v

In the winter of 1879-1880, Twain made another stab at the manuscript and succeeded in adding two more chapters, XVII and XVIII, detailing Huck's life at the Grangerfords'. The chapters were at once the funniest and the most violent he had yet written: Emmeline Grangerford's necrophilic crayon of a young lady lugubriously weeping over a dead bird with its heels up ("and underneath the picture it said, 'I Shall Never Hear Thy Sweet Chirrup More Alas!'") ironically complements the atrocious blood-bath of the Grangerford-Shepherdson feud. Brilliant as they are, however, these chapters represent the improvisations of an author who was marking time. Not only do the chapters arrest the progress of Huck and Jim's progress downstream, they separate the two runaways from one another. Not a single step is taken in these chapters toward a resolution of the moral conflict that rages in Huck's mind.

As he has been doing all along, Huck tries out a new identity at the Grangerfords'. Having masqueraded as Sarah Mary Williams at Judith Loftus's house, he now introduces himself as George Jackson (later on he will become an English valet, and still later, Tom Sawyer). However, just as his Pap's spiritual rebirth into the good graces of St. Petersburg had culminated in a quite literal Fall (dead drunk, off a porch roof), so Huck's new identities begin well but end badly. His life as George Jackson is no exception. When Huck, crying a little, covers up the face of thirteen-year-old Buck Grangerford, it is a case of the dead burying the dead, for the bloody feud ends Huck's new life as finally as it has Buck's. The test of another identity having failed, Huck goes back to Jim and the raft, which for the first time he now calls "home."

Yet this apparent tightening of the relationship between Huck and Jim merely counterbalances the powerful impression that the Grangerford family has made on Huck. White aristocrats of the Valley society (even as Nigger Jim is the black aristocrat of the raft and the river), the Grangerfords at first overawe Huck, but they are so friendly they soon succeed in making the lonesome boy feel like a member of the family. Huck's description of the Grangerfords' house lacks even the half-serious disgust for respectability and polite ways that characterized his account of the Widow Douglas's house earlier in the novel. Clearly, here was a place where Huck could have been happy: "It was a double house, and the big open place betwixt them was roofed and floored, and sometimes the table was set there in the middle of the day, and it was a cool, comfortable place. Nothing couldn't be better. And warn't the cooking good, and just bushels of it too!" As a surrogate father, Colonel Grangerford is an appealing figure, kind and courteous and honorable. "Everybody loved to have him around, too; he was sunshine most always — I mean he made it seem like good weather." In recounting Huck's happy days with Colonel Grangerford and his family, Twain was once again calling on remembrances of things past. For the Grangerford establishment was to some extent a literary recollection of the big double house on his Uncle John Quarles's farm in Florida, Missouri, "a heavenly place for a boy," where Twain had spent many summers of his youth. The portrait of the Grangerford place thus illustrates the continuing strength of the St. Petersburg image in Twain's mind. In 1879-1880 he still imagined Hannibal as a neat, white-painted, drowsy Heaven, and if the Grangerford household was many, many miles down-river, it was still within the Happy Valley of fabled memory. Huck Finn could no more renounce this Paradise than he could Nigger Jim. At the end of Chapter XVIII, Twain's novel stalled once again.

During the summer of 1880, Professor Blair believes, Twain wrote the next two chapters. In the entire canon of his work, Chapter XIX may very well be the most dazzling exhibition of the versatility of his literary genius. Huck's description of the sunrise, with which the chapter begins, is one of the two or three most perfectly controlled pieces of descriptive prose in American literature:

> Next we slid into the river and had a swim, so as to freshen up and cool off; then we set down on the sandy bottom where the water was about knee-deep, and watched the daylight come. Not a sound anywheres — perfectly still — just like the whole world was asleep, only sometimes the bullfrogs a-cluttering, maybe. The first thing to see, looking away over the water, was a kind of dull line — that was the woods on t'other side; you couldn't make nothing else out; then a pale place in the sky; then more paleness spreading around; then the river softened up away off, and warn't black any more, but gray; you could see little dark spots drifting along ever so far away — trading scows, and such things; and long black streaks —

rafts; sometimes you could hear a sweep screaking; or jum-
bled-up voices, it was so still, and sounds come so far; and by
and by you could see a streak on the water which you know
by the look of the streak that there's a snag there in a swift
current which breaks on it and makes that streak look that
way; and you see the mist curl up off of the water, and the
east reddens up, and the river, and you make out a log cabin
in the edge of the woods, away on the bank on t'other side of
the river, being a wood-yard, likely, and piled by them cheats
so you can throw a dog through it anywheres; then the nice
breeze springs up, and comes fanning you from over there, so
cool and fresh and sweet to smell on account of the woods and
the flowers; but sometimes not that way, because they've left
dead fish laying around, gars and such, and they do get pretty
rank; and next you've got the full day, and everything smiling
in the sun, and the song-birds just going it!

T. S. Eliot has hailed Hemingway for his ability "to tell the
truth about his own feelings at the moment when they exist."
Although the question of literary influence is always a tricky
one, the emotional precision of Huck's account of the sunrise
clearly indicates the author who instructed Hemingway in
the difficult art of not faking his feelings. Hemingway's celebrated tribute to *Huckleberry Finn* as the book from which all
of modern American literature derives is essentially an ac-
knowledgment of how much his own style owes to Huck
Finn's vernacular honesty.

From the sunrise description, the narrative modulates to
another picture almost equally beautiful — a nighttime glimpse
of the boy and the Negro, both naked, lying on their backs on
the drifting raft, gazing up at the stars. In an image of cosmic
loneliness, Huck and Jim's sense of how far they are from
home is quietly suggested: "We had the sky up there, all
speckled with stars, and we used to lay on our backs and look
up at them. . . . We used to watch the stars that fell, too,
and see them streak down. Jim allowed they'd got spoiled
and was hove out of the nest." The words are sad — and
something more. Beneath their poignant lyricism we catch a
barely audible whisper of foreboding: Is it possible that the

two runaways, like a "spoiled" Adam and Eve, have been ex-
pelled for their sins from St. Petersburg's heavenly nest? Can it
be that, like the arc described by the falling stars, their southward journey is also a downward one — a descent from Heaven
toward some unimaginable Hell?

Frightening questions fade with the starlight, however, and
"one morning about daybreak" the King and the Duke, the
two most celebrated con men in American literature, come
prancing on board. For the rest of Chapter XIX and all of
Chapter XX, the two frauds completely dominate the novel.
The central episode of this sequence is the King's masquerade
as a repentant sinner at the Pokeville camp meeting. The
scene is highly reminiscent of Simon Suggs at Sandy Creek,
and was indeed probably inspired by Hooper's story. Certainly
Twain's view of the camp meeting as an institution was very
close to Hooper's, for not only had Twain been raised as a good
Whig, he had also been brought up as a Presbyterian, a faith
which in Missouri in the 1830s and 1840s had suffered severely
from the depredations of the revivalistic denominations. Still,
memory did its magic work even here. The Pokeville camp
meeting, created in 1880 in Elmira, New York, is a far less
disagreeable scene than the Sandy Creek meeting, created in
the middle 1840s in East Alabama. Instead of reproducing the
saturnalia of sex, alcohol and ministerial venality that was
Hooper's story — instead of portraying human beings as so
many grotesque animals, maddened by fear, lust and superstition — Huck shows us a gullible, somewhat ridiculous, but
essentially innocent group of people. If his humor judges anyone adversely, it is the King — who is an outlaw. Unlike Simon Suggs, the King is represented as being outside of, and
morally different from, the society he gulls, and therefore
Huck's disapproval of him is not a comment on the population
of the Happy Valley. In Hooper's story, the Confidence Man
is the symbol of the age; in Chapter XX of *Huckleberry Finn,*
he is a freak.

The effect of the King and the Duke's coming aboard the

raft is to drive Huck and Jim closer together than ever, for now Huck as well as Jim is reduced in effect to being a slave who must "set to majestying" the two frauds. Once he himself is no longer free, Huck is able to see even more clearly than before what Jim is really like: "I had the middle watch, you know, but I was pretty sleepy by that time, so Jim said he would stand the first half of it for me; he was always mighty good that way, Jim was." If, however, Chapters XIX and XX establish new bonds between the boy and the Negro by in fact bonding them together in servitude, they do nothing at all to prepare us for the break that Huck must inevitably make with the people of the Happy Valley, should he decide to become Jim's liberator. Because the moral contrast between Huck and Jim on the one hand and the King and the Duke on the other is not a contrast, as certain critics have suggested, between the society of the raft and the society of the land. The King and the Duke are a part of the raft life, it must be remembered, just as Pap Finn was identified with the cabin in the woods. They represent, as Pap did, the sordidness, the cynicism, and the anarchic cruelty that are inescapable in the world beyond the pale of Eden. If Jim is the black father of the outlaw raft, the King is the white father, whose moral quality is summed up by Huck's likening him to a hog — the dirty animal that had previously symbolized Pap Finn.[8] Far from solving Mark Twain's imaginative problem, the King and the Duke compounded its difficulty. Introduced as a diversion by an author whose novelistic intentions were uncertain, they had simply made the matter of Huck's moral choice more troubling than ever. When Twain in the summer of 1880 once again threw aside the manuscript of *Huckleberry Finn*, he was no closer to figuring out how to proceed than he had been four years before.

[8] The reference to the King as a hog was omitted by Twain from the published version of the novel.

vi

With *Huckleberry Finn* perhaps permanently stalled, Twain turned to other writing tasks. Deciding that his *Atlantic* recollections of "Old Times on the Mississippi" might be worth a book if he would only combine them with some on-the-spot observations, Twain went back to the river valley of his youth in April of 1882. The resulting book, *Life on the Mississippi,* is a partial measure of the shattering disillusionment of the experience. Twain had had a brief glimpse of Hannibal fifteen years before, but as he himself admitted, the image that had lingered in his memory was of the town "I first quitted . . . twenty-nine years ago." Confronted with reality, many of Twain's long-cherished recollections of the Happy Valley vanished in a flash. As he wrote to his wife, "That world which I knew in its blossoming youth is old and bowed and melancholy now; its soft cheeks are leathery and wrinkled, the fire is gone out in its eyes, and the spring from its step." Again and again in *Life on the Mississippi* he exclaimed at how much the Valley had changed, how different everything looked. "The romance of boating is gone now," he complained. "In Hannibal the steamboat man is no longer the god."

Changes, no doubt, there had been. As Henry James would discover upon returning to New York after an absence of twenty years, childhood worlds in America are apt to be erased by the avalanche of eternal progress. Rip Van Winkle's bewildered return to the village he can no longer recognize typifies the experience of the American when he goes in search of his past. Yet one cannot help feeling that the most notable differences Twain observed between "before" and "after" were differences in the eye of the beholder. For in 1882 Mark Twain no longer was regarding the Valley of his youth from the vantage-point of memory. Emotion recollected in Hartford had produced Huck Finn's characterization of the Grangerford household as a "mighty nice family, and a mighty nice house, too"; but now, direct confrontation of the Valley culture evoked the chapter in *Life on the Mississippi* ironically entitled "The House Beautiful." In images of smothering and suffocation, of artificiality and pretense and deadness, the visitor to the Valley painted a strikingly different portrait of the life of the pre-Civil War "quality" than had Chapter XVII of *Huckleberry Finn:*

> Big, square, two-story "frame" house, painted white and porticoed like a Grecian temple — with this difference, that the imposing fluted columns and Corinthian capitals were a pathetic sham. . . . Polished air-tight stove (new and deadly invention), with pipe passing through a board which closes up the discarded good old fireplace. On each end of the wooden mantel, over the fireplace, a large basket of peaches and other fruits, natural size, all done in plaster, rudely, or in wax. . . . Under a glass French clock dome, large bouquet of stiff flowers done in corpsy white wax. . . .

In certain details the "House Beautiful" resembles the Grangerford place, yet the two houses are as different as death is from life. Similarly, Twain's *Life on the Mississippi* description of the Darnell-Watson feud is reminiscent of the account he had already given in *Huckleberry Finn* of the Grangerford-Shepherdson feud, except that the *Life* version concentrates entirely on the senseless ferocity of the bloodletting, omitting all reference to the human dignity of the participants which Huck had emphasized. Nor was the returned native able to respond as fully as he had in memory to the beauties of the river and the shore. One has only to set Huck Finn's account of the sunrise in Chapter XIX side by side with the literary hack job which is the description of a sunrise in *Life on the Mississippi* to see what happened to Mark Twain's imagination when reality replaced remembrance. "You Can't Go Home Again" is a phrase that announces a terrible defeat. It might well serve as the title of the lackluster chapters which compose Twain's record of his return to the river.

The phrase also signalizes a triumph. For oftentimes the

process of becoming disillusioned with the place where one has grown up can result in a more objective understanding of Asheville, or Salinas, or Oxford, or Sauk Center. Mark Twain gained as much as he lost in the spring of 1882.

What he gained above all else was a knowledge of what the modern South was like. Twain already thought he possessed this knowledge before he ever went back to the Valley. He was well aware, for example, that Southern society was once again under Southern direction. Thanks to Southern electoral votes, Hayes, not Tilden, had entered the White House in 1877. Shortly thereafter, Federal Reconstruction of the formerly rebellious states was liquidated. By 1880, the monolith of the "Solid South" had risen clearly into view. Thus on July 26, 1880, Wade Hampton, speaking at Staunton, Virginia, boasted that a united Dixie would deliver 138 electoral votes to the Democratic party the following autumn. The speech aroused such a storm in the press that Southern as well as Northern Democrats feared it would solidify the North for Garfield. Party headquarters therefore denied that Hampton had ever made such a speech. But as the campaign grew hotter, orators all over the South began to whip up the crowds with similar descriptions of the South's single-minded hatred of Yankee intruders and "nigger rule," and of its unanimous devotion to the ideals of Bourbon Democracy. Meanwhile, Northern Republicans were once again waving the "bloody shirt" as hard as they could. When Howells wrote to Twain in praise of Grant's denunciation of the South at Warren, Ohio, in September, he voiced the approval of many supposedly responsible Northern voters of the most patent sort of demagoguery. For the image of a puissant and unrepentant Democracy once again speaking for the South stirred emotions in Northern breasts that were easily exploited by the "patriotic" G.O.P. Twain's enthusiasm for Garfield that year was not so much a question of positive admiration for the Republican candidate as it was of negative fear of an opposition party that symbolized a resurgent Dixie.

Except, however, for a general sense of uneasiness — which subsided markedly after Garfield's victory in November — Mark Twain in 1880 did not have very many ideas about the post-Reconstruction South. He simply had not thought much about it. Then in the spring of 1882 he saw the New South firsthand.

Everywhere he went, he was impressed by "changes uniformly evidencing progress, energy, prosperity." The atmosphere was pervaded with the "wholesome and practical nineteenth-century smell of cotton factories and locomotives." New Orleans, in particular, impressed him as a "driving place commercially," "well outfitted with progressive men." Other aspects of Southern life surprised and disturbed him profoundly. In a passage written for *Life on the Mississippi,* but not included in the published version, Twain deplored the demoralizing effects on the Southern character produced by that very unanimity of public opinion about which Wade Hampton and other Southern politicians had boasted two years before. For a society which boasted of its unity was a society which feared division — whose members necessarily lived in horror of speaking their own minds:

> In one thing the average Northerner seems to be a step in advance of the average Southerner [Twain wrote], in that he bands himself with his timid fellows to support the law (at least in the matter of murder), protect judges, juries, and witnesses, and also to secure all citizens from personal danger and from obloquy or social ostracism on account of opinion, political or religious; whereas the average Southerners do not band themselves together in these high interests, but leave them to look out for themselves unsupported; the results being unpunished murder, against the popular approval, and the decay and destruction of independent thought and action in politics.[9]

Twain was also amazed to find that the Southern myth had not died with the War — that the new men of power who

[9] Copyright 1959 by the Mark Twain Company.

were industrializing the region were as fond of the chivalric panoply of pseudo-feudalism as the would-be aristocrats of antebellum days had been. Contemplating, in Richmond, Virginia, a monument to the heroic knights of the Confederacy, Henry James observed that "the bitter mixture of recantation and heresy could never have been swallowed so readily had it not been dissolved in the syrup of romanticism." In Baton Rouge, Louisiana, Mark Twain encountered similar evidence of Southern self-deception. Although the Louisiana State Capitol, "a whitewashed castle, with turrets and things — materials all genuine within and without, pretending to be what they are not," was perhaps harmless in itself, in its capacity "as a symbol and breeder and sustainer of maudlin Middle-Age romanticism" the building — Twain felt — was a disaster. Seizing on Sir Walter Scott as a convenient whipping boy, Twain denounced Scott for tempting the South to fall in love with "the duel, the inflated speech, and the jejune romanticism of an absurd past that is dead, and out of charity ought to be buried." "It was Sir Walter," he continued, "that made every gentleman in the South a major or a colonel, or a general or a judge, before the war; and it was he, also, that made these gentlemen value bogus decorations. For it was he that created rank and caste down there, and also reverence for rank and caste, and pride and pleasure in them." Scott was in fact, Twain said, "in great measure responsible" for the Civil War. In adding that Scott's ideas "flourish pretty forcefully still" he implied that the basis for a dire conflict between North and South still existed.

Twain also learned from other sources than his own observation. As he acknowledged in *Life on the Mississippi*, he had been much instructed in Southern matters by "the masterly delineator of its interior life and history," George Washington Cable. The statement lends force to Guy A. Cardwell's suggestion that Cable may very well have decisively influenced Twain's thinking about Southern society in the period immediately prior to his completion of *Huckleberry Finn*.

Although Twain was an early admirer of Cable's work —
especially of *Madame Delphine* and *The Grandissimes* — and
had had a brief conversation with him when Cable visited
Hartford in 1881, the two men did not become good friends
until the year of Twain's return to the river. When Twain
reached New Orleans, he called on Cable at his home and
they talked at length. The following fall they renewed their
friendship when Cable again came to Nook Farm. Thus in the
course of the most crucial year of his life, Twain came into
direct contact, under conditions of friendly intimacy, with a
truly powerful mind. For as Edmund Wilson has justly said,
George Washington Cable was one of "the most intellectual
Americans of his time," a man of "detached and realistic"
intelligence. Certainly his knowledge of the South was unsurpassed by any contemporary student of the subject. A native
Louisianan, Cable was an authority on Creole folklore and
language. He was also an expert on New Orleans; when the
United States Government commissioned Colonel George
Waring to gather the "social statistics of cities," Waring chose
Cable to do the New Orleans report. In 1880, the Superintendent of the Census asked Cable to make a special study of
the dialect and customs of the "Cajuns." Cable was also a
student of the political history of his native state, as well as a
bold and original sociologist. His various essays on the Negro,
eventually brought together in *The Silent South* and *The
Negro Question*, are remarkably modern. They do not have
the documentation of Gunnar Myrdal's work; nor were the
analytical concepts of twentieth-century sociology and psychology available to him; even so, his assessments of the
effect of race prejudice on Southern society, white and black,
anticipate the insights of *An American Dilemma*.

A loyal Southerner, Cable had fought for the Confederacy
during the Civil War and been wounded twice. But in the
early 1870s, as a result of much reading and thinking, he
ceased to believe in the justice of the Southern cause. Slavery
had been morally indefensible, he now felt, and the rebellion

therefore hideously wrong. He also decided that the Negro in the postwar South was the daily victim of a persecution that made a mockery of his technical freedom. Soon the literary society to which Cable belonged became aware of these ideas; when he wrote a letter to the newspapers protesting against color segregation in the horsecars and schools, all New Orleans learned of his heretical views. Cable's frankness took courage in postwar New Orleans, especially in the '70s, when the city was becoming increasingly reactionary. In 1874, the Crescent White League, a local white-supremacy organization, demonstrated that it was powerful enough to defeat the city police in pitched battle. Three years later, with Hayes in the White House, the city's carpetbag government was overthrown and a "loyal" administration installed. Independent ideas, in such an atmosphere, were simply not tolerated. Hired by the New Orleans *Picayune* as a columnist and reporter, Cable attempted to make the paper a sounding board for his views on the Negro question. Not only was he unsuccessful, but he soon thereafter lost his job. After a first horrified hearing, Cable discovered, his friends in the literary society refused to discuss his opinions with him. "With no others," he later recalled, "did I venture in those fierce days to argue, but kept a silence which I felt almost constantly ashamed of." When Cable turned to writing fiction, then, it was with the idea of expressing in imaginative and symbolic terms what he was not permitted to say directly.

Through Edward King, a *Scribner's* author who came to New Orleans in the mid-'70s on a writing assignment, Cable was brought to the attention of the *Scribner's* editors. Subsequently, the magazine published several of his stories of Creole life, and in 1879 began serializing Cable's novel, *The Grandissimes.* To the *Scribner's* people, Cable's fiction was an innocuous presentation of the quaint Louisiana past. Cable, however, knew otherwise. As he confided to his diary, "The Grandissimes contained as plain a protest against the times in which it was written as against the earlier times in which its scenes were set." There were also contemporary political implications in his short fiction. If these implications went unrecognized by New York editors, they were not lost on Cable's Southern readers. Shortly after the publication of *The Grandissimes* (1880), Cable was subjected to a scurrilous personal attack as a "nigger-lover" in an anonymously-written book. The foremost Louisiana historian of his day, Charles Gayarré, lent his prestige to the defamation of Cable's reputation in a lecture at Tulane. In 1882, Joseph Pennell visited New Orleans and found Cable to be the most hated man in the city. When Richard Watson Gilder came to the city in 1885, he asked the young Southern writer, Grace King, to explain Louisiana's hostility to such a distinguished son. "I hastened to enlighten him," she wrote later, "to the effect that Cable proclaimed his preference for colored people over white and assumed the inevitable superiority of the quadroons over the Creoles." The people of New Orleans, according to Gilder's enlightener, felt that Cable had "stabbed the city in the back . . . in a dastardly way to please the Northern press."

Contributing to the South's bitterness against him was Cable's increasing ability, born of his new prestige as a *Scribner's* author, to find audiences who would listen — or who could be forced to listen — to direct and open statements of his views. Invited by his Nook Farm friends to attend a birthday celebration for Mrs. Stowe, Cable wrote them his regrets, and then added that "I can only send you, Blessings on the day when Harriet Beecher Stowe was born." The contents of the message were soon the scandal of New Orleans. He publicly stated that in the Civil War the Northern cause had been the just one. In a commencement address at a Southern university, in a brilliant article for the *Century* called "The Freedman's Case in Equity," in another article which exposed the vicious convict lease system in the Southern states, Cable reminded the white South again and again of its moral guilt. The South repaid him for his reminders first in slander and then in ostracism. Unable to endure such treatment from the city he loved, Cable moved to the North in the mid-'8os, settling finally in Northampton, Massachusetts. He spent the rest of his long life there, a voluntary exile, but an exile, none the less.

Twain became Cable's good friend in the period between the first onslaught of slander and the culminating barrage of hate that drove him from the South forever. They talked together extensively during the time when, having published his best work of fiction, *The Grandissimes*, Cable was perfecting his major ideas on the sociology of race prejudice. Both in what he was thinking about and in what was happening to him, then, Cable was obviously a fascinating person for anyone with an interest in the South to know. No record exists as to what Cable and Twain talked about in 1882; all we know is that Twain was enthralled by their conversations. Writing to Howells, he enthusiastically reported that Cable "is a marvelous talker on a deep subject." Though Twain did not specify the subject, it is not hard to guess what it was. There can be no doubt that the topic which interested Mark Twain above all others in the year of his return to the river was Cable's specialty. That they talked long hours about life in the South, past and present, and that these talks taught Twain many things, is undeniable. In another of the passages in *Life on the Mississippi* that was cut from the published version, the author voiced his appreciation of Mrs. Trollope's courage in saying frankly what she thought about the culture of the Mississippi Valley, *circa* 1830. The words could well stand for Twain's immense admiration for Cable's willingness to speak out in criticism of the South in the face of personal threats and vile abuse:

> She found a "civilization" here which you, reader, could not have endured; and which you would not have regarded as a civilization at all. Mrs. Trollope spoke of this civilization in plain terms — plain and unsugared, but honest and without malice, and without hate. Her voice rises to indignation, sometimes, but the object justifies the attitude — being slavery,

rowdyism, "chivalrous" assassinations, sham Godliness, and several other devilishnesses which would be as hateful to you, now, as they were to her then.

It was for this sort of "photography," Twain added — and here almost certainly he had Cable's situation in mind — that "poor, candid Mrs. Trollope was so handsomely cursed and reviled by this nation. Yet she was merely telling the truth, and this indignant nation knew it." [10]

Perhaps Twain was also thinking of himself, in making that tribute. For did not his attacks, in *Life on the Mississippi,* on the modern South's continuing infatuation with the romantic anti-progressivism of Sir Walter Scott raise the possibility that he, too, would be cursed and reviled for telling the truth? Further contributing to his sense of identification with ostracized social critics was the fact that Twain was about to return to the half-finished manuscript of *Huckleberry Finn.* For Twain was ready at last to resolve Huck's moral conflict, and he intended to prepare the way for his hero's decision by passing a new and stringent judgment on the Valley society. No longer would Huck be caught between the appeals of the raft and respectability, because the Happy Valley of pleasant memory had ceased to exist in Twain's mind. With the first breath of the air of reality, hermetic St. Petersburg had crumbled to dust. In its stead, Twain would raise up the image of the society he came to know in the spring of 1882.

vii

Chapter XXI of the novel, Professor Blair suspects, was written in the spring of 1883 — exactly a year after Twain's visit to the river. It was the first sign that the long drought in his "tank" was over. Then the following summer, at Elmira, inspiration came like a flood. Soon Twain was writing to

[10] Copyright 1959 by the Mark Twain Company.

Howells that "I haven't piled up MS so in years as I have done since we came here to the farm three weeks and a half ago. Why, it's like old times, to step right into the study, damp from the breakfast table, and sail right in and sail right on, the whole day long, without thought of running short of stuff or words. I wrote 4000 words today and I touch 3000 and upwards pretty often, and don't fall below 2600 any working day." To Orion and his family Twain averred that "I am piling up manuscript in a really astonishing way. I believe I shall complete, in two months, a book which I have been fooling over for 7 years. This summer it is no more trouble to me to write than it is to lie." Shortly thereafter, the book was done.

Twain's altered view of the Valley society is immediately established in two sets of interrelated and successive chapters, XXI–XXII and XXIII–XXIV, the first four chapters written subsequent to the 1882 trip.

In Chapter XXII, Huck goes to a circus, sees a drunken man weaving around the ring on horseback, and is terribly distressed — although the crowd roars with delight. But it is not Huck's charming naïveté in not recognizing that the drunkard is a clown that Twain condemns, it is the callousness of the crowd. For this circus scene depends upon the preceding Chapter XXI, which really does involve a drunk, the drunken Boggs, who weaves down the street on horseback, shouting insults at Colonel Sherburn. When Sherburn mortally wounds Boggs, a crowd gathers excitedly around the drunkard to watch him die. Everyone is tremendously pleased — except Huck, and the dying man's daughter. By this juxtaposition of episodes, each of which contrasts the boy's sympathetic concern with the gleeful howling of the crowd, Twain lays bare the moral callousness of a society that views life romantically — that regards suffering as a circus.

The Arkansas town in which these two chapters take place is another version of Hannibal, but the place has nothing in common with the lovely, white-painted town that had sustained Twain's imagination for twenty-nine years. In contrast to the heavenly St. Petersburg he had summoned up in *Tom Sawyer*, Bricksville, Arkansas, is a squalid hole:

> The houses had little gardens around them, but they didn't seem to raise hardly anything in them but jimpson-weeds, and sun-flowers, and ash piles, and old curled-up boots and shoes, and pieces of bottles, and rags, and played-out tinware. . . . There was generly hogs in the garden, and people driving them out. . . . All the streets and lanes was just mud; they warn't nothing else *but* mud — mud as black as tar and nigh about a foot deep in some places, and two or three inches deep in *all* places. The hogs loafed and grunted around everywhere.

Images of whiteness have been replaced by images of blackness and filth; gardens no longer bloom in this fallen Eden; and everywhere there are hogs, heretofore associated not with organized society but with violent and unscrupulous outlaws. Twain once observed that the Negroes he knew as a boy feared being sold "down the river" as the equivalent of being sent to Hell, and Nigger Jim has run away precisely because of this fear. In Bricksville, the Negro's nightmare becomes the novel's reality. The 1883 version of Hannibal is a veritable Hell, populated by a company of the damned. Huck and Jim's voyage southward from St. Petersburg has in fact become — like the course of the stars that were hove out of the nest — a downward fall.

As if he were worried that the contrast between the two drunks was too subtle a condemnation, Twain chose — for the first and only time in the novel — to violate Huck's point of view in Chapter XXII and speak to the reader through another mask, in order that he might ram home his moral judgment of the society in explicit and unmistakable terms. The mask he chose to assume for this brief moment was a familiar one in Southwestern humor: the mask of a Southern aristocrat. Not, to be sure, the cool and collected Gentleman of the Whig myth, for Colonel Sherburn is self-admittedly a killer. Nor is Sherburn concerned to instruct the mob in the virtues of the temperate life. His furiously contemptuous opinion of the townspeople carries with it no hope that they will ever improve:

> Do I know you? I know you clear through. I was born and raised in the South, and I've lived in the North; so I know the average all around. The average man's a coward. In the North he lets anybody walk over him that wants to. . . . In the South one man, all by himself, has robbed a stage full of men in the daytime, and robbed the lot. . . . Why don't your juries hang murderers? Because they're afraid the man's friends will shoot them in the back in the dark — and it's just what they *would* do. So they always acquit; and then a *man* goes in the night with a hundred masked cowards at his back, and lynches the rascal. Your mistake is, that you didn't bring a man with you; that's one mistake, and the other is that you didn't come in the dark and fetch your masks.

The speech, as Professor Blair was the first to point out, is very like the passage that Twain cut from *Life on the Mississippi* about the withering-away of independent thought and action in Southern life. Sherburn's condemnation has been broadened out somewhat to make a more inclusive judgment of Americans everywhere, but it centers none the less on the degradation of human character in the monolithic South.

The point of ironic connection between Chapters XXIII and XXIV occurs in their conclusions. The last paragraph of Chapter XXIII is perhaps the most poignant moment in the entire novel, for it is here that Jim relates to Huck how his daughter, after recovering from scarlet fever, became a mysteriously disobedient child. Even when Jim had slapped her and sent her sprawling, she refused to obey his orders, but just as he was going for her again, he realized what was wrong: "De Lord God Amighty fogive po' ole Jim, kaze he never gwyne to fogive hisself as long's he live! Oh, she was plumb deef en dumb, Huck, plumb deef en dumb — en I'd ben a-treat'n her so!" On the last page of Chapter XXIV, the King and the Duke arrive at the little Tennessee town where they expect to rob the Wilks girls of their inheritance by playing the parts, respectively, of a parson and a deaf mute. When viewed beside Jim's sorrow and compassion for his deaf-and-dumb daughter, the spectacle of the two frauds talking on their hands is sickening — "It was enough," says Huck, "to make a body ashamed of the human race."

The striking difference between Huck's account of the confidence game that the King and the Duke work on the Tennessee town and the King's swindle of the Pokeville camp meeting is that the gullible townspeople now seem as subhuman as the crooks who defraud them. As Henry Nash Smith has pointed out, when the townspeople move rapidly up the street to have a look at the newly-arrived "parson" and "deaf mute," Huck likens them to soldiers marching along, thereby calling attention to their regimented minds and lives. A moment later, he refers to them as a "gang" which is "trotting along," as if they reminded him of a herd of squealing pigs. The people of what was once the Happy Valley are now not only associated with, but have actually become, the dirty animals which are the novel's leading symbol of degradation and sordidness. Huck Finn — and Mark Twain — have come a long way from St. Petersburg.

Sickened by society, Huck finds refuge in the fatherly bosom of Nigger Jim, even as Little Eva had turned to Uncle Tom. To what extent Twain had *Uncle Tom's Cabin* in mind when he conceived of the relationship between Huck and Jim can never be known, for with neighborly good manners he did not make public comments about Mrs. Stowe's famous book. We know that George Washington Cable burst into tears when he read the novel as a child; we know that the character of Uncle Tom had such a profound effect on Joel Chandler Harris that he seriously considered the novel to be a defense of slavery — on the grounds that any system which could produce such a holy man must necessarily be good; we know, indeed, the reaction of a vast number of individual Americans to *Uncle Tom's Cabin;* but not Mark Twain's. Yet Uncle Tom and little

Eva, talking rapturously about reunion in Heaven, clearly have
something to do with Huck's decision to go to Hell rather than
send Jim back to slavery: in both instances, the black man and
the white child are morally united against the organized world.
Little Eva and Uncle Tom are brought together by their unquestioning acceptance of the Will of God; Huck and Jim are
also united by their common beliefs — in the comparative
harmlessness of stealing an occasional chicken or watermelon;
in the delights of going naked in the starlight, and of smoking
a pipe after breakfast; in the undoubted existence of ghosts,
and the significance of "signs." In both novels, the child-Negro
relationship exists on a level of emotional ecstasy, the extraordinary intensity of which derived from an unappeased
longing of the author's.

For just as the religious ecstasy of Uncle Tom and Little
Eva illuminates the spiritual biography of the doubt-ridden
daughter of Lyman Beecher, so the raft life of Huck and Jim
tells us much about the emotional hunger of John Marshall
Clemens's son. Seeking for release from the emotional austerity
of the Clemens household, the young Mark Twain had turned
almost inevitably to the warm, black underworld of the slaves.
Many, many years later, Twain could still recall

> the look of Uncle Dan'l's kitchen as it was on the privi-
> leged nights, when I was a child, and I can see the white and
> black children grouped on the hearth, with the firelight play-
> ing on their faces and the shadows flickering upon the walls,
> clear back toward the cavernous gloom of the rear, and I can
> hear Uncle Dan'l telling the immortal tales which Uncle
> Remus Harris was to gather into his book and charm the world
> with, by and by; and I can feel again the creepy joy which
> quivered through me when the time for the ghost story was
> reached — and the sense of regret, too, which came over me,
> for it was always the last story of the evening and there was
> nothing between it and the unwelcome bed.

Uncle Dan'l, Twain said, was the prototype of Nigger Jim,
but as the above passage implies, Twain's memory of him was

mixed up in his mind with his response to yet another literary image of the Negro, Uncle Remus. With characteristic modesty, Joel Chandler Harris felt that the only talent he had as a writer lay in his ability to transcribe accurately the Negro tales he had been listening to — on street corners, at railroad stations, along country roads — ever since the days when, as an impoverished and illegitimate child, he had found solace in the companionship of slaves. But Mark Twain assured Harris that "in reality the stories are only alligator pears — one eats them merely for the sake of the dressing." To Twain, the most meaningful part of the Uncle Remus stories was the part that Harris had contributed — the "frame," which dramatized the relationship between Uncle Remus and the little boy who comes to listen to his stories. The comment says as much about Twain as it does about Harris. Seeking for a quality of experience they could not find in their white lives, both men sent their boy-heroes in search of the companionship and understanding of the black man. He was a mythical figure, this Negro of Twain's and Harris's, a figure out of a dream, passionate, loyal, immensely dignified — a Black Christ, in sum, but with a very human sense of humor that Mrs. Stowe's great prototype notably lacked. In Uncle Remus's cabin, or spinning down the big river at night with Nigger Jim, there were beauty, and mystery, and laughter.

"It needs no scientific investigation," Harris wrote in the preface of his first book, "to show why [the Negro] selects as his hero the weakest and most harmless of all animals, and brings him out victorious in contest with the bear, the wolf, and the fox." Nor is any scientific investigation necessary to understand why Twain's and Harris's boys were drawn so irresistibly toward the black storyteller. In a world of wolves and foxes — and hogs — he was a bulwark and a refuge. The cave in *Tom Sawyer*, that vast, subterranean realm of darkness, was a place of ambivalent meaning: a place of magical excitement, full of mysterious chambers with exotic names, a dream-world where one could find the love of a young girl and buried treasure; yet death was down there, too, in the lurking presence of an "underground man" whose skin was not white; all in all, it was safer for Tom Sawyer to return to the white-painted Heaven above. But by the summer of 1883, the "cavernous gloom" of Uncle Dan'l's cabin had come to figure in Mark Twain's mind as a lonely boy's only haven. When the moment comes for Huck to choose whether to live by the precepts of his society-trained conscience or in spite of them, a Valley of Bricksvilles can offer no comparable image of love and warmth to his vision of the black man: "I see Jim there before me all the time: in the day and in the night-time, sometimes moonlight, sometimes storm, and we a-floating along, talking and singing and laughing." Unlike Tom Sawyer, Huck does not flee the "underground man"; he joins him.

viii

When Moses led the Israelites to freedom he also moved toward his prophesied appointment with death; *Huckleberry Finn* likewise moves simultaneously toward triumph and tragedy. For the liberation of Jim inexorably enforces the tragic separation of the boy and the Negro. Throughout the long, final sequence at the Phelps farm,[11] the information is withheld from the reader that a repentant Miss Watson has freed Jim on her deathbed. Yet it is perfectly clear from the mo-

---

[11] The Phelps farm is another version of John A. Quarles's farm at Florida, Missouri, but it is a "one-horse" affair by comparison with the Grangerford establishment. Nothing more clearly illustrates the effect of the 1882 trip on the images of Mark Twain's memory than the difference in size and attractiveness between the "before" and "after" portraits of the Quarles farm. As Twain observed to Howells in 1887, "When a man goes back to look at the house of his childhood it has always *shrunk*; there is no instance of such a house being as big as the picture that memory and imagination call for. Shrunk how? Why, to its correct dimensions: the house hasn't altered; this is the first time it has been in focus." Although Twain did not visit the Quarleses in 1882, the general effect of the trip was to deflate all his childhood memories.

ment that Tom Sawyer arrives that something is terribly wrong. Although Huck works night and day to liberate Jim from the locked-up cabin, the two of them are never really "in touch" again. They have become strangers to one another. Evidently, Mark Twain was only capable of imagining Huck and Jim's relationship as existing in the condition of slavery and under the aspect of flight — as an "underground" affair — although he tried very hard to imagine it otherwise. Hating to bring the story of the two runaways to a close, striving vainly to recreate the intense emotion that had lifted the middle section of the novel into the most memorable idyll in American literature, Twain prolonged and prolonged the final sequence into by far the longest — and the least successful — in the book.

Even the humor is not up to par. In certain moments, as Huck (masquerading as Tom Sawyer) and Tom (masquerading as his half-brother Sid) go cavorting through Aunt Sally's house, it is possible to believe that we are back once again in the high-spirited, comic world of *The Adventures of Tom Sawyer*. But Aunt Sally is Aunt Polly with a difference — the difference created by Twain's 1882 trip:

> "Good gracious! anybody hurt?"
> "No'm. Killed a nigger."
> "Well, it's lucky; because people sometimes do get hurt."

Huck and Tom are no longer playing in Heaven; a shadow has fallen across their boyish good fun, stilling the reader's laughter.

If the Phelps farm sequence fails as humor, perhaps it succeeds as anguish. For Huck is pathetically reluctant to see his beautiful dream of the raft and the river come to an end. In "Chapter the Last" he responds excitedly to Tom Sawyer's gorgeous schemes for running Jim "down the river on the raft, . . . plumb to the mouth," and for having "howling adventures amongst the Injuns over in the Territory, for a couple of weeks or two." Having turned his back on society by refusing to turn his back on Jim, Huck seeks to avoid the terrors of lonesomeness by sticking close to the colored man. Preparing to light out for the Territory at the end of the novel, he seems almost jaunty at the prospect of a reunion there with Jim and Tom Sawyer. We may well wonder, however, if his jauntiness is not simply boyish bravado — or a mask for the author's bewildered sense of loss, growing out of his awareness of the final and terrible truth about his book: which is that *Huckleberry Finn* proposes, in W. H. Auden's words, the incompatibility of love and freedom.

In *Tom Sawyer Abroad*, Twain would try to write *Huckleberry Finn* all over again, with Jim and Huck aloft with Tom Sawyer in a balloon, instead of floating downstream on a raft. And he just couldn't do it. Throughout the book's tiresome length, Huck and the colored freedman are never really together in any meaningful sense. Huck is wrapped up in Tom Sawyer's schemes, while the sorrowing, compassionate figure of the slave in *Huckleberry Finn* is barely recognizable in the minstrel-show darky of the later book. In one of the numerous sequels to *Huckleberry Finn* that Twain obsessively sketched out in his later years, Jim has somehow been caught again, and Huck fantastically plans to free him by changing places with him and blacking his face, as if by making Huck a Negro Twain hoped to bridge the gulf that now separated "son" from "father." But this desperate masquerade also proved to be imaginatively unworkable, and Huck and Jim remained forever separated. It is scarcely necessary to know that in still another contemplated sequel Twain envisioned Huck as a broken, helplessly insane old man in order to sense that at the conclusion of *Huckleberry Finn* Huck's voyage has become, for all his superficial jauntiness, as doomed to defeat as Captain Ahab's, and that in lighting out for the Territory without Jim beside him he flees with "all havens astern."

CHAPTER X

The Volcano — Part III

And now the stranger stepped back one pace, took off his soldier-cap, tossed it into the wing, and began to speak with deliberation, nobody listening, everybody laughing and whispering. The speaker talked on unembarrassed, and presently delivered a shot which went home, and silence and attention resulted. He followed it quick and fast with other telling things; warmed to his work and began to pour his words out, instead of dripping them; grew hotter and hotter, and fell to discharging lightnings and thunder — and now the house began to break into applause, to which the speaker gave no heed, but went hammering straight on; unwound his black bandage and cast it away, still thundering; presently discarded the bob-tailed coat and flung it aside, firing up higher and higher all the time; finally flung the vest after the coat; and then for an untimed period stood there, like another Vesuvius, spouting smoke and flame, lava and ashes, raining pumice-stone and cinders, shaking the moral earth with crash after crash, explosion upon explosion, while the mad multitude stood upon their feet in a solid body answering back with a ceaseless hurricane of cheers, through a thrashing snowstorm of waving handkerchiefs.

— *Life on the Mississippi*

THE HERO who emerges in Twain's major fictions of the late '8os and early '9os is a lonesome stranger, wandering in search of a lost Paradise. Like Twain's earlier heroes, he is an "innocent," in that the ways of society are not his ways; but instead of being alienated from the group by his boyish inexperience, he is an adult who is set apart by his extraordinary knowledge. There is a familiar generosity and compassion in his spirit —

and a new harshness as well; somewhere, somehow, iron has entered his soul. If he would be a liberator, he is also a destroyer, ready to tell the facts that will ruin a man's life, or even to kill him, if need be. Although at times he resembles gentle Huck, he also calls to mind Colonel Sherburn, the desperado Slade, and the instigator of "The Recent Carnival of Crime in Connecticut."

His appearances are by no means entirely confined to fiction. Wherever one looks in Twain's later essays and correspondence, one soon comes across this man, usually standing apart from the crowd in an attitude of defiance which scarcely conceals his longing to be its leader. His presence can be felt in a letter to Howells, written in 1887: "How stunning are the changes which age makes in a man while he sleeps. When I finished Carlyle's French Revolution in 1871, I was a Girondin; . . . and I lay the book down once more, and recognize that I am a Sansculotte! — And not a pale, characterless Sansculotte, but a Marat." "The United States of Lyncherdom," a late essay, celebrates three men, and they are all the same defiant, Marat-like fellow: Savonarola, who could "quell and scatter a mob of lynchers with a mere glance of his eye"; a "brave gentleman" remembered by Twain from Hannibal days, who derided and insulted a mob and drove it away; and a "noted desperado" he had once seen in Nevada, who made "two hundred men sit still, with the house burning under them, until he gave them permission to retire." That Twain's descriptions of this hero were projections of the crowd-defying genius whom he himself wished to be is suggested by his rueful admission in "Purchasing Civic Virtue" that he lacked the "necessary moral courage" to stand up before an audience and denounce it. The metaphorical description of the "stranger" in *Life on the Mississippi,* who brings the crowd to its feet with the volcanic fury of his invective, reveals even more about the later Twain's ambitions. For in the last quarter century of his life, Mark Twain habitually talked about himself as a volcano.

The volcano metaphor was meaningful to Twain first of all

because it recalled a vivid experience of his young manhood. In Hawaii, in the 1860s, he had made a special, two-day journey to see the volcano of Kilauea. "I have seen Vesuvius since," the narrator of *Roughing It* declares, "but it was a mere toy, a child's volcano, a soup-kettle, compared to this. . . . Under us, and stretching away before us, was a heaving sea of molten fire of seemingly limitless extent. The glare from it was so blinding that it was some time before we could bear to look upon it steadily. It was like gazing at the sun at noonday. . . ." In the years after *Huckleberry Finn,* when writing became for him a means of releasing a seething inner pressure, Twain had cause to remember Kilauea. Preparing a mock-serious introduction to a collection of scorching letters he had written but never mailed, Twain suggested the following epistolary formula for the angry man: "He is not to *mail* this letter, he understands that, and so he can turn on the whole volume of his wrath; there is no harm. He is only writing to get the bile out. So to speak, he is a volcano: imagining himself erupting does no good; he must open up his crater and pour out in reality his intolerable charge of lava if he would get relief." [1] Thus did Kilauea become the later Twain's symbol of himself as a writer. So frequently did he refer to himself in volcanic terms in the years after *Huckleberry Finn* that when Bernard DeVoto put together a posthumous collection of Twain's animadversions he felt that the most appropriate title was *Mark Twain in Eruption.* Writing with "a pen warmed up in hell," the later Twain vented his spleen against a nation which gave him less and less to believe in. If his critiques of American society are both unsystematic and in places woefully undeveloped, they are full of brilliant flashes; and his attacks on Yankee imperialism and social conformism still rank among the most effective satiric commentaries ever written on the moral quality of life in the United States.

The most enduring achievement of the pen warmed up in

[1] Copyright 1959 by the Mark Twain Company.

hell, however, was the creation of a new fictional persona to replace the lonely boy who had gone off to the Territory. Like his creator, this new hero is also a volcano, on fire with a sense of the surging possibilities of life, and yet possessed of a terrible power — and willingness — to wipe out anyone who stands in his way. In the Southwestern tradition, the volcano was the terrible image of a rebellious Negro and an exploding Union: for Mark Twain, the volcano is both a symbol of chaos and of the possibility of a better world.

ii

An early memorandum on *A Connecticut Yankee in King Arthur's Court* reads as follows: "He mourns his lost land — has come to England & revisited it, but it is all changed & become old, so old! — & it was so fresh & new, so virgin before. . . . Has lost all interest in life — is found dead next morning — suicide." [2] Twain's terrible sense of loss that resulted from his 1882 trip to the river is easily recognizable in these fatalistic lines, thus prompting the question: Does the Yankee's journey to Arthurian England symbolize the doomed effort of a Twain hero to get back to the Happy Valley? If it does, then there is something radically wrong with the popular theory that *A Connecticut Yankee* is a happy book which triumphantly celebrates American democracy as a Heaven-on-earth.

According to this theory, the novel expresses Twain's growing sympathy with the political and economic aspirations of the masses; his faith in a machine civilization and his pride in America's industrial accomplishment; his hatred for the ignorance and superstition of the Middle Ages and the Catholic Church; and his patriotic desire to twist the British lion's tail, a desire lately inflamed by Matthew Arnold's criticism of Gen-

[2] Copyright 1959 by the Mark Twain Company.

eral Grant's memoirs and of certain vulgar aspects of American life. Even a sensible critic like Kenneth R. Andrews, ordinarily attuned to the ambivalences of Mark Twain's mind, says of *A Connecticut Yankee* that the novel asserts Twain's approval of the society of his time "unmistakably and enthusiastically." Individual sentences in the novel seem to lend this interpretation weight, but they do so only if their context, both within the book and within the over-all context of Twain's writings, is ignored. Like his Yankee hero, Twain was a passionately loyal American, but by the late '80s his revolt against the Republican party had blossomed into a wholesale contempt for America's business civilization. The nation's institutions, he said, had fallen into rags which were totally unable "to protect the body from winter, disease, and death." For all the quotations about the glories of industrial democracy, et cetera, that can be gleaned from the book, Twain's early memorandum on the despairing suicide of the novel's hero testifies to the somberness of the imagination which created *A Connecticut Yankee*.

In many ways, the novel is the most "Southwestern" book Twain ever wrote, and the first evidence of this is that it begins with a frame. Starting with an encounter between "Mark Twain" and "a curious stranger" in Warwick Castle, the novel leads us by degrees deep into a dream. As the story proper begins, we feel that sense of being in a strange and topsy-turvy world where things are familiar, and yet not, which is one of the most distinctive qualities of the dream-state. Thinking that he recognizes contemporary Bridgeport, the dreaming narrator is told that the town is King Arthur's Camelot. On closer inspection, however, the place turns out to look very much like Bricksville, Arkansas, in the days when Huck Finn was a boy: "The streets were mere crooked alleys, unpaved; troops of dogs and nude children played in the sun . . . ; hogs roamed and rooted contentedly about, and one of them lay in a reeking wallow in the middle of the main thoroughfare." The crazy impression that the stranger's journey into the medieval past has also transported him simultaneously to the pre-Civil War Southwest is reinforced in a multitude of ways — by the Crockett-like tall tales which the knights of the Round Table are forever spinning; by the "Southern" emphasis of Arthur's courtiers on personal honor and the immaculate virtue of fair ladies; and by the fact that a large segment of the population is held in involuntary servitude. The very characteristics of the Valley society which in Twain's view Mrs. Trollope had every right to denounce — "slavery, rowdyism, 'chivalrous' assassinations, sham Godliness"— precisely define the Arthurian world into which the stranger from Connecticut wanders.

He is a strange man, this stranger. Although a Yankee mechanic from Hartford, Hank Morgan speaks with disconcerting familiarity of Arkansas journalism, steamboating, and sunsets on the Mississippi, while his narrative style makes him sound like a grown-up Huck Finn. Except that Hank is Huck with a vengeance. The gentle boy who was so ashamed of the human race that he seceded from society has grown into an aggressive adult who wishes not to escape from a fallen Eden, but rather to uplift it, who dreams — inside his own dream — of turning Bricksville-like Camelot into a St. Petersburg with modern conveniences. And yet despite his Utopianism, he has a relentless and unforgiving contempt for the human race. In Hank's curious view, the people whom he proposes to help are animals who aren't worth the trouble: "Finally it occurred to me that these animals didn't reason," he says. "Why, they were nothing but rabbits," he says. "The people had inherited the idea that all men without title . . . were creatures of no more consideration than so many animals, bugs, insects, whereas I had inherited the notion that human daws who can consent to masquerade in the peacock-shams of inherited dignities and unearned titles, are of no good but to be laughed at." From that last quotation it is possible, of course, to extract an endorsement of democracy, and critics have done so, but the imagery in which the endorsement is cast reflects a view of humanity as degraded beyond the power of any political system to redeem it. Hank Morgan, unlike the narrators of the Southwestern tradition, makes no moral distinctions between the Gentleman and the Clown, but in democratically consigning everyone, regardless of social rank, to the category of human daws the Yankee can hardly be described as the triumphant voice of American egalitarianism.

Anesthetized by his contempt, Hank Morgan is able to laugh uproariously at the spectacle of human suffering. In *A Connecticut Yankee,* the detached and callous joking that was one of the distinguishing marks of the Southwestern tradition abruptly re-emerges. To be sure, much of the humor in the novel follows the usual Twain formula of drawing attention to the minor discomforts of the innocent abroad — Hank Morgan trying to scratch an itch while wearing a suit of armor, for example. But some of the jokes are shockingly cruel. "There are times," the Yankee says, "when one would like to hang the whole human race and finish the farce," a vengeful wisecrack indeed, and one which serves as the prelude to a number of exceedingly sadistic pranks. By profession a maker of guns, revolvers, and cannon — which he significantly calls "labor-saving machinery"— Hank Morgan is a Sut Lovingood with all the latest weapons at his disposal, a backwoods prankster with technological know-how.

Nevertheless, this strange man from Hartford has entered history in order to redeem it. He desires to give the people a "new deal" (a phrase which Franklin Roosevelt did *not* get from *A Connecticut Yankee*), and the drama of the novel consists in his attempt to create a new and better society, a Heavenly City of machines, in backward Camelot. If the Happy Valley no longer existed in the past, perhaps it could be re-created in the future, bigger and better than ever.

Discovering that King Arthur is an "extinct volcano," the Yankee mechanic comes to power by displaying an assortment of nineteenth-century tricks, most of them volcanic in nature.

"I made about three passes in the air, and then there was an awful crash and that old tower leaped into the sky in chunks, along with a vast volcanic fountain of fire that turned night to noonday. . . . It rained mortar and masonry the rest of the week." With the resources of a kingdom now under his command, he secretly creates the modern world, and the way in which he describes his creation is of the utmost significance: "It was fenced away from the public view, but there it was, a gigantic and unassailable fact — and to be heard from yet, if I lived and had luck. There it was, as sure a fact and as substantial a fact as any serene volcano, standing innocent with its smokeless summit in the blue sky and giving no sign of the rising hell in its bowels." Standing for the creative flux of a new and better life, Hank Morgan's volcano image also implies a hellish instrument of destruction, to be used against all contemptible creatures who forcibly resist Utopia. As it did in the United States in the 1850s, the volcano in Arthurian England prophesies a civil war between the old order and the new.

For with the introduction of democratic institutions and technological marvels, England is divided in two: the Yankee versus the chivalric knights, "hard unsentimental common-sense and reason" versus a feudalistic romanticism. When the war comes, it is horrible. Volcanic explosions now cause more than mortar to rain down: "It resembled a steamboat explosion on the Mississippi; and during the next fifteen minutes we stood under a steady drizzle of microscopic fragments of knights and hardware and horseflesh." Finally, the struggle ends — with the Yankee victorious. "Slavery was dead and gone," he says exultantly, and "the march of civilization was begun. How did I feel? Ah, you never could imagine it." Schools, mines, and factories come out into the open; the telegraph, the telephone, the phonograph, the typewriter, and the sewing machine are introduced; the Round Table is now employed for "business purposes." Progress, energy, and prosperity have become a reality.

If Twain had concluded his novel with this rosy, postwar picture, *A Connecticut Yankee* would take its place beside Edward Bellamy's *Looking Backward* and Howells's *A Traveler from Altruria* as one of those bright prophecies of a brave new world a-coming which flooded the American literary market in the closing decades of the nineteenth century. For in a troubled era, many Americans turned to Utopian fictions for reassurance, and Twain might well have tailored his novel to the popular taste of the moment, as he had done some years earlier in *The Prince and the Pauper*. But Twain conceived of *A Connecticut Yankee* as his farewell to literature, and he wrote it according to the requirements of his personal vision of history, without regard for the market place. "What saves history from triviality," Salvador de Madariaga has said, "is that in its core it is a tragedy"; what saves *A Connecticut Yankee* from being a trivial book is its awareness of that fact. The novel therefore belongs in American literature not with the shallow prophecies of Bellamy and Howells, but alongside *The Education of Henry Adams*.

iii

That Twain should have heard, as Adams did, the sound of doom in the humming of the dynamos is at first glance a surprising fact, especially when one considers the personal history of Mark Twain during the decade in which he conceived and wrote *A Connecticut Yankee*. It was in the '80s that Twain's lifelong enthusiasm for machines reached its apogee.

From the day that Mark Twain first grasped the wheel of a steamboat and felt the power that machines could deliver into a man's hands, he had been an inveterate inventor of gadgets. He also invested money numerous times in the brain children of other men. An engraving process called the Kaolotype, a steam-railway brake, a hinged pants button, a self-pasting scrapbook, a patent steam generator, a steam pulley, a new method of marine telegraphy, a new kind of watch, a new kind of mechanical organ, all these things and many, many more claimed the attention, the money, and the dreams of Mark Twain. Then, in the '80s, he became more deeply involved than ever before, both financially and emotionally, in a grandiose scheme of mechanical perfection.

In the year 1880, Twain purchased two thousand dollars' worth of stock in the Paige typesetting machine, then being brought to completion in the Colt arms factory in Hartford. Soon he put his name down for another three thousand dollars' worth. Five years later, the machine was still not workable, but by this time Twain's faith in it had grown into an obsession. James W. Paige, the inventor of the typesetter, he believed to be "a poet; a most great and genuine poet, whose sublime creations are written in steel." When Paige offered him a half-interest in the machine in exchange for thirty thousand dollars, Twain eagerly accepted. In 1886, the year in which Twain began to work on A Connecticut Yankee, Paige came to him for another four thousand dollars. Twain supplied it, and at the rate of three to four thousand dollars every month thereafter, poured his fortune into the "most wonderful typesetting machine ever invented." Offered a half interest in the Mergenthaler linotype in exchange for his interest in the Paige patents, Twain loftily refused. Once the Paige machine was on the market it would bring in annual rentals, Twain calculated, of fifty-five million dollars.

Meantime, Twain was rapidly running out of money. (At Christmastime, 1887, for example, he was able to send his sister only fifteen dollars because, as he wrote to her, he was "a little crowded this year by the type-setter.") The completion of the machine thus became a race against the exhaustion of Twain's funds. All through 1888, while Twain worked steadily and hard on A Connecticut Yankee, Paige and the master mechanics he had assembled around him in Pratt and Whitney's shops (the scene of the operations had been shifted from the Colt factory some time before) seemed tantalizingly close to finishing the machine. Finally, in January of 1889, the long task was completed. "The machine is finished!" Twain wrote to a London publisher. "This is by far the most marvelous invention ever contrived by man. And it is not a thing of rags and patches; it is made of massive steel, and will last a century." To Orion he exclaimed, "It's a cunning devil, is that machine! . . . All the other inventions of the human brain sink pretty nearly into commonplace, contrasted with this awful mechanical miracle. Telephones, telegraphs, locomotives, cotton gins, sewing machines, Babbage calculators, Jacquard looms, perfecting presses, Arkwright's frames — all mere toys, simplicities! The Paige Compositor marches alone and far in the lead of human inventions." "In two or three weeks," he added as an afterthought, "we shall work the stiffness out of her joints and have her performing as smoothly and softly as human muscles, and then we shall speak out the big secret and let the whole world come and gaze." In two or three weeks, however, the machine was breaking types, and Paige tore it apart again to see what the trouble was. Once more, Twain had to reach into his pocket every month for another three thousand dollars; with his other hand he wrote the concluding chapters of *A Connecticut Yankee*.

In the fall of 1880, after he had finished reading page proofs on the novel, Twain attempted to sell one hundred thousand dollars in Paige stock to Senator John P. Jones, in order to raise additional funds for the insatiable machine. Neither Jones, nor any other capitalist, was interested. With all of his financial resources committed, and unable to raise any outside aid, Twain was now irrevocably headed down the road that would take him away from his comfortable life in Hartford, bankrupt both him and the publishing firm he controlled, and bring him at last to that bitter December day in Paris in 1894 when he learned that the Paige machine had definitively failed. "It hit me like a thunder-clap," he wrote to his Standard Oil friend H. H. Rogers. "It knocked every rag of sense out of my head, and I went flying here and there and yonder, not knowing what I was doing, and only one clearly defined thought standing up visible and substantial out of the crazy storm-drift — that my dream of ten years was in desperate peril and . . . [that] I must be there and see it die." "Don't say I'm wild," he added some hours later. "For really I'm sane again this morning."

This final, agonizing episode in the history of Mark Twain and the typesetter took place well after his completion of *A Connecticut Yankee*. Up to the point of finishing the book and well beyond it, Twain continued to believe in James W. Paige and his wonderful machine, and Hank Morgan's excited plans for improving the world through technological ingenuity undoubtedly reflect that belief. Indeed, it may very well be that Paige partially inspired the character of Hank Morgan, who in his nineteenth-century identity, after all, was a superintendent of mechanics in a Connecticut arms factory. (Trooping back and forth, in 1885, between Paige's workshop in Hartford and his Nook Farm desk, did not Twain begin to wonder what the world would be like if it were run by a poet whose sublime creations were written in steel? And was it not then that he decided to write a novel on the subject?) As he moved, however, toward the conclusion of *A Connecticut Yankee*, Paige and his typesetter may have begun to have a somewhat less exhilarating effect on Twain's creative imagination. "A cunning devil," was now his name for the machine; having drained him of so much of his wealth, having tantalized and frustrated him a thousand times, it is a wonder he did not call the thing a Frankenstein's monster. The early memorandum that Twain wrote on *A Connecticut Yankee* suggests that right from the beginning he conceived of Hank Morgan's story as a tragedy: like Veblen, Twain believed that the modern technologist could create the world anew, but doubted that society would permit him to do so. In the final chapters of the novel, however, the tragedy becomes something more than simply the downfall of a genius who could not sell his up-to-date ideas to an animalistic people. It becomes the story of a man who is the victim of his own inventions. The steamboat catastrophe with which the cub pilot's education had concluded flowers horribly in *A Connecticut Yankee* into a machine-created cataclysm in which no one is spared, including Hank Morgan, as if Twain now sensed that the Paige typesetter was uncontrollable — that it not only could not be stopped from breaking types, but that it would end by smashing his very life to bits. Translating a foreboding sense of personal disaster into a public one, Twain envisioned the world-wide explosions of the mechanically marvelous twentieth century.

When the war of the future comes, and the "sheep" swarm down upon them from all sides, Hank Morgan and his sidekick Clarence fight back with all the latest weapons, including Gatling guns, dynamite, and electrified fences. The story of their last stand is quintessentially Twainian: their only allies in the struggle against a depraved society are boys — "a darling fifty-two" of them; their place of refuge (how could it be otherwise?) is a cave. Fifty-two Tom Sawyers in a cave, commanded by a "curious stranger," mowing down the enemy, electrocuting him, drowning him, blowing him sky-high in volcanic explosions, until the stench from twenty-five thousand corpses seeps into the cave and the boys (no longer as lucky as Tom Sawyer) all die of asphyxiation, while the Yankee — transposed once more to the nineteenth century — cries out one last time for the Paradise he has lost, and then falls back dead: this, in Mark Twain's history, is the way the world ends.

iv

Although *Pudd'nhead Wilson* lacks the dream-frame of *A Connecticut Yankee*, it is no less unreal a story. The composition of this weird book has a strange history, which Twain has related:

258

Originally the story was called "Those Extraordinary Twins." I meant to make it very short. I had seen a picture of a youthful Italian "freak" — or "freaks" — which was — or which were — on exhibition in our cities — a combination consisting of two heads and four arms joined to a single body and a single pair of legs — and I thought I would write an extravagantly fantastic little story with this freak of nature for hero — or heroes — a silly young miss for heroine, and two old ladies and two boys for the minor parts. I lavishly elaborated these people and their doings, of course. But the tale kept spreading along, and spreading along, and other people got to introducing themselves and taking up more and more room with their talk and their affairs. Among them came a stranger named Pudd'nhead Wilson, and a woman named Roxana; and presently the doings of these two pushed up into prominence a young fellow named Tom Driscoll, whose proper place was away in the obscure background. Before the book was half finished those three were taking things almost entirely into their own hands and working the whole tale as a private venture of their own — a tale which they had nothing at all to do with, by rights.

With two stories growing like two heads out of the same body, Twain decided to split them in half, the farcical story of the twin-monster becoming "Those Extraordinary Twins," while the doings of Roxy, Tom Driscoll and the "stranger" turned into the novel we know as *Pudd'nhead Wilson*.

The farce has very little to recommend it. Twain's efforts to be funny about the physical deformities of human beings generally were not very funny — for example, the jokes in *Huckleberry Finn* about Joanna Wilks's harelip — and the relentlessly worked-out situation-gags about the twin-monster are as tiresome as they are tasteless. The farce is worth mention only because of its relevance to one of the most important themes in all of Twain's work: the twinhood, or more broadly, the switched-identity theme.

The theme does not always concern twins, although twins predominate. Sometimes triplets, or simply a single individual with a talent for masquerading, may be involved. The transpositions of identity may be sexual, or racial, or social, in nature. The drowned woman dressed up in a man's clothes whom Huck momentarily thinks is his Pap; Nigger Jim disguised as a "sick A-rab," his black skin painted a dead, dull, solid blue; Injun Joe's appearance as a white man; Huck Finn's experiments with a variety of identities; the double masquerade brought off by the prince and the pauper; these are all variations on a central and abiding concern of Mark Twain's art. There is, indeed, hardly a book in the long shelf of Twain's published writings in which he does not play with the idea of switched identities; one can believe that he chose his *nom de plume* as much for its connotation of doubleness as for its evocation of steamboat days. Twain's unpublished manuscripts are also rich with examples of his preoccupation. Stories or notes for stories about identical triplets who deceive people into thinking they are one and the same person — or about white boys who black their faces and pull on woolly wigs — or about men like "Wapping Alice" who masquerade as women ("Why he unsexed himself was his own affair" [3]) — or about girls who love to wear men's clothes, *à la* Joan of Arc — can be found in abundance in the Mark Twain Papers. When these documents are added to the published work, they make an exceedingly significant design.

In Mark Twain's early fiction, the ability to switch identities is a means of release, a way of learning about the world, a talent that leads toward freedom and self-realization. Gradually, the twinhood theme becomes a nightmare. In Mark Twain's later writings, the protagonist often finds that he has been locked up inside the wrong identity and can't get out again, or that he is in some way tied to another individual in an attachment from which there is no release, this side of the grave. Thus if the prince and the pauper both profit by their exchange of roles, Hellfire Hotchkiss, the young heroine of one of Twain's later — and unpublished — fictions, is a tragic sexual misfit: "She trained with the boys altogether, and found in their rough play and tough combats and dangerous enterprises the contentment and joy for which she had long hungered. . . . All alone she learned how to swim, and with the boys she learned to skate. She was the only person of her sex in the county who had these accomplishments." At fifteen, she "ranked as the strongest 'boy' in the town"; whereas her boy friend, Thug Carpenter, is a "genuwyne female girl, if you leave out sex and just consider the business facts." In her agony at being so cruelly trapped, Hellfire cries, "Oh, everything seems to be made wrong, nothing seems to be the way it ought to be. Thug Carpenter is out of his sphere, I am out of mine. Neither of us can arrive at any success in life, we shall always be hampered and fretted and kept back by our misplaced sexes, and in the end defeated by them." [4]

"Those Extraordinary Twins" is another instance of the later, tragic phase of the twinhood theme. For although the story maintains a farcical tone for most of its length, it becomes at the end a harsh and brutal extravaganza. Luigi and Angelo, the two halves of the twin-monster, have radically different personalities. Angelo is a sober-sided, teetotaling, church-going reformer; Luigi is a hotheaded, hard-drinking atheist. (Given the political myths on which Mark Twain was raised, it is not surprising that when they go into politics sober Angelo becomes a Whig, while hotheaded Luigi joins the Democrats.) Yet they are incapable of surviving apart — and this is their tragedy. When Luigi is hanged for committing a crime, his execution inexorably finishes off Angelo as well. The situation-gag to end all is that you can't hang one man without hanging his brother, too. It is a grim joke which in *Pudd'nhead Wilson* forms the heart of the novel.

v

The locale of the novel, as of the farce out of which it grew, is another version of the town in which Mark Twain spent his

[4] Copyright 1959 by the Mark Twain Company.

boyhood. As the shock of the 1882 trip faded into the past, there were times when the vision of the Happy Valley came flooding back into Twain's imagination. His late autobiographical reminiscence of the Quarles farm at Florida, Missouri, and a letter of 1887 to the daughter of the old Hannibal jeweler — in which he wrote that the act of remembering "that old day" in Hannibal made him feel "like some banished Adam who is revisiting his half-forgotten Paradise and wondering how the arid outside world could ever have seemed green and fair to him" [5] — are both examples of what one might call Mark Twain's re-invention of his memories. But such nostalgic moments were rare. In *Pudd'nhead Wilson*, he could no longer even bring himself to call the town St. Petersburg. Instead, it is called Dawson's Landing. (Soon Twain would be referring to the town as Hadleyburg — a play, possibly, on Hadesburg — and eventually, as Jackassville.) After a savagely ironic description of the town's white-painted loveliness in the opening pages — a description which F. R. Leavis has incomprehensibly called a sign of the inward grace of Dawson's Landing — the novel's major theme is introduced in the form of a variation of the joke about killing half a twin-monster:

> "I wish I owned half that dog."
> "Why?" somebody asked.
> "Because I would kill my half."

As Perry Miller has pointed out, this little witticism could hardly have been considered new when *Pudd'nhead Wilson* was published. Well before the Civil War, it had appeared in Porter's *Spirit of the Times,* and from there had been picked up and reprinted in Lewis Gaylord Clark's *Knickerbocker.* To Porter and Clark and their circle of Whig friends, the grotesque, sly, and violent humor of the joke must have served as one more proof that Jacksonian America lacked polish, not

[5] Copyright 1959 by the Mark Twain Company.

to say moral perfection: their point of view toward this clown-ish witticism was one of detached and complacent amusement. In appropriating the joke, Twain kept the lines, but altered the character of the joker, thereby transforming the social effect of his remarks from a defense of gentility to an attack on it. The joker in *Pudd'nhead Wilson* is a New Yorker by birth, a college man, and the graduate of "a post-college course in an Eastern law school." The object of ridicule in Twain's version of the joke is not this intellectually superior stranger, but the respectable society of Dawson's Landing, which is too lit-eral-minded and unimaginative to see that he is not speaking seriously. Taking the stranger's words at face-value, the towns-people conclude that he must be a fool, but their nicknaming him "Pudd'nhead" and their subsequent boycott of his law practice are in fact a comment on their own stupidity. In forcing us to see the joke from the stranger's point of view, Twain struck back at an America which had always taken *him* at face-value as a lighthearted entertainer.[6]

Directed outward toward an uncomprehending and Philis-tine nation, the joke also points inward toward the heart of the novel. Every jest, Shaw tells us, is an earnest in the womb of time; Pudd'nhead Wilson's misunderstood witticism is a prophecy of the ensuing tragic action.

As the tragedy opens, two babies, one white, the other one/thirty-second black (and therefore by "law and custom" a Negro and a slave) are sitting face to face in a little wagon. Their resemblance to a twin-monster is sufficient to recall to mind Pudd'nhead Wilson's joke of a few pages before. "I wish I owned half that dog." Can a man really "own" another living being? If you "own" the black half of a black-and-white baby wagon, can you shoot it, or maim it in any way, without hurt-ing the white half as well? Is the human race any more divis-

[6] *Pudd'nhead Wilson*, it is worth remembering, was written during the period when Twain decided to publish *Joan of Arc* anonymously, on the grounds that the book would not be accepted as a serious work if it were known that he had written it.

ible than a dog? Are not two babies in a wagon as much of a unity as the single child whom King Solomon proposed — much to Nigger Jim's horror — to cut in two? Such questions remind us once again of Cable's influence on Twain, for these are the problems with which Cable's fiction of the late '70s and early '80s was vitally concerned. *The Grandissimes*, for example, dramatizes the ironies of white-black interrelationships in ways which surely must have been instructive to Twain, while the old priest in *Madame Delphine* makes a remark which constitutes a perfect gloss on *Pudd'nhead Wilson:* "We all participate in one another's sins. There is a community of responsibility attaching to every misdeed. No human since Adam — nay, nor Adam himself — ever sinned entirely to himself. And so I never am called upon to contemplate a crime or a criminal but I feel my conscience pointing at me as one of the accessories."

The crime in *Madame Delphine* is that of a quadroon mother who renounces her daughter so that the daughter may marry a white man. *Pudd'nhead Wilson* is concerned with a similar but graver offense. The slave woman, Roxy, gives up her child out of love, so that he can have a chance to live in the white man's world. Fearing the possibility of her son's being sold "down the river," Roxy at first believes that she can thwart fate only by drowning both the child and herself. Deciding to dress for the occasion, she dons a gaudy, curtain-calico dress, a turban, and a lurid ribbon, until she looks — as Twain says in a deliberate phrase — like a "volcanic irruption of infernal splendors." For Roxy is truly one of Twain's volcanoes, at once a liberator and a destroyer, a cunning and ruthless idealist who does not hesitate to kill in order to save. Slipping one of the white child's gowns on her own baby, she is overcome by their resemblance to one another; after a brief hesitation, she switches them in the cradle, moving about as she does so "like one in a dream."

The nightmare begins twenty years later. In a haunted house, in the dead of night, arrogant Tom Driscoll, Yale man,

scion of the Dawson's Landing aristocracy, and descendant
of Virginia gentlemen, sits helpless while a Negro mammy,
glooming above him "like a Fate," declares that she is his true
mother. To represent Tom's response to this shattering blow,
Twain turned to an inevitable image:

> A gigantic eruption, like that of Krakatoa a few years ago,
> with the accompanying earthquakes, tidal waves, and clouds
> of volcanic dust, changes the face of the surrounding land-
> scape beyond recognition, bringing down the high lands, ele-
> vating the low, making fair lakes where deserts had been, and
> deserts where green prairies had smiled before. The tremen-
> dous catastrophe which had befallen Tom had changed his
> moral landscape in much the same way. Some of his low places
> he found lifted to ideals, some of his ideals had sunk to the
> valleys, and lay there with the sackcloth and ashes of pumice-
> stone and sulphur on their ruined heads.

Like the anti-Semite who turns out to be "the Jew," the
young blueblood who has always scorned the Negro as a
"beast" finds that he is the very thing he most despises. And
his mother's attempt to console him is the final twist of the
knife: "You ain't got no 'casion to be shame' o' yo' father, I kin
tell you. He wuz the highest quality in dis whole town —
ole Virginny stock. Fust famblies, he wuz. Dey ain't another
nigger in dis town dat's as high-bawn as you is. Now den, go
long!"

Tom Driscoll is one of Mark Twain's best-drawn characters.
A sort of evil Tom Sawyer, he represents the romantic imagination of boyhood gone finally and irrevocably sour. But with the
single exception of Huckleberry Finn, the finest character in
all of Twain's fiction is volcanic Roxy. She is not, it must be
said, entirely an original creation — her personality comes too
close to that of Cassy in *Uncle Tom's Cabin* to be mere coinci-
dence. In appearance, Cassy and Roxy are nearly identical —
strong, beautiful, and nearly white; in personality, they are
both proud, imperious, and as ruthlessly capable of wielding
a knife as any man; sexually promiscuous, they are also fiercely

devoted mothers who are prepared to sacrifice everything for the well-being of their sons. Striking as these similarities are, however, there are also significant differences between the two characterizations. Adhering to the formulas of the sentimental novel, Mrs. Stowe transformed Cassy toward the close of *Uncle Tom's Cabin* into a devout Christian and a doting grandmother who sends her son off to a life of happiness in Africa. Twain disdained such dishonest compromises. Roxy is a greater character than her prototype, first of all because Twain was more faithful to the tragic limitations imposed on the Negro woman's mind and morals by the institution of slavery: Roxy never reforms. Roxy, too, has much more emotional depth than Cassy. Cassy is a somewhat flat character, a character who is illuminated from without, by the white spotlight of her creator's New England conscience. Mrs. Stowe's understanding of her is a detached understanding; she sees Cassy as an object lesson; she is sorry for her; and there she stops. Roxy, by contrast, is a startlingly vital character with whom Mark Twain seems to have been emotionally involved. Portrayed alternately as immensely desirable and luridly threatening, as if Twain were not so much creating a character as projecting an inner conflict, she has the daemonic magnetism of a figure of myth, or of dreams. In the fantastic scene where she looms up before Tom Driscoll in the haunted house and reclaims him as her son, we feel ourselves in contact not with the "reality" of the Negro slave, but with the guilt, the fears, and the illicit desires of the antebellum white South. From these emotions the adult Mark Twain had never shaken himself free. Whether Mark Twain ever fantasied, as so many Southern boys from time immemorial have done, that his real mother was a Negro mammy, we do not know; but a passage in Twain's notebook demonstrates that this son of the Old South had extremely ambivalent feelings about a black mistress, if not about a black mother. Long after he had left Missouri, the image of a sexually complaisant Negress continued to haunt Mark Twain's dreams:

In my dream last night I was suddenly in the presence of a negro wench who was sitting in grassy open country, with her left arm resting on the arm of one of those park-sofas that are made of broad slats with cracks between, and a curve-over back. She was very vivid to me — round black face, shiny black eyes, thick lips, very white regular teeth showing through her smile. She was about 22, and plump — not fleshy, not fat, merely rounded and plump; and good-natured and not at all bad-looking. She had but one garment on — a coarse tow-linen shirt that reached from her neck to her ankles without a break. She sold me a pie, a mushy apple pie — hot. She was eating one herself with a tin teaspoon. She made a disgusting proposition to me. Although it was disgusting it did not surprise me — for I was young (I was never old in a dream yet) and it seemed quite natural that it should come from her. It was disgusting, but I did not say so; I merely made a chaffing remark, brushing aside the matter — a little jeeringly — and this embarrassed her and she made an awkward pretence that I had misunderstood her. I made a sarcastic remark about this pretence, and asked her for a spoon to eat my pie with. She had but the one, and she took it out of her mouth, in a quite matter-of-course way, and offered it to me. My stomach rose — there everything vanished.

As Bernard DeVoto has observed, the slavewoman in *Pudd'nhead Wilson* is the only sexy female in all of Twain's fiction. Charged with the vital energy of Twain's black dream-girl, Roxy is an adulterous Eve in the sordid garden of Dawson's Landing.

By comparison with Roxy, Pudd'nhead Wilson is a rather remote figure. The principal cause of his remoteness is that in writing this novel Twain once again abandoned first-person narration, with the result that the stranger-hero is a much less vivid presence in the reader's mind than Hank Morgan or Huck Finn. The first-person, vernacular style was a sign of the narrator's own vibrant self, no matter the deadly horrors of which he told; by the time he wrote *Pudd'nhead Wilson*, Mark Twain was no longer prepared to offer his readers even this solace. The narrative style of Twain's last manner is cold, implacable, and impersonal. Further contributing to

Pudd'nhead's remoteness is the fact that his connection with the Tom-Roxy drama is only peripheral, so that he is offstage for long periods of time. Our continuing awareness of his personality is kept up largely through the aphorisms from his "Calendar" which serve as chapter epigraphs. Designed, as Twain sardonically explained, for "the luring of youth toward high moral altitudes," these maxims show Twain once again making fun of Benjamin Franklin's *Poor Richard* — except that now the parody constitutes not only a criticism of a prudential approach to life, but of life itself: "Whoever has lived long enough to find out what life is, knows how deep a debt of gratitude we owe to Adam, the first great benefactor of our race. He brought death into the world." Pudd'nhead, being an adult, cannot humble the world with a childish travesty of its solemn plans and advice, as Tom Sawyer could. His satirical sayings are unrelievedly bitter; in his destructive words one can find no echo of childhood's high spirits, by way of hope for the human race. Pudd'nhead Wilson's laughter is one long cry of pain.

Only toward the close of the novel does Pudd'nhead at last move to the front of the stage and become the dominant figure in the society which has for so long rejected him. With his superior intelligence, he is able to penetrate a bewildering series of disguises: his exposure of the fact that the "Negro woman" who has murdered one of the town's leading citizens is in reality a man, Tom Driscoll, whose entire life has been a masquerade in whiteface, is a *tour de force* of the detective's art. But finally, Pudd'nhead Wilson is a helpless man. His superior intelligence is powerless to compete against the accumulated weight of history, so that while he is capable of solving a particular problem which society defines as a crime, he can do absolutely nothing about the more legal forms of social murder. His testimony at the trial sends the false Tom Driscoll to jail and imprisons him once again in a black identity, but his volcanic revelations do not really free the true Tom from being a Negro slave — for how can a man be free who has never been permitted to learn the meaning of the term? "He could neither read nor write, and his speech was the basest dialect of the negro quarter. His gait, his attitudes, his gestures, his bearing, his laugh — all were vulgar and uncouth; his manners were the manners of a slave." The chapter in which these words appear is the last one in the novel, and it is headed by a maxim which reads, *"October 12, the Discovery. It was wonderful to find America, but it would have been more wonderful to miss it."* To Pudd'nhead Wilson, a Mosaic liberator who can only enslave, the Promised Land is a lie.

CHAPTER XI

Apocalypse

All through the book is the glare of a resplendent intellect
gone mad — a marvelous spectacle.

— MARK TWAIN's opinion of Jonathan
Edwards's *Freedom of the Will*

THE unpublished Papers of Mark Twain are the broken ruins
and unfinished monuments of a great talent. To go poking
about amongst them is an appalling experience. For they
record, these shards, the steep descent of a richly humorous
imagination into black despair.

Thanks largely to the scholarship of Albert Bigelow Paine,
the factors overtly responsible for the darkening of Twain's
mind in his later years are familiar enough: the failure of the
Paige typesetter; the bankruptcy of the publishing firm that
Twain controlled and the loss of his personal fortune; the discovery that his daughter Jean was an epileptic; the sudden
death, from meningitis, of his daughter Susy, whom Twain
adored as he did no one else on earth; his wife's slow decline
into permanent invalidism. To a man who celebrated youth,
old age brought a rain of hammer blows.

To his private losses was added an ever-growing sense of
public tragedy, for Twain at the close of the 1890s shared
the conviction of many sensitive Americans that the *fin-de-
siècle* was the end of the world as they had known it. "The
lust for money," Twain wrote in 1897, was now "the rule of

life" in the United States.[1] The spirit of the country, he felt, had become hard and cynical. In a period which produced Frederick Jackson Turner's elegy to a vanished frontier, Stephen Crane's *Maggie*, Brooks Adams's apocalyptic theory of history, and Thorstein Veblen's analysis of the predatory habits of the new ruling classes, Mark Twain depicted, in fragmentary fictions, a degraded civilization sliding toward final disintegration.

As was true of the later Kipling, Twain in his old age was fascinated by the idea of revenge. Perhaps writing stories about people who lose someone they intensely love, and who then seek revenge against society for their loss, was somehow a consolation to a grief-stricken and bitter man. The revenge theme crops up here and there in the Mark Twain Papers as early as the middle '80s; a decade later, the manuscripts are full of it. An early example is the story of a man who is married to a rich woman whom he has ceased to love. Under cover of a different identity, he pays court to a young girl, becomes infatuated with her, and forthwith murders his wife by plunging "a long wire, sharp-pointed, as thick as a crochet-needle," into her armpit.[2] Thereafter, he is pursued by a nameless and implacable avenger who had been very dear to the dead woman. Betrayal, violence, and revenge: these are the elements of this curious story. In different combinations they reappear in the Twain papers again and again, with ever-increasing frequency. In "An Extraordinary Case," we learn of a brilliantly gifted but cowardly man who cannot bring himself to kill the man who has seduced and then scorned his beloved sister. The coward is, however, a master of male and female disguises, and he shadows the seducer wherever he goes, eventually entering his house as an employee. At the point where the story breaks off, he has decided to repay the seducer in kind by running off with his daughter. Still another example of this type of story — and perhaps the

[1] Copyright 1959 by the Mark Twain Company.
[2] Copyright 1959 by the Mark Twain Company.

most bizarre tale of revenge Twain ever wrote — tells of a bitter old bachelor who forces the daughter of a woman he has vainly loved to cut off her hair, wear the clothes of a lynched colored man, and marry another girl. Meanwhile, Kate Wilson (the woman who had jilted the bachelor) also becomes an avenger, after she is deserted by her smooth-talking lover who has got her with child. Going about with a smile on her face, but "entertaining a volcano inside," she vows to take her revenge on the male sex by breaking the heart of every man who comes her way.[3] Like the iron-hearted mother in "A Double-Barreled Detective Story" (published in *Harper's Magazine* in 1902), who pledges her son's entire career to the pursuit and harassment of her former husband (by way of revenge for his having tied her to a tree when she was pregnant and ordered his bloodhounds to tear all her clothes off), Kate Wilson is a formidably strong-willed and implacable woman; if her daughter is forced to masquerade as a man, it is Kate who seems truly masculine in her unswerving determination to get even with a world she despises. A preoccupation with the reversal of sexual roles — with the dominance of the female and the weakness of the male — is one of the most striking characteristics of modern American fiction: from Henry James to Dos Passos, in the works of Dreiser and Willa Cather and Frank Norris and Edith Wharton, the reversal theme is strongly present. But nowhere in twentieth-century American writing are "male" women and "female" men more in evidence than in the fiction of Mark Twain's final period, nor does any modern writer make more clear than Twain does that sexual reversal stands for the disintegration of all traditional values.

The only male in the Mark Twain Papers who matches the female in vindictive passion is that dark angel of destruction, the Negro avenger. In the year 1885, Twain recorded the following prophecy in his notebook: "America in 1985.

---

[3] Copyright 1959 by the Mark Twain Company.

(Negro supremacy — the whites under foot.)" [4] Emphatically, the prophecy had nothing to do with the ancient Southern argument for keeping a tight rein on the blacks. Rather, it was the speculation of a man whose disgust with respectable, white America had reached the point where he was pleased to entertain thoughts of its destruction. The Negro avenger of the Mark Twain Papers is a figure with whom the author to a large degree identified. Thus in the "George Harrison Story" we are introduced to a Negro slave named Jasper, who threatens to expose the respectable Harrison as a criminal unless the white man does whatever the Negro commands him to do. "You's a slave!" Jasper cries out in triumph —

. . . dat's what you is; en I lay I'll learn you de paces! I been one, en I *know* 'em; slave to de meanest white man dat ever walked — en he 'uz *my father*, en I bought my freedom fum him en paid him for it, en he took 'vantage of me en stole it back; en he sold my mother down de river, po' young thing, en she a cryin' en a begging him to let her hug me jist once mo', en he wouldn't [let her]; en she say "cruel cruel," en he hit her on de mouf, God damn his soul! — but it's my turn now; dey's a long bill agin de [dam] [dam] low-down ornery white race, en you's a-gwyneter *settle* it.[5]

Reminiscent of Melville's "Benito Cereno" — particularly in the scene where Jasper, acting the perfect slave in the presence of an unsuspecting third person, waits on his white master at table and coerces him by covert gestures and whispered threats into looking happy and eating with appetite — the "George Harrison Story" differs from Melville's masterpiece in that it is as much concerned with the psychology of the Negro aggressor as of the white victim, whereas "Benito Cereno" tells us much more about Captain Delano's and Don Benito's minds than about Babo's. In his disaffection from America, an aging Mark Twain more and more looked at life from a "Negro" point of view.

[4] Copyright 1959 by the Mark Twain Company.
[5] Copyright 1959 by the Mark Twain Company.

ii

The Mark Twain Papers also tell of strange and fantastic voyages to the end of time. Twain, of course, had been writing about voyages all his life. *The Innocents Abroad, Roughing It, Huckleberry Finn, Life on the Mississippi, A Tramp Abroad, A Connecticut Yankee, The Prince and the Pauper, Tom Sawyer, Detective* and *Tom Sawyer Abroad* are all travel books, in their several ways. And from the somnolent trip around Tahoe in *Roughing It,* to the sleepwalking pilot in "Old Times on the Mississippi" who takes a hitch at the wheel without waking up, to Hank Morgan's arrival in Camelot, these voyages partook of the quality of dreams. When Huck Finn, after losing Jim in the fog, wakes up to find himself spinning stern first down an unfamiliar and "monstrous big river," his first impulse is to believe that he is dreaming, and in a sense he is: having drifted past the junction of the Ohio with the Mississippi, Huck and Jim are now fleeing with the illogicality of dreams ever deeper into slave country. Like the drunken boat of which Rimbaud dreamed, the raft gets out of their control, and the helpless runaways go booming downstream on the June rise of the mighty river. That they are headed due South recalls an earlier American dream-book, Poe's *Narrative of Arthur Gordon Pym,* for the greatest American writer of Southern origin before Mark Twain also had visions of a boy on a ship caught in a Southerly current, albeit Gordon Pym is borne toward Antarctica, rather than Arkansas. In the Mark Twain Papers, the dream-like elements of Huck and Jim's voyage become more pronounced than ever. Twain's later voyagers find themselves helplessly adrift in a phantasmagoric universe, a million miles from reality. The resemblances between *Arthur Gordon Pym* and *Huckleberry Finn* are perhaps superficial, but the voyages recorded in Twain's unpublished manuscripts are startlingly Poe-like in their weird symbolism and psychological atmosphere.

274

In his notes for a projected novel, for example, we find Twain writing that "this voyage must be a dream." As the story was to begin,[6] a man named Edwards falls asleep, after having spent some time examining a single drop of water in a microscope. Suddenly, a mysterious stranger appears. He calls himself the Superintendent of Dreams, and he proposes to provide the Edwards family with a ship and a crew for a long ocean voyage. Launched on the deep, the ship plunges through heavy seas and spitting snow flurries. Even the captain of the vessel is unsure where they are, except that they are in Northern waters. A "whale with hairy spider-legs to it" — one of the many "strange, uncanny brutes" with which the sea is filled — tries to ram the ship. The heavens are black, day and night: not even a single star lights the empty sky. This shipboard-world is a nightmare, surely, and yet the Edwardses are not quite sure whether they are awake or asleep. When the Superintendent of Dreams asks them, *"Are you quite sure it is a dream?"* they are unable to answer him. Eventually, Mrs. Edwards ceases altogether to believe in the existence of her waking life on land. When the ghastly "spider-squid" devours the captain's son, she insists that the incident has really and truly happened.

Six years later, the nightmarish voyage still goes on. Mutinies have taken place — led by the ship's carpenter — and the Edwardses have had another child. The ship is attacked by a spider-squid and a couple of passengers are swept overboard. The blind squid searches out the ship once more and again attempts to destroy it. Another mutiny is put down. The ship encounters another vessel, *The Two Darlings*, which then disappears in a blinding snowstorm, with the Edwardses' baby on board. The ship gives chase — but in vain. Phantom vessels are sighted, but never *The Two Darlings*. The passengers grow old; their hair turns gray; the Edwardses are

---

[6] Certain episodes in this novel — which Bernard DeVoto has called "The Great Dark" — were actually written out, but for the most part it consists of notes.

broken in spirit by their loss. Toward the end of the tenth year, the ship enters a region of "disastrous bright light" (presumably the field of the microscope's reflector). The heat produced by the light causes intense suffering. The water changes color; terrible beasts, which swarm in the Glare, are so maddened by the poisonous water that they attack one another as well as the ship. The sea dries up and the passengers long for death. *The Two Darlings* is sighted on the rough ocean floor, but everyone on board is dead, including the baby, and the corpses have been mummified by the heat. The ship's captain goes mad, as does the mutinous carpenter. Some of the crew are killed in a brawl, while others die of thirst. The oldest Edwards child is killed by a stray bullet fired in the course of the brawl. A daughter of the Edwardses fails in health. Finally, everyone dies, save Mr. Edwards and a loyal Negro named George.[7]

The hot water, the white light, the violence, the madness, the ship full of corpses, the terrifying snowfall, the fact that one of the mutinies is led by a "brute named Peters," are all details which are remarkably reminiscent of *Arthur Gordon Pym*. But above all, it is the sense that Twain's projected novel conveys of a world going out of control which brings the story of the Edwardses close to Poe. As in the case of Pym's voyage, the journey of the Edwardses carries them across tropic seas toward chaos.

The story of the Edwardses makes no specific mention of the South Pacific Ocean, as does *Pym*, but there can be little doubt that it was this watery region of the globe which furnished Twain with some of the novel's key images. For in a time of personal crisis, Mark Twain had sought out the South Seas, as Henry Adams had done a few years before. In the aftermath of the Paige typesetter's final fiasco, Twain had embarked on a round-the-world tour which he hoped would revive his spirits as well as his bank account. In August, 1895, having crossed the continent to Vancouver, British Columbia, he boarded a ship bound for Australia, and from there went on to India. *Following the Equator,* the travel book which came out of the experience, is a sorry affair, the only uninteresting travel book Twain ever wrote. It is noteworthy only for the mordant maxims from "Pudd'nhead Wilson's New Calendar" which it contains, and for occasional passages such as this:

> The passengers were sent for, to come up in the bow and see a fine sight. It was very dark. One could not follow with the eye the surface of the sea more than fifty yards in any direction — it dimmed away and became lost to sight at about that distance from us. But if you patiently gazed into the darkness a little while, there was a sure reward for you. Presently, a quarter of a mile away you would see a blinding splash or explosion of light on the water — a flash so sudden and so astonishingly brilliant that it would make you catch your breath; then that blotch of light would instantly expend itself and take the corkscrew shape and imposing length of the fabled sea-serpent, with every curve of its body and "break" spreading away from its head, and the wake following behind its tail clothed in a fierce splendor of living fire. And my, but it was coming at a lightning gait! Almost before you could think, this monster of light, fifty feet long, would go flaming and storming by, and suddenly disappear. And out in the distance whence he came you would see another flash, and another and another and another, and see them turn into sea-serpents on the instant; and once sixteen flashed up at the same time and came tearing toward us, a swarm of wiggling curves, a moving conflagration, a vision of bewildering beauty, a spectacle of fire and energy whose equal the most of those people will not see again until after they are dead.

Porpoises, glowing with phosphorescent light, disporting themselves on a dark night in the vast spaces of the South Pacific: "a fine sight," indeed. When such sights were transformed by Twain's tortured imagination from a travel book narrative into fiction, sea serpents became whales with spidery legs, the glow of phosphorescent light in dark seas became burning oceans, and voyages to Australia became journeys to the end of time. Coming upon Jonathan Edwards's *Freedom of the Will* late in life, Twain remarked that the book seemed illuminated by the glare of a resplendent intellect gone mad; it is a statement which might very well be made about the story of the Edwardses. (There is, indeed, a fair possibility that Twain gave the family the name Edwards with malice aforethought. In any event, the spider held over the fiery pit which Jonathan Edwards likened to the human condition is certainly the ancestor of the spidery monsters who fight and die in the boiling ocean of Twain's novel.) In the insane world of his final fictions, Twain imagined human society as a ship, struggling through frightful seas.

It is a journey from which there is no escape. Huck Finn wished to sustain his dream-like voyage for as long as possible; not so the Edwardses. To them, their trip is a nightmare, inside which they are forever imprisoned, as are the poor passengers in a story called "The Enchanted Sea-Wilderness," whose ship is blown southward through "wild seas," until it is finally caught in the trap of the "Everlasting Sunday," where there is no current, and no wind, and no sound — except the frantic booming of the useless compass ("We came to believe that it had a soul and that it was in hell"), and where all passing ships are freighted with human corpses that look so natural one might almost think they were alive.[8] (Here again one thinks of *Pym*.) In "An Adventure in Remote Seas," Twain told a story that might once have been a Tom Sawyer romance, except that the familiar images of boyish adventure have here been twisted into gruesome symbols of horror. A nameless ship runs into a snowstorm in remote Southern waters —"in that vast empty stretch of ocean which lies southwest of Cape Horn." [9] Managing to weather the blast, the captain and his crew go ashore on a deserted island, where they discover a cave. Inside the cave are bushels of gold in Spanish coins. The captain and one of the crew, whose Christian name

[8] Copyright 1959 by the Mark Twain Company.
[9] Copyright 1959 by the Mark Twain Company.

is not given, but who is known as "the Finn," kiss the coins and fondle them, they are so happy to be rich. At the point where the story breaks off, they discover that while they have been in the cave their ship has blown away in a storm. If "the Finn" is in fact Huck, then the fabulous "Territory" for which he lit out so long ago stands revealed as a desert waste where he will die a hideous death.

iii

Was there a God in such a world as Twain now portrayed? The Superintendent of Dreams, that enigmatic figure in a slouch hat, was *he* the ruler of the universe? Perhaps God was a cosmic version of the twinhood fantasy: "so atrocious in the Old Testament, so attractive in the New" — was he not, Twain asked, the "Jekyll and Hyde of sacred romance?" [10] Or possibly He was the misanthrope called Godkin who appears in one of the late manuscripts. If so, then God was a white man, and He was as loathsome a creature as Pap Finn:

> His complexion . . . was ghostly, spectral, ghastly. It was wholly colorless. And that was not all; that was not the marvel — far from it. It was the *kind* of pallor — that was the miracle; for this was a pallor which had never bleached-out a human face before, either in life or subsequently; it would have added a new terror to death. It was the cold, hard, smooth, polished, opaque, tintless and horrible white of a wax-figure's hands. There was no beard, and there were no eyebrows. . . . Out of this dreadful mask looked a pair of sloe-black eyes.[11]

Whoever He was, Twain was certain of one thing: God, he averred, lacked a sense of humor. For this reason if for no other, Twain was a God-hater. When it came to the mysterious

10 Copyright 1959 by the Mark Twain Company.
11 Copyright 1959 by the Mark Twain Company.

strangers of the cosmos, he preferred Satan, who knew how to laugh.

In February, 1897, Twain recorded in his notebook that he had had a dream in which he tried to sell his soul to Satan. The following June he wrote a note to himself: "Satan's boyhood — going around with other boys & surprising them with devilish miracles." [12] Almost a year and a half later, in November, 1898, Twain dashed off a five-hundred-word sketch of a boy named "little Satan, jr.," a schoolmate of Huck Finn's and Tom Sawyer's. This sketch was expanded, probably during 1899, into the first version — the so-called Hannibal version — of *The Mysterious Stranger*. The Satanic hero of the novel is Twain's final persona: once more, his hero is a boy, a handsome boy of fifteen, who calls himself by a most curious name — Forty-four. Certainly Twain wished the name to indicate the strangeness of the boy. Henry Nash Smith has suggested that it may also signify that Twain thought of his alien hero as a Jew.

Growing up in a provincial Missouri town, Mark Twain never knew what a Jew was, until one day two of them were enrolled in the Hannibal school. As he recalled the experience in his *Autobiography,* Twain remembered that . . .

> It took me a good while to get over the awe of it. To my fancy they were clothed invisibly in the damp and cobwebby mold of antiquity. They carried me back to Egypt, and in imagination I moved among the Pharaohs and all the shadowy celebrities of that remote age. The name of the boys was Levin. We had a collective name for them. . . . We called them Twenty-two — and even when the joke was old and had been worn threadbare we always followed it with the explanation to make sure that it would be understood, "Twice Levin — twenty-two."

Twice twenty-two — forty-four. Reinforcement for this explanation of the stranger's curious name is furnished by two of Twain's unpublished stories, "Newhouse's Jew Story," and

[12] Copyright 1959 by the Mark Twain Company.

"Mr. Randall's Jew Story," both of which concern a young man who risks his life in a duel with a riverboat gambler in order to save a Negro girl from being delivered into the gambler's hands. Both liberators are explicitly described as Jewish — the result, in all likelihood, of Twain's all-but-automatic association of slave-liberators with the Moses story. By the same associative process, he gave his final hero a name which conjured up Egypt and the Pharaohs in his mind, for the most important fact about Twain's Satan is that he wishes to be Moses.

An exotic stranger in Hannibal, young Forty-four is further differentiated from the rest of the community by his animal characteristics. In appearance, Forty-four looks as "prim en slick en combed up nice as a cat." Furthermore, he can see in the dark, can talk "cat-talk," and "mouse-talk" as well.[13] (This "grand natural animal talent" of Forty-four's is the distinguishing mark of several of Twain's late heroes, including the youthful avenger in "A Double-Barreled Detective Story," whose nose is as sensitive as a bloodhound's. Conversely, some of his other late heroes are animals with human characteristics, for instance the "Telegraph Dog" who can bark the Morse code, and the cat named Belshazzar who is the author of a book. Exuberantly, the men along the Southwestern frontier had once boasted that they were brutes; in the despairing tag-end of a comic tradition, Mark Twain asserted that only animals were truly heroic, and that "humane" was the most misleading word in the English language. Forty-four is Davy Crockett à rebours.) But if the Hannibal version succeeds in establishing the strangeness of Twain's new hero, it does not last long enough for us to see what Twain intended to make of his hero's peculiarities. Forty-four comes to town; proves himself a precocious scholar; rescues some people who are marooned in a blizzard; expresses the wish that man might be freed from his conscience (or the "Moral Sense," as Forty-four calls it); and that is all. Feeling his way along,

13 Copyright 1959 by the Mark Twain Company.

Twain was working toward the imaginative statement that could serve as his valedictory; the Hannibal version of his novel was the crucial first step in the right direction, but nothing more than that.

Another version, attempted some time later, produced several new characters, including Father Adolf, a dissolute, profane, and malicious priest with "fishy eyes" and a "purple fat face." [14] It also endowed the hero — now known as Philip Traum — with far more awesome powers than those with which Forty-four had dazzled the town. Not only can the boy talk to the animals in their own language, he is now able to create them, with a few swift movements of his hands. Traum also wishes to rid humanity of the Moral Sense, for he believes that it is the Moral Sense which has turned man into a beast infinitely more cruel and savage than the "Higher Animals."

Around 1902, Twain wrote the so-called "Print Shop" version of the novel. The hero is here known as "Number 44, New Series 864,962" — the serial number probably indicating Twain's sense of how many times he had attempted to get the book right. Number 44 looks like a singed cat, can speak cat language, and in an idle moment turns a lady's maid into a house cat named Mary Baker G. Eddy. With magnificent ease, he invents a printing machine that works entirely without human assistance. He insists — as Philip Traum also had done — that reality is a dream. The story terminates with a trip backward in time from Hannibal to the Garden of Eden, and from there into the "empty and soundless world" beyond.[15]

The version of the novel that the world reads was written in 1905-1906, although the ending was chosen by Albert Bigelow Paine some time after Twain's death out of a heap of fragments in the Twain Papers. The published version was by no means the last attempt that Twain made on the novel, which probably means that he never did succeed in writing it to his own satisfaction. Even so, the novel clearly belongs

[14] Copyright 1959 by the Mark Twain Company.
[15] Copyright 1959 by the Mark Twain Company.

in the second rank of Twain's major works — below *Huckleberry Finn*, of course, and inferior as well to "Old Times on the Mississippi," but on a par with *Tom Sawyer* and *Pudd'nhead Wilson* and *A Connecticut Yankee*. As for the ending selected by Paine, it was a brilliant choice. (Paine had his limitations, but less than justice has been done to him in the last quarter of a century of Twain scholarship. His biography of Twain, particularly the latter two volumes, will never be superseded, and his contribution to *The Mysterious Stranger* shows that there were times, at least, when he genuinely understood the mind of the man to whom he was so devoted.)

This time the locale of the novel is not Hannibal, but Eseldorf — Jackassville — in medieval Austria. Like Hank Morgan's Camelot, however, the town is American to the core. Eseldorf is really another portrait — a final portrait — of the Happy Valley. The village drowses, as did Tom Sawyer's home town, in peace and contentment; a splendid river washes its front, in a manner reminiscent of "Old Times on the Mississippi." "Eseldorf," says the boy-narrator in a familiar phrase, "was a paradise for us boys." The Christian name of the wise and good old priest whom the boys "all loved best" echoes the saintly place-name that Twain had long ago bestowed on the heavenly village of his lost youth: Father Peter. Everything, in sum, is just as it was in Twain's books of the 1870s — and yet not. White paint had been the symbol of St. Petersburg's innocence, but Father Peter's symbolic color is black — the color of his priestly garb. (In an earlier version of the book, Twain had signified the gentle goodness of this man by calling him Mr. Black.) In Eseldorf as in St. Petersburg, the "black man" is an outcast, the difference being that in *The Mysterious Stranger* the moral implications of excluding him are no longer blithely ignored, as they were in *Tom Sawyer*. When the townspeople put Father Peter in jail, Eseldorf lives up to its name as a community of asses.

Once the priest is imprisoned, the plot of *The Mysterious Stranger* becomes the familiar Twain story of an attempted liberation. Father Peter's would-be liberators are Theodor Fischer (the boy-narrator) and his playmates, and a youthful, Satanic stranger who calls himself Philip Traum. The boys, however, have none of the old-time inventiveness of Tom Sawyer; their lack of spirit, indeed, makes them seem like the wan ghosts of Huck and Tom. As for Traum, although he possesses supernatural powers, he is basically helpless. He can talk to cats; can travel effortlessly through space and time; can create living people out of mudballs; and knows everything about everyone, past, present, and future. Even so, he cannot really free Father Peter from the town jail, for the simple reason that the entire world is a prison-house. Wherever Traum and the boys go on their prodigious flights through history, they encounter only slaves and prisoners, serving out one variation or another of the same inexorable sentence. Mocked by his supernatural endowments, the stranger can only laugh in the face of a world he cannot change; laugh "enough to make a person sick to hear him"; laugh in a way Mark Twain wished *he* could, and could not. Watching, with an "evil chuckle," the cruel spectacle of the human comedy, the stranger reminds us, in his aloofness and detachment, of the Self-controlled Gentleman of the Southwestern tradition, except that Satan is a puppeteer who cannot, finally, control the puppets. At the end of the show, the Stranger speaks to his audience not of temperance and harmony, but of universal destruction: "There is no God," he says, "no universe, no human race, no earthly life, no heaven, no hell. It is all a dream, a grotesque and foolish dream." For the author of *The Mysterious Stranger* had nothing left to believe in. The past had failed him, and so had the present; as he looked about him, so ran a notebook entry of 1902, he saw a formerly great civilization eaten away with "moral rot." [16] Facing the twentieth century, Twain envisioned something even grimmer than Eliot's waste land — an utter blank. "Nothing," Satan exclaims to Theodor Fischer, "nothing exists but you. And you

[16] Copyright 1959 by the Mark Twain Company.

are but a *thought* — a vagrant thought, a useless thought, a homeless thought, wandering forlorn among the empty eternities!"

The statement appalls the boy, as well it might, yet the astonishing fact is that the stranger also tells Theodor that his terrible revelation has "set you free." Paradoxically, the destroyer of Theodor's world turns out to be the boy's liberator; Satan is really Moses, after all. For having annihilated a despicable universe, the Stranger enjoins the youth to build the world anew. The words of his plea, delivered against a backdrop of smoking chaos, ring in our ears today with an urgency which has by no means diminished with the years: "Dream other dreams, and better!"

Acknowledgments

IN the 1930s, when F. O. Matthiessen's *American Renaissance* and Perry Miller's *The New England Mind* were both in the works and there was a sense in the air that the study of American literature was at last coming into its own, three authoritative studies of American humor appeared: Walter Blair's *Native American Humor,* Constance Rourke's *American Humor,* and Bernard DeVoto's *Mark Twain's America.* It is a tribute to the factual and imaginative richness of these books that they remain — in particular, Miss Rourke's — as influential today as they were a quarter of a century ago. The present volume dissents from all three authorities in fundamental ways, but it would be a mistake to assume that I am unaware of how much I owe to them. Without their investigations to guide me, I cannot imagine how my own could have been conducted.

Among more recent critics of Mark Twain, I have found Henry Nash Smith the most informative and Leslie Fiedler the most provocative. Edmund Wilson's *New Yorker* piece on George Washington Harris, read at a time when I was just starting to formulate my ideas about pre-Civil War Southwestern humor, meant a very great deal to me, as, indeed, Wilson's literary criticism always has. Erich Auerbach's *Mimesis,* especially his discussion of the Roman historians, taught me to understand that mutations in the literary style of Southwestern humor were reflections of changes in the social order of the antebellum South.

Henry Nash Smith, in his capacity as Literary Editor of the

Mark Twain Estate, was extremely kind to me during the summer I spent in Berkeley going through Twain's unpublished papers, and he has cheerfully allowed me to continue imposing on him ever since. His assistant, Frederick Anderson, pointed out to me many items I would otherwise have missed, was patient with my questions, and in general was the most helpful librarian I have ever encountered. Portions of my manuscript were improved by the suggestions of William Abrahams, Walter Jackson Bate, Seymour Lawrence, Harry Levin, Ernest L. Lynn, Elizabeth Williams Miller, and Kenneth B. Murdock. To Perry Miller I owe a special debt. On the basis of a lecture he heard me deliver on *Huckleberry Finn*, he encouraged me to write this book, and I have benefited from his criticism and advice at every step of the way. I am grateful to my friends Alice Cooper and Alan Heimert for their willingness to share with me their own ideas about Davy Crockett, Huck Finn, Southern Whiggery, and other relevant matters. My researches in California and elsewhere were made possible by grants from the Harvard Foundation for Advanced Study and Research and the American Council of Learned Societies. I have acknowledged my profoundest indebtedness on the dedication page.

INDEX

INDEX

INDEX

College of William and Mary, 5
Collinson, Peter, 21
Colloquial style, the, 149, 155, 161-162, 219
Colton, Calvin, 81
Compromise of 1850, 114-115
Confidence Man, the, *see* Clown, the
Congreve, William, 8, 12
Conkling, Roscoe, 201
Conrad, Joseph, 23
Cooper, James Fenimore, 26, 37, 164
  Home as Found, 37
  Prairie, The, 26
Crane, Stephen, 24, 271
  Maggie, 271
Craven, Avery, 21
Crescent White League, 233
Crèvecœur, Michel Guillaume Jean de, 150
Crockett, Davy, 32-45, 68, 69, 86, 92, 281
  Almanacs, 43-45, 94
  Autobiography, 32-33, 42
  Colonel Crockett's Exploits and Adventures in Texas, 68
Curtis, George William, 150, 201

DEMOCRACY, THE, 132, 198, 200, 201-202, 229; for pre-Civil War period, *see* Jacksonian revolution
Des-Bouverie, Sir Edward, 10
DeVoto, Bernard, 216, 248, 267, 275n., 286
  Mark Twain in Eruption, 248
  Mark Twain's America, 286
Dickens, Charles, 24, 76, 209
Dickinson, Emily, 106
Dixon, George Washington, 42
Dos Passos, John, 272
Douglas, Stephen A., 140
Dreiser, Theodore, 169, 272

EDDY, MARY BAKER, 282
Edwards, Jonathan, 270, 278
  Freedom of the Will, The, 270, 278
Eliot, T. S., 219, 224, 284
Emerson, Ralph Waldo, 26, 59n. 97, 179, 204
Everett, Edward, 59

FAULKNER, WILLIAM, 56, 70, 98, 111, 137, 143, 221
  "Bear, The," 98
  Sound and the Fury, The, 221
Fiedler, Leslie, 286
Fielding, Henry, 63
  Joseph Andrews, 63
  Tom Jones, 63
Fields, W. C., 179
Fink, Mike, 30-31, 73, 91-92
Fisher, Miles Mark, 106
Fitzhugh, George, 130
  Cannibals All!, 130-131
Fitz-William, Richard, 14, 15, 16
Flint, Timothy, 23, 24, 25, 27, 28
Force Bill, 53
Forster, E. M., 192
  Passage to India, A, 192
Foster, Charles H., 108
Frame device, the, 64-65, 68, 78-80, 82, 92, 133, 145-146, 155, 242, 250
Franklin, Benjamin, 7, 10, 11, 12, 189-190, 206, 268
  Autobiography, 190
  Way to Wealth, The, 190
Franklin, John Hope, 86

GARFIELD, JAMES A., 201, 229, 230
Garrison, William Lloyd, 110
Gayarré, Charles, 234
Gentleman, the, 17, 19, 29, 42, 47-48, 61, 64-72, 78-80, 83-84, 85, 91, 92-94, 97-99, 103, 115, 118-